125 Cookies
to Bake, Nibble, and Savor

Elinor Klivans

125
Cookies

to Bake, Nibble, and Savor

Broadway Books   New York

BROADWAY

125 COOKIES TO BAKE, NIBBLE, AND SAVOR. Copyright © 1998 by Elinor Klivans.
All rights reserved. Printed in the United States of America. No part of this book may be
reproduced or transmitted in any form or by any means, electronic or mechanical, including
photocopying, recording, or by any information storage and retrieval system, without written
permission from the publisher. For information, address Broadway Books, a division of
Bantam Doubleday Dell Publishing Group, Inc., 1540 Broadway, New York, NY 10036.

Broadway Books titles may be purchased for business or promotional use or for special sales.
For information, please write to: Special Markets Department, Bantam Doubleday Dell
Publishing Group, Inc., 1540 Broadway, New York, NY 10036.

BROADWAY BOOKS and its logo, a letter B bisected on the diagonal, are trademarks of
Broadway Books, a division of Bantam Doubleday Dell Publishing Group, Inc.

Library of Congress Cataloging-in-Publication Data

Klivans, Elinor.
125 Cookies to Bake, Nibble, and Savor / Elinor Klivans. — 1st ed.
p.   cm.
Includes bibliographical references and index.
ISBN 0-7679-0154-1 (hardcover)
1. Cookies.   2. Make-ahead cookery.   I. Title.
TX772.K58   1998
641.8′654—dc21   98-10234
CIP

FIRST EDITION

Designed by Ralph Fowler

98 99 00 01 02 10 9 8 7 6 5 4 3 2 1

To Jeffrey, Laura, and Peter

forever cheering me on

and helping me find

the power within

Contents

ACKNOWLEDGMENTS   ix

INTRODUCTION   1

2   Everyday Cookie Baking Techniques

6   Baking Equipment

11   Cookie Ingredients

15   Freezing and Shipping Cookies

19   The Frozen Pantry

27   Kid Easy Cookies

38   Slice and Bake Cookies from the Freezer

51   Shortbread

68   Butter Cookies and Crisps

82   Sugar and Spice Cookies

94   Chocolate Chip Cookies and Bars

107   Brownies

117   Bars with Chocolate or Nuts

130   Bars with Fruit

146   Cookie Sandwiches and Filled Cookies

165 Meringues, Macaroons, and
     Parisian Macaroon Sandwiches

180 Tassies, Tea Cakes, and Truffles

193 Especially for Holidays

212 Savory Cookies

MAIL ORDER SOURCES 224
BIBLIOGRAPHY 225
INDEX 226

Acknowledgments

Judith Weber, my agent, who always knows exactly the right thing to say and do.

Harriet Bell, my editor, who took such extraordinary care of this book down to the last detail and knew how to make my cookies "fly." I'm so fortunate to have an editor who is wise as well as nice.

Sonia Greenbaum and Jane Mollman, my copy editors, who checked this book so carefully.

Quentin Bacon and Suzie Smith, the brilliant photographer and meticulous food stylist who captured the essence of these cookies.

Thank you to the finest of all publishing teams at Broadway Books; especially Roberto de Vicq de Cumptich, an art director who is a creative genius; Caitlin Connelly, my enthusiastic publicist; Caitlin's superorganized assistant, Lisa Bullaro; Janice Race, fellow baker and production editor; and Alexis Levenson, for so much able and prompt assistance.

My husband, Jeff, who is a genuine cookie lover, always ready to climb the next mountain with me and help me up.

My daughter, Laura, who sends me so much encouragement with every recipe she proofreads.

My son, Peter, who conscientiously proofread my recipes and baked so many of them that his friends' party invitations now feature "desserts by Peter."

My parents, Selma and Lester Wishnatzki, who brought me up in a house filled with cookies and love.

Helen Hall, whose good taste and wise opinions help make my recipes better, and Reg Hall, who helps me understand the food chemistry so I can pass it on.

I want to thank the companies who supplied information and the business people who offered their expertise: Bruce Stillings and The Chocolate Manufacturers and Confectionery Association, John Park of Park Appliance, and everyone at the General Electric Company consumer answer phone.

A big thank you to my circle of supporters and encouragers: Valerie Baker, Melanie Barnard, Flo Braker, Sue Chase, Susan Derecskey, Susan Dunning, Natalie and Harvey Dworken, Lisa Ekus, Carole and Woody Emanuel, Barbara Fairchild, Betty and Joe Fleming, Mutzi Frankel, Karen and Michael Good, Kat and Howard Grossman, Heather Harland, Carolyn and Ted Hoffman, Kristine Kidd, Alice and Norman Klivans, Mom and Dad Klivans, Susan Lasky, Robert Laurence, Rosie and Larry Levitan, Gordon Paine, Joan, Graham, and Ella Phaup, Dale Mudge, Janet and Alan Roberts, Pam and Stephen Ross, Julia Schultz, Louise and Erv Shames, Gail Venuto, Elaine and Wil Wolfson, Jeffrey Young, and the family and friends who shared so many of their cookies with me.

Introduction

We have a cookie division of labor at our house. I bake and freeze the cookies; my husband, Jeff, takes charge of our daily allotment. At dessert time he chooses cookies from the freezer and arranges them on a plate. One day, I looked down at that plate of cookies and realized it was my family's legacy. I remembered my Grandmother Sophie for her butter cookies and the cookie legacy she left our family. I saw my mother as forever young as we rolled strudel together. I thought of Jeff's Grandmother Tillie baking hundreds of her chocolate chip raisin cookies in her big old-fashioned Midwestern kitchen, and my Uncle Howie, the family cookie inventor, baking his new butterscotch bars. My own chocolate chip cookies were there to transport me back to a time when anything could be cured by eating a chocolate chip cookie.

When I think about my childhood, it centers around cookies. Before I was old enough to read a recipe, I had a special stool so that I could reach the counter and pat out cookies beside my mother. I carried a box of my mom's cookies to every holiday party, and school days meant finding the cookie she put in the bottom of my lunch bag. When my dad had a birthday, his "birthday cakes" were always platters of cookies. If I stayed home sick from school, my mother baked pecan crescents; and when I went to college, she mailed mandel bread. When I started dating my future husband, she put him on her cookie list. She must have had a sixth sense that he was the one, because he was the only man I ever dated who made that list.

My first apartment had a small under-the-counter refrigerator with a tiny freezer section just large enough to hold a package of cookies. We lived in nine apartments during our first four years of marriage, but each one had some sort of freezer, and the cookies in them made each one seem like home. I've passed along our cookie traditions to my children by baking cookies for them, with them, and now watching them make cookies for their friends, schoolmates, coworkers, and me. Even my husband bakes now. Although he often cooks other parts of our meals, he never baked cookies until he made his own Super S'more cookies when I was busy with other recipes. It's never too late to become a cookie baker.

For twelve years, I worked as a pastry chef in a restaurant where we served ice cream and homemade cookies every night. I baked cookies weekly and stored containers in the freezer so that they were fresh each night. Those years of cookie baking gave me a chance to experiment with new ideas and try many of the recipes that I had clipped and saved for years. My cookie list grew. When friends heard I was writing a cookie book, even the few who never baked cookies had family recipes to share with me. Their cookies arrived in the mail while recipes came on the fax and via e-mail. Through the cookies, I renewed friendships and made new ones. I was surprised at the response, but cookies do that.

While writing this book, I held my first cookie exchange party. I asked friends and neighbors to bring cookies and a story to share, as well as an empty box for taking cookies home. They carried their own traditions in those boxes of cookies, bringing cookies that their great-grandmothers had baked, ones that had comforted them through sad times, and others that had celebrated joyous times. Some friends baked cookies only for holidays, some baked them regularly, and some brought versions of the first cookies they had ever baked; but everyone had fun baking them and everyone had a cookie story.

Although I find cookies the easiest desserts to bake, I include some recommendations with almost every recipe. These words of good advice explain a term, tell where to find an ingredient that might not be easily available, try to anticipate questions that might come up, and just prevent problems. When I've questioned a step in a recipe, or someone has asked me about the directions in a recipe, that becomes part of my good advice. If you read, "watch these cookies carefully at the end of their baking time," that means I answered the phone for just one minute and burned the bottoms. When I add "be careful not to burn yourself," it means I burned myself or almost did, and I don't want it to happen to you.

Now my family is scattered around the country, but when I fill a Pecan Tassie my mother is gently warning me not to add too much filling; when I bake Gingerbread People, my daughter, Laura, is next to me with her tiny fingers making the raisin faces on her gingerbread family; and as I spoon out any kind of chocolate chip cookie, there's my son, Peter, sneaking extra chocolate chips into the dough. Like mother like son.

Although this book is complete, I keep baking cookies and the ideas keep coming. Friends continue to share recipes, uncles call with new suggestions, the freezer is stocked, and the cookie welcome mat is always out.

Everyday Cookie Baking Techniques

Techniques for cookies are similar to those for general baking, but you will use fewer of them, and they are all easy. Understanding how to perform a technique and why it's done is the key to good results. If you know how to cream soft butter with sugar to achieve a smooth texture, melt chocolate so it combines easily with other ingredients, and check that cookies are baking properly, you'll be pulling batch after batch of perfect cookies out of your oven.

Creaming Fats and Sugar

Creaming fat and sugar together beats air into them and forms a smooth mixture that combines easily with other ingredients in a recipe. The fluffy, light-colored mixture that results from thorough creaming is full of air cells

that expand and lighten cookies somewhat as they bake. Most of the sugar crystals do not dissolve during creaming, and their rough texture helps to hold in the air. Soften butter, margarine, or vegetable shortening to room temperature, 65°F to 75°F, before creaming.

Beating Eggs

Some bars, macaroons, and meringue cookies require beaten eggs or egg whites. When eggs are beaten, they form a foam that is filled with air cells. This foam lightens as the heat expands the air cells during baking.

Whole eggs and egg yolks are beaten until their color lightens and they thicken. When eggs are beaten with sugar, the mixture becomes denser and the foam more stable.

When egg whites are beaten, they form a delicate foam. (Because acid helps to stabilize egg white foams, cream of tartar is often beaten with them.) Egg whites will not whip properly if they come in contact with fat. As long as the egg whites do not contain any egg yolk, and the mixing bowl and utensils are clean and absolutely free of fat, there should be no problem.

Properly beaten egg whites are shiny and will form a soft point or peak if you dip in a spoon and lift it out. At the soft peak stage, the moving beaters form smooth, curving lines in the egg whites. Egg whites at the soft peak stage look creamy; they combine smoothly and easily with other mixtures. It is preferable to underbeat egg whites slightly rather than to overbeat them. Overbeaten egg whites look lumpy and dull and form big clumps if you try to fold them into another mixture.

I beat egg whites with an electric mixer on low speed until the cream of tartar is dissolved. Then I increase the speed to medium and beat until soft peaks form. I find it's easier to check the egg whites and control the results on medium rather than on high speed. A hand mixer works fine, but it takes longer to beat the whites to soft peaks than a standing mixer does.

Adding sugar to beaten egg whites stabilizes the foam just as it stabilizes an egg yolk foam. After sugar is beaten in, the mixture thickens and can be baked into crisp meringue cookies. Begin adding sugar just as the egg whites reach the soft peak stage. Add it slowly so the egg whites have time to absorb it. Adding one tablespoon of sugar every thirty seconds is a good practice. Egg whites beaten with sugar form firm peaks if you dip in a spoon and lift it out.

Folding

When a light mixture is to be combined with a heavy mixture, fold the two together gently with a rubber spatula so as not to push the air out of the lighter mixture and break up the air cells. When I mix meringue cookies I fold part of the lighter meringue into the heavier nut mixture to lighten it; then I fold in the remainder. Use the spatula to dig down to the bottom of the bowl and bring the two mixtures up and over each other. Use a large bowl and turn it as you fold so that the mixtures blend quickly.

Softening Ingredients

A smooth cookie dough requires soft shortening. Cold, hard butter forms small lumps, so you won't get the even-textured cookies that soft butter produces. Softened cream cheese combines smoothly with other ingredients to produce a creamy filling for bars. Properly softened butter or cream cheese gives easily if pressed. On a warm day butter softens in about one hour, but softening can take up to three hours in a cold kitchen. Don't try to speed the process by heating the butter.

Peeling, Toasting, and Grinding Nuts

Toasting nuts improves their flavor. Try toasting some nuts, then taste both the toasted nuts and untoasted ones; you'll notice the difference. When almonds, pine nuts, and hazelnuts are toasted, the flavor of the nut actually changes. I toast nuts by spreading them in a single layer on a baking sheet and baking them in an oven preheated to 325°F. Walnuts and pecans should bake about eight to ten minutes; pine nuts about ten minutes until golden; blanched, sliced, or slivered almonds about twelve minutes until golden; and blanched whole almonds and hazelnuts about fifteen minutes until golden. Just before the nuts are ready, you should smell a pleasant aroma of toasting nuts. Pistachio and macadamia nuts are normally sold roasted.

Since hazelnuts must have their skins removed before they are used for baking, try to buy blanched (peeled) hazelnuts. If the hazelnuts need to be blanched, fill a saucepan with enough water to cover the nuts and bring the water to a boil. Add the hazelnuts and boil for five minutes. Drain the hazelnuts, immerse them in cold water for several minutes to cool, drain again, and peel the nuts with a small sharp knife. The skins will come off easily, and the nuts will dry out when they toast. If the hazelnuts are not toasted immediately, dry them with a clean dish towel and refrigerate or freeze them.

I chop nuts by hand with a large sharp knife, which gives me control over the size. (A food processor invariably grinds some of the nuts rather than chopping them.) Finely chopped nuts should be $1/8$ inch in size and coarsely chopped nuts between $1/4$ inch and $3/8$ inch in size. When I need ground nuts, I use a food processor fitted with the steel blade. Processing the nuts with some of the sugar or flour from the recipe allows them to become finely ground without forming a paste.

Melting Chocolate

The key to melting chocolate is to melt it slowly, using gentle heat. The cocoa butter in the chocolate should melt, but not the sugar. Cocoa butter is one of the few fats that is solid at room temperature; it doesn't soften, as butter will. At 92°F cocoa butter and, in turn, chocolate, begin to melt. When it reaches body temperature (98.6°F), the chocolate melts; it should be completely melted by the time its temperature reaches 113°F. At higher temperatures, the sugar in chocolate can melt and burn, causing the chocolate to become grainy and lumpy. Since this window between the melting temperature and the scorching temperature is small, gentle heating is essential. Be careful that the chocolate is not subjected to sudden bursts of high heat from steam or boiling water,

which can shock and scorch it. Stirring the chocolate and removing it from the heat as soon as it melts will assure smoothly melted chocolate.

To melt chocolate, chop large pieces of chocolate into approximately $1/2$-inch pieces so it melts evenly. When melting chocolate with other ingredients such as butter, put everything in a heatproof container, a small saucepan, or the top of a double boiler. Place the container over very hot or barely simmering water and stir until the mixture is smooth. Keep the heat about low medium and turn it down if steam forms. Remove the chocolate mixture from over the hot water as soon as it is melted. White chocolate should be melted in a nonreactive container (Pyrex glass or stainless steel containers are nonreactive; aluminum is not).

When melting chocolate by itself, I do so in the oven, which requires no stirring. I preheat the oven to 175°F, cut the chocolate into $1/2$- to $3/4$-inch pieces, and put it in an ovenproof container. Remove the chocolate from the oven as soon as it is melted. You are not heating the chocolate to 175°F, since you remove it from the oven as soon as it melts, long before it reaches that temperature. The oven supplies dry, gentle warmth, making it difficult for the chocolate to burn even if left in the oven an additional minute or two. The familiar one-ounce squares of baking chocolate do not need to be cut, but will take longer to melt than small pieces. Oven melting usually takes at least ten minutes, depending on the amount of chocolate to be melted and the size of the pieces. A microwave oven can be used to melt chocolate. I don't own one, but manufacturers supply directions for melting chocolate.

Preparing Baking Pans

I line baking sheets with parchment paper or one of the newly available nonstick liners. Lined baking sheets do not have to be greased.

Cookies that spread thin during baking can benefit from being baked on a slick nonstick liner, but generally parchment paper and nonstick liners are interchangeable. I often bake one pan of cookies with a nonstick liner and one with parchment paper and notice no difference.

When baking pans for bars or brownies need to be greased, I use the same shortening to grease the pan that I use in the recipe. If bars have a graham cracker crust or bottom that would be difficult to remove from the pan neatly, line the pans with heavy aluminum foil that extends over the ends of the pan. After the bars cool, use the overhanging ends of aluminum foil to lift the bars out of the pan. They cut into neat slices and slide easily off the foil.

Baking Cookies Properly

Cookie doughs are quite forgiving if mixed longer than necessary or handled too much. It's when they bake that they require your close attention. With their high sugar content and small size, they can burn if baked even a few minutes longer than specified. This is easily prevented if you watch the cookies carefully as the end of their baking time nears. Underbaking is better than overbaking. Cookies continue to bake slightly as they sit on a warm baking sheet or as they cool. A slightly underbaked soft center is preferable to a burned bottom. Brownies and bars, since they are more like thin cakes, are less apt to burn if baked a few minutes too long, but you don't want them dry and crumbly. The thicker the cookie or bar, the lower the temperature at which I bake it. (Too high an oven temperature could burn the edges or bottom before the inside is done.) Thin, crisp cookies often require higher temperatures. The higher the oven temperature the more often you must check the cookie. Lifting a cookie with a spatula to check the bottom may break one cookie but save a whole pan.

To bake cookies evenly, reverse the baking sheets during baking. Since cookie dough takes time to heat in the oven and begin its cooking, I wait to reverse the sheets until the cookies have been in more than half of their baking time. If the total specified time is fifteen minutes, I would reverse the baking sheet in the oven after eight or nine minutes.

Sometimes a pan of cookies must wait its turn to bake if you're making a large batch. It's more efficient to form all of the cookies at the same time. Most cookies are fine if they sit on their baking sheet while others bake, as long as the sheet wasn't warm. In that case, the dough begins to melt, the cookies will bake unevenly, and baking times are affected.

When baking more than one sheet at a time, adjust the oven racks carefully and reverse the baking sheets top to bottom and front to back about halfway through the baking time. Often one pan of cookies bakes faster than the other. If I'm baking a type of cookie that burns easily or requires a high oven temperature, I bake one sheet at a time on the middle rack.

Kitchen Temperatures

Although it's not always possible to have kitchen temperatures at the desired 65°F to 75°F, baking can be adjusted to accommodate variable room temperatures. If your kitchen is cold, allow additional time for butter and cream cheese to soften and for ingredients to melt, and even additional baking time if the cookie dough or baking pans are cold. Cooling times for all types of cookies are affected by kitchen temperatures. Pine Nut Toffee Bars firm more quickly in a cool winter kitchen than in a warm summer one. Cold weather is an ideal time to roll out cookie dough and know it won't stick to the rolling surface. (Maybe that's why the holidays fall in the winter, when you want to roll and cut fancy shapes from cookie dough.) If you are preparing crusts or flaky cookies in a warm kitchen, chill the shortening pieces in the freezer for about thirty minutes and take care not to overwork the dough. When glazes are slow to thicken and cool and chocolate toppings won't firm, try refrigerating them to speed up the cooling process.

Coating Cookies with Powdered Sugar

I coat cookies or dust bars with powdered sugar after they cool thoroughly but before I freeze them. Then they're ready to serve when they defrost. Warm cookies would melt powdered sugar. If the powdered sugar needs freshening due to humid conditions or from the cookies being moved in the freezer, it's simple to do a quick dusting before serving.

Baking Times

The shorter a baking time, the more important a minute or two of time in the oven becomes. Most cookies bake quickly, and baking times must be treated as recommenda-tions. So many variables affect how long cookies should bake that opening the oven to check them is the best policy. Ovens vary in their performance and temperature accuracy, doughs may be at different temperatures when put into the oven, or pan measurements and the weight of the pan may differ from what is called for in a recipe. Other considerations are the position of the pan in the oven, how many pans are being baked at once, and how full the pans are.

To test brownies or soft bars, insert a tooth-pick into the center. When the toothpick comes out clean, the bars are done. Remember, an overbaked brownie or bar also yields a clean toothpick, so don't wait too long to test them. Moist dense brownies or bars may have a few crumbs clinging to the toothpick when it is removed. Cookies are done when they reach a certain color, golden or light brown, or when their edges turn light brown. Some cookies are ready when they feel firm to the touch. And trust your nose—if you smell something burning, check it fast. I think of each oven as having a personality that I have to get to know before I can judge how it will bake my cookies.

Baking Equipment

The list of equipment for baking cookies consists largely of basic kitchen items. All that's needed are several rectangular and square pans and baking sheets; bowls and measuring utensils; an accurate oven; and a few wire cooling racks. An electric mixer, although not essential, makes mixing easy. Experience has taught me to buy the best equipment available. Handles break off inexpensive metal measuring cups and lightweight baking sheets bend and warp. I've bought both kinds and have learned that good-quality pans and utensils pay for themselves by lasting indefinitely and dependably turning out well-baked cookies. What follows is what I find indispensable and what I find comes in handy.

Baking Pans

Using heavyweight baking sheets and baking pans avoids burned cookie bottoms and overbrowned edges on bars. I've found heavy aluminum to be the best material for these pans.

The baking pan measurements given in the recipes are the inside measurements of the pan. The size of baking sheets for cookies is not crucial, but they should not touch the oven walls, so that air can circulate in the oven. For bars and brownies, use the size pan specified in the recipe. Using a different size will affect the baking time and often change the final result. Too small a pan can cause the batter to overflow as it rises during baking, and too large a pan can cause dry brownies.

BAKING SHEETS/COOKIE SHEETS

Although I use the two terms interchangeably, I consider cookie sheets to have flat sides or ones no more than $1/2$ inch high and raised ends for removing them easily from the oven. Standard sheets suitable for home ovens range from about 15×12 inches to about 18×14 inches.

As I've searched for the perfect baking sheet, I've assembled quite a collection. All of the pans are heavyweight but there the similarity ends. They're dark or shiny, have nonstick or plain metal finishes, and have 1-inch-high sides or just rims at the ends that curve upward to grasp when removing them from the oven. From all of these choices, there are two baking sheets that I always pull out first. Both of them are shiny, heavy aluminum pans. Shiny finishes deflect heat so cookie bottoms are less likely to burn, and the aluminum absorbs heat evenly so cookies bake evenly. One has 1-inch-high sides and measures 18×12 inches. It is also known as a baker's half sheet and I bought it at a kitchen shop. The second pan is flat except for curved rims at each end and measures 18×14 inches. Both allow for air circulation around baking cookies. They're available from Bridge Kitchenware, listed in the mail order section at the back of the book. Since I always use a baking liner, it's not important to me whether a baking sheet has a nonstick finish.

Jelly roll pans are baking sheets with a 1-inch rim around all sides; they are used for baking cookies and some bars. Their measurements range from about $15^{1}/_{2} \times 10^{1}/_{2}$ inches to about 17×12 inches.

PANS FOR BROWNIES AND BARS

Rectangular and square pans for brownies or bars should be heavyweight aluminum, preferably with a nonstick coating, and have 2-inch-high sides. The sizes I use are $8 \times 8 \times 2$ inches, $9 \times 9 \times 2$ inches, $11 \times 7 \times 1^{3}/_{4}$ inches, and $13 \times 9 \times 2$ inches. I have noted the few recipes where 1-inch-high sides are acceptable. It's useful to own two pans in each size, so recipes can be doubled.

PIE PANS

Several of the shortbreads bake in 9-inch or 10-inch diameter heavyweight aluminum pie pans.

Electric Mixers

I tested all of these recipes with my KitchenAid mixer that has a 5-quart bowl. This mixer comes with a flat beater for beating, a wire whip for whipping, and a dough hook for kneading yeast dough. However, it is a considerable investment, and other standing countertop mixers will work fine in any of my recipes. Handheld mixers also work well for mixing cookies, and are especially good for mixing small amounts. Handheld mixers are less powerful than standing countertop electric mixers, so recipes usually require slightly longer beating times at a slightly higher mixing speed. Some double recipes of firm cookie doughs are too heavy to mix with less powerful handheld mixers; they should be mixed in separate batches.

Food Processors

Buy a machine with a large capacity and a powerful motor that can handle all jobs.

Freezers

Until we moved to Maine, I had never owned an upright freezer. For many years I used a side-by-side refrigerator/freezer combination, but there is no question that a freestanding freezer, which is opened infrequently and has its own temperature control, will maintain a more constant, colder temperature than a refrigerator/freezer combination and is preferable for storing frozen foods. If you lack space for a full freezer, a compact under-the-counter freezer is often a good solution. If freezer space is limited, try setting aside one small shelf or section of the freezer for cookies. It's surprising how many cookies can be frozen in a small space.

Ovens

Temperatures will vary about ten degrees within the oven, with the upper third and rear of the oven usually being the warmest. If your oven thermometer and oven thermostat register more than a ten degree difference, or if your cookies suddenly begin burning or underbaking during their normal baking period, the oven should be recalibrated. Even when they are calibrated to the correct temperature, different ovens will bake cookies faster or slower, so baking times are approximate and visual tests for doneness should be applied.

When you are baking in a standard oven, remember to reverse the sheets front to back and from lower rack to upper rack during the baking to ensure even browning. Be careful to avoid overloading the oven; you want the air to circulate properly. The middle shelf of the oven provides the most even temperature. Some cookies do not bake evenly if you try to bake two pans (on upper and lower shelves) at the same time. The solution is to bake one pan at a time on the middle rack.

My oven bakes with either convection or standard heat. Since most household ovens are the standard type, I tested all of these recipes using my oven as a standard oven, but I recommend baking with convection heat if you have it. Convection ovens have a fan that circulates the air in the oven to produce even heat throughout. Baking sheets seldom need to be rearranged for even browning, and cookies bake evenly. For convection baking, I follow the baking instructions for a recipe but lower the oven temperature 50°F. If cookies normally bake at 350°F, bake them at 300°F. Some manufacturers claim baking times will be shortened, but I find them to be the same as for standard oven baking.

Saucepans and Double Boilers

I use stainless steel saucepans, which will not react with acidic foods. They have either a copper- or aluminum-clad bottom to help the pans conduct heat evenly. My small saucepan holds one quart, the medium saucepan holds two quarts, and my two large saucepans hold three and four quarts, respectively.

My 2-quart saucepan has an insert to convert it into a double boiler. If you don't have a double boiler, heat a small amount of water in a 4-quart saucepan and place a 2-quart nonreactive saucepan filled with whatever needs to be heated over the 4-quart saucepan. The rim of the smaller saucepan must rest on the rim of the larger saucepan. It is easy to see the water in the saucepan below and prevent it from boiling or producing steam, which could harm a delicate ingredient like chocolate.

Scales

A scale with a removable bin on the top rather than a flat top is practical for kitchen use. (The bin holds whatever food must be weighed without the food rolling off the top of the scale.) I find a scale that measures in ounces or grams useful.

Thermometers

I use four kinds of thermometers—oven, freezer, food, and candy. I use a mercury oven thermometer to check my oven accuracy about once a week. My appliance repairman advised me that a mercury thermometer is most accurate for checking ovens. I leave a freezer thermometer in my freezer and adjust the freezer control to maintain a freezer temperature between 0° and 8°F. I use an instant-read food thermometer to measure temperatures from 0° to 220°F. Since this thermometer does not have to be clipped on the side of the pan, there is no worry about knocking the thermometer off the pan as you stir. Instant-read food thermometers are also useful for checking the temperature of ingredients, such as soft butter or hot milk. These thermometers actually register a temperature within ten to fifteen seconds, which is fast but not really instantaneous, so wear an oven mitt for protection from heat or steam. For measuring higher temperatures, I use a mercury candy thermometer. (Cookie techniques seldom require measuring these higher temperatures.) This candy thermometer can also double as an oven thermometer for temperatures up to 400°F. Do not leave it in the oven for a long period of time or in an oven set for a higher temperature than the thermometer is set to measure, since the glass tube can break if the thermometer overheats. I use Taylor thermometers; they are high quality and readily available.

Utensils

The following utensils and small tools are the ones I find useful to have on hand.

COOKIE CUTTERS

Cookie cutters are inexpensive and fun to collect. I use star and heart cutters most often and have several sizes of each. My box of assorted cutters has such holiday shapes as a bunny, four-leaf clover, tree, and gingerbread person. A set of alphabet cutters is useful for cutting out words for birthdays or good wishes.

COOLING RACKS

I use rectangular cooling racks with thin cross-woven wires. They support cookies without digging into soft ones. One rectangular rack usually holds one pan of cookies. When I cool bars or brownies in their pans, I place the pans on cooling racks so that air circulates and the bars cool evenly.

GRATERS

I use a four-sided box grater for grating citrus zest and chocolate. This type of grater rests securely on the counter. The tiny teardrop holes are best for grating zest. After I began teaching dessert classes around the country, I realized that some four-sided graters don't have teardrop holes. When you buy a box grater, check to see that it has one side with large holes and one side with these little teardrop holes.

KNIVES

I use a small, sharp paring knife with a 4¹/₂-inch blade to loosen bars and brownies from their pans, but a large chef's knife with an 8-inch blade works well for cutting them evenly.

MEASURING SPOONS AND CUPS

Have two sets of measuring spoons available, one for dry ingredients and one for wet ingredients. For accurate measuring, use dry measuring cups to measure dry ingredients and liquid measuring cups to measure liquid ingredients. It may sound obvious, but it makes a difference when measuring. Measure dry ingredients by filling the cup and leveling the top with a thin metal spatula. I sift dry ingredients after I measure them. For liquids, use cups with clear markings and place the cup on a flat surface when measuring. Liquid measuring cups in 1-, 2-, and

4-cup sizes are good to have on hand. Dry measuring cups are sold in sets of four gradations.

MIXING BOWLS

When I refer to small mixing bowls, they have a 2- to 3-cup capacity; medium a 6-cup capacity; and large, a 2- to 5-quart capacity. It is preferable to use a bowl that is too large rather than one that is too small. Pyrex bowls are heatproof and chip resistant, and I have been using the same set for over twenty-five years. Stainless steel bowls are easy to clean, will not react with ingredients, and are virtually unbreakable. I do not recommend plastic mixing bowls because they can absorb odors and fat.

MIXING SPOONS

Have at least one wooden spoon to use when cooking sugar to a high temperature. Since wood is a poor conductor of heat, a wooden spoon will not draw heat from a mixture, nor will it melt the spoon. For general mixing, I have several heatproof plastic mixing spoons that do not absorb odors as wooden spoons might.

BAKING PAN LINERS

I rarely butter or wash my baking sheets. It's not that I'm sloppy, but I line baking sheets with liners so that cookies don't stick to them; the sheets stay clean through repeated bakings. Parchment paper or the newly available nonstick liners work well. Parchment paper usually comes in rolls or large sheets and can be cut to fit baking pans. Discard it after each baking and line pans with clean paper. There are two types of nonstick liners to ensure that cookies never stick to the pan. Thin nonstick liners can be cut to fit baking sheets, or more expensive, thick Silpat nonstick liners can be bought finished in two sizes to fit most baking sheets. Both of them can be wiped clean and used repeatedly. Both liners are available from *King*

Arthur Flour Baker's Catalogue and Silpat liners are available from Bridge Kitchenware, listed in the mail order section at the end of the book. I recommend trying them.

Most ovens hold only two baking sheets. When baking more than two sheets of cookies, ready the remaining cookies on a piece of parchment paper or nonstick liner and slide them onto baking sheets as soon as the pans cool. Use pans with flat sides so the cookies stay in place when moved onto the sheet.

PASTRY BAGS AND PASTRY TIPS

I use Ateco cloth pastry bags with a plastic-coated lining that makes them easy to clean. Dry the pastry bags on a sunny windowsill to prevent them from developing a musty odor. A 16-inch pastry bag is a good all-purpose size. Clear plastic disposable pastry bags are another option; they are available from Bridge Kitchenware, listed in the mail order section at the end of the book. Ateco also makes good quality pastry tips that do not rust easily. Round tips with $3/8$- and $1/2$-inch openings are the ones I use most often. I prefer 2-inch-long pastry tips to the 1-inch-long size.

PASTRY BRUSH

Buy a good quality pastry brush that will not drop its bristles on your cookies. A brush 1 inch wide with 2-inch bristles is a useful size.

ROLLING PINS AND ROLLING SURFACES

I prefer a fixed rolling pin, without ball bearings but with handles. For a rolling surface, I use a freestanding white ceramic Corning Counter Saver with hard rubber feet. The surface remains cool; it measures a substantial 18 × 16 inches; it is lightweight; and it can be washed in the kitchen sink. When I'm not using it for rolling, it doubles as an extra cutting surface. I bought it at a local kitchen design center, but kitchen shops and department stores are another source.

SPATULAS

Use rubber spatulas to scrape bowls clean and fold mixtures together. I have a long narrow metal spatula with a 9 × 1-inch blade for lifting bars from pans and smoothing the top of firm cookie dough after I spread it in a pan. An offset spatula, which looks like a pancake turner with a long blade, is useful for sliding cookies off a baking sheet. I use a rigid pastry scraper to loosen shaped cookies from a rolling surface. The stainless steel blade is 5 × 3½ inches and does not have sharp edges.

STRAINERS AND SIFTERS

To strain fruit and sift dry ingredients, especially cocoa powder, I use a fine mesh strainer with a 7-inch top diameter; it holds about 4 cups of dry ingredients. It is easy to clean and does a fine job. When I want to remove every small seed from a fruit, I clean the strainer and strain the fruit a second time. I sift dry ingredients onto a large piece of wax paper to save cleaning an additional bowl. I have a flour sifter with a rotary handle, but if I use it to sift cocoa powder, it must be cleaned, a tedious chore.

WHISKS

Stainless steel sauce whisks are invaluable for whisking mixtures smooth.

Cookie Ingredients

Ten years ago, I couldn't find white chocolate in the Maine village (population 5,000) where I live. Now I can choose from at least three quality brands in my market. My local natural food store carries ten types of nuts and three varieties of dried apricots alone. Camden is not an isolated example. All around the country good and sophisticated ingredients are readily available and something like white chocolate has become commonplace. Any of the ingredients for these cookies should be as easy to find in your town as they are in my small village, so you can use your time for baking rather than shopping. There is a list of mail order sources at the end of the book, just in case you find it necessary to order an ingredient or some equipment.

Most cookies have short ingredient lists, so substituting something for natural flavorings, pure chocolate, or the correct shortening is go-ing to be noticeable. When butter makes up a large proportion of a cookie dough, changing the fat is going to affect the taste considerably, and not for the better. On the other hand, substituting butter for a vegetable shortening will alter the preferred texture of a cookie, and adding jumbo eggs instead of large eggs could produce a cookie that spreads all over the pan. The ingredients below are what I use when I bake cookies. Good ingredients make good cookies.

Butter, Shortening, and Oils

Unsalted butter should be used in all of the recipes requiring butter, and corn oil margarine with salt in any recipe that calls for margarine; I store both in my freezer to keep them fresh. Using unsalted butter allows you to control the exact amount of salt added to a recipe. I use Crisco for vegetable shortening and corn or canola oil for recipes requiring oil. Crisco is available in convenient bars that have markings for easy measuring. Check to see that the shortening is plain and not butter-flavored. Room temperature butter or margarine should test between 65°F and 75°F; check it once with a food thermometer to see exactly how it looks and feels at this temperature.

I often use margarine or vegetable shortening for the fat in spice cookies. The spices can mask any butter flavor, and margarine or vegetable shortening produces the crisp exterior and soft interior textures that I look for in a spice cookie.

Chocolate

In the United States, the Food and Drug Administration sets the requirements for each type of chocolate; each must contain a certain amount of chocolate liquor. Unsweetened chocolate is chocolate liquor and is required to contain 50 to 58 percent cocoa butter. Unsweetened cocoa powder is chocolate liquor with some of the cocoa butter pressed out, and it must contain from 10 to 22 percent cocoa butter.

European standards differ from ours and comparisons are difficult to make, but the United States requirements for sweet chocolate are based on the amount of chocolate liquor as follows:

SEMISWEET CHOCOLATE
15 to 35 percent chocolate liquor

BITTERSWEET CHOCOLATE
at least 35 percent chocolate liquor

MILK CHOCOLATE
at least 10 percent chocolate liquor with added milk solids

White chocolate contains cocoa butter, sugar, milk solids, and flavorings. The Food and Drug Administration is currently working on a standard of identity for white chocolate and has issued temporary permits that allow some white chocolate products containing cocoa butter to be labeled white chocolate rather than white confectionery coating.

European companies usually list the cocoa butter (cocoa fat) content of their chocolate, and you can use this to judge if the type of chocolate is suitable for the dessert you plan to bake. For instance, if a European chocolate has 40 percent cocoa butter, it is at the low end of United States bittersweet chocolate requirements and could be used for a recipe that calls for semisweet or bittersweet chocolate.

I choose the same chocolate for baking that I enjoy eating. Try buying several brands of quality chocolate to taste. Choose the ones that you prefer and then use them in your cookies. The following brands of chocolate are the ones I use most in my baking, and the ones I used to test the recipes in this book:

UNSWEETENED CHOCOLATE
Baker's, Nestlé, and Guittard

SEMISWEET CHOCOLATE
Baker's, Guittard, Dove Bar, and Callebaut

BITTERSWEET CHOCOLATE
Guittard, Lindt, and Callebaut

SEMISWEET CHOCOLATE CHIPS
Nestlé and Guittard

MILK CHOCOLATE
Lindt, Dove Bar, and Callebaut

WHITE CHOCOLATE
Callebaut, Lindt, and Baker's Premium White Chocolate Baking Squares

WHITE CHOCOLATE CHIPS
Ghirardelli Classic White Chips and Guittard Vanilla Milk Chips

UNSWEETENED COCOA POWDER
Droste or Hershey's European Style
(both are Dutch process)

If stored properly, unsweetened and dark chocolate can be stored for as long as a year. I wrap chocolate tightly in plastic wrap, then in aluminum foil, and store it in a cool, dark place. Ideally the storage temperature should range between 60°F and 70°F. Milk chocolate and white chocolate contain milk solids and thus are more perishable. I store milk chocolate and white chocolate tightly wrapped in a cool, dry place up to 1 month or freeze it for up to six months. To freeze chocolate, break any large blocks into one-pound pieces and wrap tightly in plastic wrap and heavy aluminum foil. Defrost the wrapped chocolate in a cool, dry place at room temperature to prevent moisture from forming. If moisture condenses on chocolate, some of the sugar can dissolve and produce sugar bloom, which forms an undesirable crusty, grainy surface on the outside of the chocolate. Sugar bloom is different from fat bloom, which occurs when chocolate is exposed to warm temperatures. Here the cocoa butter melts slightly, then firms again, and a whitish film forms on the outside of the chocolate. Aside from appearance, fat bloom doesn't harm the chocolate, but it does indicate that chocolate has not been shipped or stored under ideal conditions. During warm weather, taste chocolate before using it, especially milk chocolate or white chocolate, to verify that it still has a good, fresh chocolate taste.

Tightly sealed unsweetened cocoa powder that is stored at room temperature will keep in good condition for up to two years.

Citrus and Citrus Zest

Use fresh citrus juice for all of the recipes. Citrus zest is the rind of the fruit without any of the bitter white pith. Before grating zest from citrus fruit, wash the fruit with warm water and dry it.

Cream and Milk

Heavy whipping cream contains from 36 to 40 percent butterfat. Cartons may be labeled "heavy whipping cream," "whipping cream," or "heavy cream." I use the term *heavy whipping cream.* I use heavy whipping cream for whipped cream toppings and fillings. For other recipes light whipping cream, which has slightly less fat, works fine.

Light whipping cream contains from 30 to 36 percent butterfat and is the cream that I use most often. Cartons may be labeled "light whipping cream" or "whipping cream," which is the designation I use.

I have noted on the recipes if the recipe requires a particular milk or if any fat content milk is suitable.

Buttermilk is low-fat or fat-free milk that has been cultured with bacteria. It has a thick texture and slightly sour taste. I use fat-free buttermilk in my recipes.

Condensed milk is sweetened milk that has been heated to evaporate some of its water and thicken it. It is available in full-fat, low-fat, and no-fat versions. I use them interchangeably in the recipes that call for condensed milk and find they all work well. I did notice when I checked the nutritional information on the can that the calorie difference between full-fat and no-fat condensed milk is quite small.

Eggs

Large eggs are used in the recipes in this book. Cold eggs are easier to separate, and bacteria are less likely to multiply in an egg that is kept cold.

If you have egg whites left over from a recipe, freeze them for up to three months. Put them in a clean, grease-free plastic freezer container, leaving at least an inch of air space, press plastic wrap onto the surface of the egg whites, and cover tightly. Label with the date and the number of egg whites in the container. I defrost the covered egg whites overnight in the refrigerator. I do not freeze or store leftover egg yolks. Either use them immediately or discard them. Fortunately, eggs are one of the less expensive baking ingredients.

Flavorings and Spices

Always use pure vanilla extract. It would be better to omit vanilla than to use an artificial substitute. I tested the recipes with McCormick vanilla extract, which is readily available. Pure almond extract, containing oil of bitter almond, is now available in my supermarket. I used McCormick pure almond extract for testing these recipes. It adds a pleasant almond flavor to cookies, and doesn't leave that aftertaste that almond extract prepared from chemicals can.

Although cookie recipes seldom include liqueur, several of the bars and the Milk Chocolate and Almond Praline Truffles call for liqueur as a flavoring. Too much liqueur can cause a bitter taste, so I add it sparingly.

I use decaffeinated, freeze-dried instant coffee granules to add coffee flavoring to desserts. To dissolve the coffee, mix equal parts of hot liquid and instant coffee.

Use fresh spices and store them tightly covered. Storage times and conditions for different spices vary; a simple way to check to see if a spice is fresh is to taste it. If it is stale, it will add little or no taste to a dessert. Although I used supermarket cinnamon to test the recipes, extra fancy China Tunghing cinnamon, an exceptionally strong sweet cinnamon, and extra fancy Vietnamese cassia cinnamon, a strong spicy cinnamon, are worth trying. The Vietnamese cassia cinnamon is closest to the supermarket version, but has a sweeter and stronger cinnamon flavor. Both are available from Penzey's Spice House Ltd. (see page 224).

Preserved ginger is young shoots of ginger that are cooked and preserved in a thick sugar syrup. The pieces of ginger become soft and candied from the process. Raffetto Stem Ginger in Syrup is the brand most commonly found in the United States. Preserved ginger is expensive, but it adds an unmatched quality to the Grasmere Crisp Ginger Shortbread. I noticed on a recent trip to England that preserved ginger costs about a third as much there as it does in the United States, but it's a lot less expensive to buy it here than to fly to England.

Flour

I tested the recipes using either unbleached all-purpose flour, cake flour, or whole wheat flour. Cake flour contains less gluten than all-purpose flour; it is usually packaged in two-pound boxes. A combination of all-purpose flour and cake flour produces an especially tender cookie. Whole wheat flour contains wheat germ, and should be stored in the refrigerator to prevent the fat in the wheat germ from turning the flour rancid. The combination of all-purpose flour and whole wheat flour in the Grasmere Crisp Ginger Shortbread adds a nutty taste and crisp texture. Store flour tightly covered, and keep it dry.

Leavening Agents

Air, steam, baking soda, and baking powder leaven these cookies. Air is beaten into doughs and batters, and the liquid in doughs and batters produces steam during baking. Baking soda and baking powder are ingredients that, when activated in some way, produce carbon dioxide gas cells in a batter or dough. These gas cells, like tiny bubbles or air pockets, form during baking and lighten the batter or dough.

Baking soda or sodium bicarbonate is an alkaline leavening that is activated when it is combined with an acid ingredient like sour cream, molasses, or buttermilk. If kept dry, baking soda can be stored indefinitely.

Baking powder contains baking soda (alkaline), plus an acid ingredient, and is activated when combined with a liquid. Double-acting baking powders contain two acid ingredients, one activated by liquid and one activated by heat. I use double-acting baking powder. Store baking powder tightly covered, and do not use it past the expiration date on the can.

Nuts

I use blanched almonds (without skins), unblanched almonds (with skins), pecans, walnuts, hazelnuts, macadamia nuts (preferably unsalted), unsalted roasted cashew nuts, lightly salted peanuts, unsalted roasted pistachio nuts, and pine nuts. Generally, the new crop of nuts appears in supermarkets from September to December; this is a good time to buy a year's supply. Store the nuts in the freezer in a tightly sealed heavy-duty freezer bag or plastic freezer container. Fresh nuts can be stored for a month in the refrigerator, but the freezer is best for longer storage.

Sugars

Four types of sugar are used in the recipes: granulated sugar, superfine granulated sugar, brown sugar, and powdered sugar. Superfine granulated sugar has a finer crystal size than granulated sugar. It forms an especially smooth mixture when blended with butter and produces a fine-textured, tender shortbread. Brown sugar contains molasses, with light brown sugar having less molasses than dark brown sugar. Powdered sugar, or confectioners' sugar, is granulated sugar that has been ground to a powder. Cornstarch is added to powdered sugar to prevent caking, but it's still a good idea to sift powdered sugar before using it to remove any lumps. Store all sugar tightly covered and in a dry place; brown sugar should be stored in a tightly sealed plastic bag to preserve its moisture.

Lyle's Golden Syrup is cane sugar syrup produced in England. In some recipes where the flavor of the syrup is noticeable, I prefer it to light corn syrup. Use the same quantity if you substitute one for the other. Lyle's Golden Syrup is stocked with the corn syrup or pancake syrups in my supermarket.

Freezing and Shipping Cookies

If ever a dessert was designed for baking, freezing, and mailing, it's cookies. Most cookies have the low moisture content required for successful freezing, take up little space in the freezer, wrap easily for freezer storage, and defrost quickly. Although many cookies retain their quality when kept at room temperature for a few days, the freezer allows you to store them for as long as three months and have one or a dozen "freshly baked" cookies ready whenever you want them. There is no chance for crisp cookies to become soft from humidity, for frostings to melt from heat, or for any cookie to lose its fresh taste. It is important to understand what happens when cookies freeze, to know the best way to protect them in the freezer, and to defrost them properly. Some of the following information was previously published in *Bake and Freeze Chocolate Desserts,* and is repeated here for your convenience.

Freezer Temperatures

Try to keep your freezer temperature as close to 0°F as possible. Most home freezers are designed to maintain a temperature between 0°F and 8°F. I keep a freezer thermometer in the back of my freezer and adjust the thermostat as necessary. Try to keep temperature fluctuations to a minimum by opening the freezer door as little as possible and not adding a lot of unfrozen items to your freezer at the same time.

Wrapping Cookies for Freezing

Wrapping cookies carefully before freezing them is such a simple task that you might overlook its importance. The air in the freezer is dry and has a natural inclination to pull moisture from any food that it comes in contact with. If you think about how your skin feels after a winter of dry, cold weather, you'll understand what the concentrated cold, dry freezer air could do to a poorly wrapped cookie. This dry air will find any hole in the packaging or gap in a seal and draw the moisture out of your carefully prepared cookies. The "freezer burn" with which we are all familiar is an example of what happens to food that has been exposed to dry freezer air and has had the moisture sucked out of it. Since it is impractical to package cookies in a vacuum, some moisture will be lost, but good packaging holds this loss to a minimum.

Your carefully prepared desserts are worth spending a few extra pennies on the best supplies for wrapping them. I use heavy-duty freezer bags, heavy aluminum foil, plastic wrap, rigid plastic freezer containers, and metal tins. This supply list is short, but it offers maximum protection from air, moisture, and odors. Heavyweight aluminum foil is so easy to use that I prefer it to the polycoated freezer wrap that requires tape for sealing. Square or rectangular containers that can be stacked take up less room in your freezer than round containers. Saran Wrap, made from polyvinylidene chloride, is the plastic wrap rated as having the best barrier against water and odor transmission. Do not reuse bags from the produce department, which are too lightweight to offer protection.

Packaging cookies properly is quite simple. Plain cookies, brownies, bars, truffles, small tarts, and individual cakes should be individually wrapped in plastic wrap, then placed in a metal or rigid plastic container and covered tightly. Use clean plastic containers that are free of any odors. Clean and dry coffee or shortening tins work fine for containers. Wrapping individual cookies in plastic wrap before putting them in a container rather than just stacking them in makes an enormous difference. It may seem time-consuming, but it actually takes only a few minutes to add this protection from the air that is inevitably trapped in the container, so the desserts won't pick up off flavors or develop the dreaded "freezer taste." If cookies aren't sticky, wrap several together. I pack cookies for gift-giving in attractive metal tins and freeze them, ready to deliver. Brownies or bars are less likely to break than crisp cookies if moved around in the freezer, so they can be wrapped in plastic wrap, then sealed in heavy-duty plastic freezer bags. Large pieces or a whole pan of bars and brownies should be tightly wrapped with plastic wrap, then with a layer of heavy aluminum foil. The plastic wrap fits smoothly against the bars and forms a tight seal, while the heavy aluminum foil provides a strong barrier against moisture and resists punctures. Check your packages to make sure the contents are covered completely and that containers are sealed tightly. Cookies, tea cakes, or bars with frosting or soft toppings should be put in the freezer to firm the soft top before being wrapped.

Labeling Cookies

Whenever I open my freezer and see the labels on all those packages and containers, I'm reminded of how important it is to mark each one. It takes only a few extra seconds to label packages with the date and contents. There is always a roll of masking tape and a pen in my kitchen drawer, so I'm never tempted to put off labeling. Plastic freezer bags usually have a white area where you can write information with a ballpoint pen or felt tip marker. Since a cold, moist surface is difficult to apply a label to or to write on, label packages before they go into the freezer.

Defrosting Cookies

Although defrosting cookies is a no-work task, these recommendations should be helpful.

Generally, if cookies will be served cold, defrost them in the refrigerator, and if they will be served at room temperature, defrost them at room temperature. Keep cookies wrapped or in covered containers while they defrost; that way, the moisture that forms as they defrost forms on the wrappings, not on the cookies.

Most cookies take about one or two hours to defrost, but times can vary even for the same type of cookie. Room temperatures change with the seasons, and the warmer the room the shorter the thawing time. Even your refrigerator will be colder on a winter day than on a summer day, and cookies may require more time to defrost. Thick bars such as Key Lime Bars take longer to

defrost than thin lace-type cookies. After baked cookies defrost, they're ready to serve. Each of the recipes gives specific storage suggestions.

Preventing the Cookie Crumbles

If such a job existed, I could be a professional cookie mailer. Once I realized many years ago that cookies were an easy dessert to ship successfully, I've sent off hundreds of cookie packages. I mail cookies for any reason—birthdays, holidays, cheer-up packages, edible thank-you notes, or just no-excuse cookie surprises. With all of this mailing experience, I've devised some packaging techniques to ensure that my cookies arrive undamaged and tasting fresh.

Choosing the Best Cookies to Ship

Most cookies travel well if packed properly. The only types of cookies that I don't try to mail are delicate crisp ones that break easily such as Cashew Lace Crisps or Almond Tuiles, or the few that require refrigeration such as Key Lime Bars. Some cookie fillings, especially chocolate ones, melt in warm temperatures and are best saved for cool weather shipping. Some types of cookies are less likely to crumble during shipping than others. Soft brownies and bars seldom break unless they're actually crushed, but shortbread, wafer, and cookie sandwiches need to be packed with care. If a cookie can be stored without refrigeration for at least three days without losing any flavor, it's usually a good choice for mailing.

Packing Cookies to Arrive Safely

The two secrets of good cookie packaging are to use plenty of packing material and to double-box all packages. Start your packing by choosing one or two rigid plastic containers or tins large enough to hold the cookies for mailing. Find a sturdy carton that will hold the cookie containers and a generous amount of packing material. For crisp or wafer cookies, put two cookie bottoms together and wrap them in plastic wrap. Wrap sticky cookies, brownies, and bars individually in plastic wrap. Fill the bottom of the cookie container with a layer of crumpled wax paper about $3/4$ inch thick. Stack the wrapped cookies in the container, putting a piece of wax paper between each cookie layer to prevent shifting. Fill any air spaces with crumpled wax paper. Leave 1 inch of space at the top of the container and fill this with crumpled wax paper. The container should be full but not packed tightly. Seal the container tightly and tape the top with masking tape to secure it. Wrap the container carefully in newspaper, using enough paper to make a layer about 1 inch thick that provides a uniform cushion around it. To pack the carton, add a cushion of crumpled newspaper or packing material to the bottom. Place the cookie container or containers in the carton. The cookie container should not touch the sides or top of the carton. Add crumpled newspaper or packing material around the cookie container until it fits securely in the carton. This produces a cushioned container inside a cushioned box that offers excellent protection. I enclose a note that lists the contents so that cookies aren't accidentally thrown away with the packing material. Seal the carton with package sealing tape, and rest assured that you've given your cookies a good sendoff.

Ship by the Best Method

Overnight delivery is a good choice, but it's expensive and not always necessary. If the cookies will remain fresh for up to three days, try the priority mail service from the post office, or check shipping schedules with United Parcel Service. To avoid having my cookies sit in some warehouse over a weekend, I ship perishables on a Monday or a Tuesday. In a pinch, I'll gamble on a Wednesday, but without using overnight service, it's risky.

Carrying Cookies Around

I transport cookies often. They go to friends, picnics, and even get packed in my luggage. When taking cookies somewhere by car, I transport them wrapped securely in a covered container. Then I never have cookies sliding around the back seat. After I arrive with my cookies, it's easy to arrange them on serving plates. To pack cookies in my luggage, I package them carefully in a rigid container with plenty of wax paper, just as if I were going to mail them. Remember to tape the top of the container so that it doesn't come open in your suitcase, and cushion the container with clothes. Packed this way, my cookies have traveled around the world and arrived safely.

The Frozen Pantry

y freezer is an extension of my pantry, except that instead of flour and sugar, it's filled with crusts, sauces, and fillings. If I have a pan of butter crust for some bars or a container of Caramel Filling ready in my freezer, I know that I can whip up a batch of cookies at a moment's notice.

Some of these components can become complete desserts. If I bake a pan of Butter Pastry for Tassies from my freezer and fill them with some defrosted Lemon Curd, I can have instant lemon tarts. Many of the items don't even require defrosting. Pastry crusts hold their shape well when baked frozen, Nut Pralines can be added to cookies directly from their freezer container, and frozen crusts for bars only need to bake a few minutes longer than freshly made crusts.

When preparing one of these items for a recipe, try making a double quantity and freezing the extra share for later. It takes about the same time to prepare and clean up a double recipe as a single batch, and you'll be off to a good start for the next baking day.

This list of timesavers is short, but they make cookie baking as easy as opening your freezer door.

Chocolate Truffle Sauce, Filling, and Glaze

utter, cream, chocolate, and vanilla—a winning combination if ever I heard one. That's all it takes to produce this versatile chocolate mixture. If cooled until thickened, it becomes a fudge filling for cookie sandwiches or a chocolate glaze for bars, and warmed it's a rich fudge sauce. When whipped, the mixture turns into a creamy filling for truffles and tassies. It's a great example of keeping it simple and using good ingredients.

MAKES ABOUT 1 CUP

> ¹/₂ cup whipping cream
> 1 tablespoon unsalted butter
> 1 cup (6 ounces) semisweet chocolate chips or semisweet chocolate, chopped
> ¹/₂ teaspoon vanilla extract

Put the cream and butter in a medium saucepan and heat over medium-low heat until the cream is hot and the butter is melted. The hot cream mixture will form tiny bubbles and measure about 175°F on a food thermometer. Do not let it boil. Remove the pan from the heat. Add the chocolate and let it soften in the hot cream mixture for about 30 seconds. Add the vanilla and whisk the sauce until it is smooth and all of the chocolate is melted.

Good Advice: Stir the chocolate gently into the hot cream mixture so that it doesn't splash out of the pan. *To Freeze:* Pour the sauce into a plastic freezer container, leaving 1 inch of space at the top. Cover loosely and cool for 1 hour at room temperature. Press a piece of plastic wrap onto the top of the sauce and cover the container tightly. Or, divide each recipe of sauce between 2 plastic containers. Label with the date and contents. Freeze up to 2 months. *To Serve:* Defrost in the covered container overnight in the refrigerator. Warm the sauce in a medium saucepan over low heat, stirring frequently. Cool the mixture and use as directed in the recipes. If you need the sauce in a hurry and don't have time to defrost it, run hot water over the covered container to loosen the sides and transfer the frozen sauce to a heatproof container. Place over (but not touching) barely simmering water and warm, stirring often. Leftover sauce can be stored up to 2 weeks in the refrigerator.

Press-in Butter Crust for Bars

This tender butter crust forms the base for many bars. The dough is mixed with an electric beater until crumbs form, then pressed into the bottom of the baking pan—no rolling whatsoever. Granulated sugar, brown sugar, or powdered sugar works equally well as the sweetener, and I usually choose to match the sugar called for in the filling.

CRUST FOR 8 × 8 × 2- OR 9 × 9 × 2-INCH PAN

1 cup unbleached all-purpose flour
$^1/_4$ cup granulated sugar, powdered sugar, or packed light brown sugar
$^1/_8$ teaspoon salt
8 tablespoons (1 stick) cold unsalted butter, cut into 8 pieces

CRUST FOR 13 × 9 × 2-INCH PAN

$1^1/_2$ cups unbleached all-purpose flour
6 tablespoons granulated sugar, powdered sugar, or packed light brown sugar
$^1/_8$ teaspoon salt
12 tablespoons ($1^1/_2$ sticks) cold unsalted butter, cut into 12 pieces

Butter the bottom and sides of the baking pan of your choice. Put the flour and granulated sugar, powdered sugar, or light brown sugar and the salt in the bowl of an electric mixer and mix on low speed just to blend the ingredients, about 10 seconds. Add the butter. Increase the speed to medium and mix until fine crumbs form, about 1 minute. (Some large crumbs, about $^1/_4$ inch in size, will remain.) Transfer the mixture to the prepared pan and press it evenly over the bottom.

Good Advice: Using cold butter produces the desired crumbly dough. You can mix it with a pastry blender, but I prefer an electric mixer, which takes about 1 minute. **To Freeze:** Press plastic wrap firmly onto the crust. Wrap with heavy aluminum foil, pressing the foil tightly around the edges of the pan. Freeze up to 1 month. Do not defrost the crust before baking.

Cookie Crumb Crusts for Bars

ookie crumb crusts make an appropriate choice for bars. They go well with fruit, chocolate, or nut flavors, and they keep recipes simple. I buy prepared graham cracker crumbs or use a food processor to grind plain chocolate wafers to crumbs, add melted butter and any appropriate spices, and press them into the pan of my choice. Although the baking time is short, it's an important step that produces a crisp crust.

GRAHAM CRACKER CRUST FOR 13 × 9 × 2-INCH PAN

2 cups graham cracker crumbs
$^3/_4$ teaspoon ground cinnamon
7 tablespoons unsalted butter, melted

THICK GRAHAM CRACKER CRUST FOR 9 × 9 × 2-INCH PAN

$2^1/_4$ cups graham cracker crumbs
$^3/_4$ teaspoon ground cinnamon
8 tablespoons (1 stick) unsalted butter, melted

CHOCOLATE WAFER COOKIE CRUMB CRUST
FOR 8 × 8 × 1- OR 8 × 8 × 2-INCH PAN

$1^3/_4$ cups chocolate wafer cookie crumbs
4 tablespoons ($^1/_2$ stick) unsalted butter, melted

1. Position a rack in the middle of the oven and preheat the oven to 300°F. Line the pan of your choice with heavy aluminum foil, letting the foil extend over the ends of the pan. Butter the bottom and sides of the aluminum foil.

2. Put the cookie crumbs and cinnamon, if used, in a large bowl and mix together. Add the melted butter and stir until the crumbs are evenly moistened with the butter. Transfer the crumbs to the prepared pan. Using your fingers, press them evenly over the bottom and $^1/_2$ inch up the sides of the foil. Press chocolate crumbs only over the bottom of the pan. Bake the graham cracker crumb crust for 8 minutes and the chocolate crumb crust for 10 minutes. Cool the crust thoroughly before filling or freezing it. Crumb crusts can be baked a day ahead, covered, and stored overnight at room temperature.

Good Advice: I use Nabisco Famous Chocolate Wafers to make chocolate cookie crumbs. **To Freeze:** Press plastic wrap tightly onto the cooled crumb crust. Cover the pan with heavy aluminum foil and press the foil tightly around the edges of the pan. Freeze up to 1 month.

Butter Pastry for Tassies

his tender butter pastry is similar to a cookie dough. I use it for lining mini-muffin tins to make small individual tart crusts. The pastry is comfortable to work with and tolerates mixing a bit longer than necessary, as well as repeated rolling.

PASTRY FOR 24 MINI-MUFFIN TINS

1 large cold egg
$1/2$ teaspoon vanilla extract
1 cup unbleached all-purpose flour
$1/4$ cup cake flour
$1/3$ cup powdered sugar
$1/2$ teaspoon baking powder
$1/8$ teaspoon salt
8 tablespoons (1 stick) cold unsalted butter, cut into 8 pieces

1. Have ready 2 nonstick mini-muffin tins with 12 openings each.

2. Put the egg and vanilla in a small bowl and mix with a fork just to blend. Put the flours, powdered sugar, baking powder, and salt in the large bowl of an electric mixer and mix on low speed just to blend the ingredients, about 10 seconds. Add the butter and mix until most of the butter pieces are the size of peas, about 2 minutes. The mixture will look crumbly and the crumbs will vary in size. With the mixer running, add the egg mixture. Beat until the dough clings together and pulls away from the sides of the bowl, about 20 seconds. It will look smooth and have a golden color.

3. Form the dough into a round disk about 6 inches in diameter. Wrap in plastic wrap and refrigerate until firm, for at least 1 hour or overnight.

4. Remove the dough from the refrigerator and unwrap it. If it is too hard to roll, let it sit at room temperature for about 15 minutes until it softens a bit. Lightly flour the rolling surface and rolling pin. Roll the dough out $1/8$ inch thick. Don't flip it over while rolling, but lift and turn it several times to prevent it from sticking. Dust the rolling surface and rolling pin with more flour as necessary.

5. Cut the dough into $2^3/4$-inch circles. Gather the dough scraps together and roll and cut them. You should have 24 circles. Place a circle in each mini-muffin tin and gently press the dough into the bottom and against the sides. It will have a smooth edge and sit $1/4$ inch above the lip of each opening. Repeat with the remaining dough circles.

To Freeze: Wrap each filled tin tightly with plastic wrap, then with heavy aluminum foil. Label with the date and contents. Freeze up to 2 months. Once the pastry is frozen, the tins can be stacked. **To Bake the Pastry Blind:** Preheat the oven to 400°F. Unwrap the frozen pastry. Press a small piece of heavy aluminum foil into each frozen crust, covering the edges. Fill the foil with raw rice, dried beans, or metal pie weights. Place the pans on a baking sheet. Bake for 10 minutes. Carefully remove the pie weights and aluminum foil. The edges will be brown. Reduce the oven temperature to 350°F. Bake about 10 minutes more, or until the bottom is firm and looks dry. If you are filling the pastry with a filling that doesn't require baking, cool the crust thoroughly before adding the filling.

Lemon Curd

Lemon curd is a thick lemon butter sauce that makes a filling for Lemon Tassies, is spread in the middle of Lemon Macaroon Sandwiches, or can be mixed with whipped cream for a quick lemon cream filling. It never freezes firm, so you can keep a container in the freezer and scoop out just what you need when you're ready to use it. The only difficulty with making lemon curd is that the egg whites cook faster than the yolks and form undesirable white bits that must be strained out. After trying for years to figure out the solution, I found the answer in the most unlikely place. 🏃 I was having my hair cut when my hairdresser, Mary Jane Duncan, said she had inadvertently beaten the ingredients together for the lemon curd recipe from *Bake and Freeze Desserts* before cooking them, and the Lemon Curd came out smooth and didn't need any straining. I myself was straining at the bit to get home and try her new method. It works; the curd is smooth, velvety, and has nary a white bit floating around anywhere.

MAKES ABOUT 2 CUPS

> 6 tablespoons ($^3/_4$ stick) soft unsalted butter
> 1 cup sugar
> 2 large eggs
> 2 large egg yolks
> $^1/_2$ cup fresh lemon juice
> 1 teaspoon grated lemon zest

1. Put the butter and sugar in the large bowl of an electric mixer and beat on medium speed until the mixture is fluffy and lightens from a yellow to a cream color. Add the eggs and yolks one at a time. Beat for 1 more minute. Mix in the lemon juice. The mixture will look curdled.

2. Put the mixture in a medium saucepan and cook over medium-low heat, stirring constantly, until the mixture looks smooth. The curdling disappears as the butter melts. Increase the heat to medium and cook, stirring constantly, until the mixture thickens, leaves a path on the back of a spoon, and measures 170°F on a food thermometer. Stir the sauce often where the bottom and sides of the saucepan meet to prevent burning. Do not let the mixture boil. Remove from the heat and stir in the lemon zest.

3. Pour the lemon curd into a plastic freezer container, leaving at least an inch of space at the top. Press plastic wrap onto the surface and chill the curd in the refrigerator. It will thicken further as it cools.

VARIATION   **Orange Curd:** Use the following ingredients and follow the directions for preparing lemon curd: 8 tablespoons (1 stick) soft unsalted butter; 1 cup sugar; 2 large eggs, and 2 large yolks; $^1/_3$ cup fresh orange juice; 2 tablespoons fresh lemon juice; and tablespoon grated orange zest. This makes about 2 cups.

To Freeze: Cover the chilled curd tightly. Label with the date and contents. Freeze up to 2 months.
To Use: Spoon the necessary amount of Lemon Curd from the container and defrost it in the refrigerator for about 2 hours or overnight, until it is spreadable.

Caramel Filling

his may be a simple mixture of cooked sugar and cream, but it has a multitude of uses. It forms ribbons of caramel inside and a sticky caramel glaze on top of Banana Caramel Brownies, it can be mixed with nuts for a filling for Caramel Cashew Bars, and when warmed becomes an instant rich sauce for pouring over ice cream. When caramelizing the sugar, just watch it carefully so it doesn't burn and you will have no trouble. As my son, Peter, recently told me when I was impressed by a caramel dessert he made, "Once you practice making caramel a few times, it's easy."

MAKES ABOUT 2 CUPS

1^1/$_2$ cups whipping cream
2 cups sugar

1. Heat the cream in a small saucepan and keep it hot, about 150°F if measured with a food thermometer, without boiling it. The mixture will form tiny bubbles around the edge of the pan.

2. Put ^{1}/$_2$ cup water and the sugar in a 4-quart heavy-bottomed saucepan. Cover and cook over low heat until the sugar dissolves, about 5 minutes, stirring occasionally. Remove the cover, increase the heat to medium-high, and bring to a boil. Boil until the sugar melts, caramelizes, and turns a dark golden color, about 5 minutes. Watch the sugar carefully and stir it with a wooden spoon occasionally to be sure it cooks evenly and all of it caramelizes. Remove from the heat.

3. Slowly and cautiously add the hot cream to the hot sugar. The mixture will bubble up, so be careful. Return the saucepan to low heat and cook, stirring with the wooden spoon, until the caramel is completely dissolved and the mixture is smooth. The caramel mixture is ready to use, or it can be covered and refrigerated up to 2 weeks or frozen up to 2 months.

VARIATION   To make Coffee Caramel Sauce, dissolve 2 teaspoons instant decaffeinated coffee granules in the whipping cream. Heat the dissolved coffee with the cream in the small saucepan.

Good Advice: As the sugar cooks, it may crystallize and harden. Keep cooking it and the mixture will become smooth when the sugar melts and caramelizes.   Use a wooden spoon to stir the caramel. It will not retain heat and burn you as a metal spoon could.   Cook caramel in a large saucepan so that the mixture doesn't bubble up out of the pot. **Doubling the Recipe:** Use a large saucepan, about 8-quart size, for a double recipe. **To Freeze:** Pour the warm sauce into a plastic freezer container or divide it between 2 such containers, leaving at least an inch of space in the top. Loosely cover and cool for 1 hour at room temperature. Press plastic wrap onto the surface of the caramel sauce and chill thoroughly. Cover the container tightly. Label with the date and contents and freeze up to 2 months. **To Serve or Use:** Defrost in the refrigerator overnight, or at room temperature for about 5 hours. Put the filling in a medium saucepan and warm it over low heat just until it pours easily.

Nut Pralines

Cooking sugar to the caramel stage and combining it with nuts produces praline. Although praline looks as if it's complicated to make, it's really just a simple process of melting and cooking the sugar to a dark golden color. There isn't even the usual concern about the sugar crystallizing and turning grainy, since caramelized sugar is cooked to such a high temperature that it loses its ability to recrystallize. The only time I ruin a batch of praline is when I don't watch it carefully and the sugar burns. Then I must discard it and start over, but it's just a bit of sugar and a little time. The one caution is not to splash any of this very hot sugar on yourself. 🏃 After praline cools and hardens, it can be crushed into small pieces or ground in a food processor. The crushed praline can bake into a crunchy topping for cookies or brownies while ground praline can flavor frostings and truffles. Although almonds and hazelnuts are the traditional nuts used for praline, any nut can benefit from being coated with the caramelized sugar.

MAKES 2 CUPS

³/₄ **cup sugar**
1 cup nuts, such as blanched slivered almonds, unsalted cashew nuts,
    toasted skinned hazelnuts, unsalted chopped macadamia nuts,
    roasted unsalted pistachio nuts, pecans, or walnuts

1. Lightly oil a metal baking sheet.

2. Put the sugar in a large, heavy frying pan or medium saucepan, preferably with a nonstick finish, and cook over low heat. Stir occasionally with a wooden spoon to be sure the sugar melts evenly. When it begins to melt, increase the heat to medium and cook the melted sugar to a light golden color. Add the nuts, stirring with the wooden spoon to coat them completely with the caramelized sugar, about 1 minute. The mixture will turn a slightly darker golden color. Immediately pour the praline onto the prepared baking sheet and spread it with the wooden spoon. Be careful; the mixture is very hot. Cool the praline until it hardens and is cool to the touch.

3. Break the praline into 1- to 2-inch pieces. Wrap several pieces of praline in heavy aluminum foil. Crush the praline with a clean mallet, rolling pin, or meat pounder into approximately ¹/₄- to ³/₈-inch pieces. Repeat with the remaining praline. To prepare praline powder, transfer the crushed praline to a food processor fitted with a metal blade and process just until the praline forms a powder. Overprocessing can turn it into a paste. Use the same day or freeze.

Good Advice: It is easy to melt the sugar evenly if you cook it in a nonstick pan. 🏃 Stir smaller nuts or chopped nuts constantly after you add them to the sugar, since they burn easily. The larger the nut, the less the praline will spread when you pour it onto the baking sheet to cool. 🏃 Brush away loose skins from pistachio nuts before adding them to the sugar. **To Freeze:** Put crushed or ground praline in a plastic freezer container. Press plastic wrap onto the praline. Cover the container tightly and freeze up to 3 months. Praline can be used directly from the freezer. Spoon out the amount needed and return the rest to the freezer.

Kid Easy Cookies

Most cookies are so easy to prepare that for a while this chapter was growing as fast as Jack's beanstalk. I finally trimmed the list by including only cookies that met three criteria. They had to mix together quickly, be virtually foolproof, and be easy to form. Children can easily make these cookies with some supervision, but they're for kids of all ages. Any of these cookies would make a good choice for one's first foray into cookie baking.

The cookies range from sophisticated Chocolate Truffle Squares to a butter-filled shortbread to the Sticky Tiffin Bar specialty that traveled from the far north of England. Graham crackers, pecans, marshmallows, and milk chocolate make a cookie version of the campfire treats you made as a child. Even my husband, Jeff, who is normally a cookie taster, not a cookie baker, bakes Super S'mores. Uncle Howie's brown sugar and butterscotch chip bars continue my uncle's tradition of coming up with new versions of our family chocolate chip cake. This time he's turned the cake into a butterscotch-fudge bar. My sister, Susan, contributed a contender for easiest cookie in the book, her three-ingredient oatmeal bars. When you want homemade cookies fast, you'll find yourself turning to these pages as often as I do.

Sticky Tiffin Bars

ne of the best vacations Jeff and I ever took was a walking holiday with our English cousins in the Lake District of northern England. Each day, after a fortifying English breakfast, we would pack ordnance survey maps to guide us along woodland streams, up rolling fells (hills) to mountain lakes, and across grassy sheep meadows where we clambered up and over "kissing" stiles. We planned each walk to finish around midafternoon, just in time for a traditional English tea. ❧ One afternoon, we stopped at The Kirkstone Galleries at Skelwith Bridge. The shop displays Kirkstone, a green slate native to the area, and there's a tearoom with about twenty homemade sweets to choose from. I spotted these Tiffin Bars right away, but even after eating them, we weren't sure what was in them—we just knew they were different from anything else we had tasted. On the way out, I asked the host what they were and he promptly replied, "Just grated chocolate, golden syrup, currants, and biscuits." No measurements, no baking times, no pan sizes, no details, but at least I knew the ingredients. My Tiffin Bar experiments began as soon as we returned home while their taste was fresh in my memory. These take about ten minutes to put together and are as sticky and full of chocolate, currants, and cookies as I remembered.

MAKES 20 BARS

$^1\!/_2$ cup Lyle's Golden Syrup
1 cup (6 ounces) miniature semisweet chocolate chips
$^1\!/_2$ cup currants
20 Social Tea cookies (about $1^1\!/_3$ cups), broken in approximately $^1\!/_2$-inch pieces
1 tablespoon vegetable shortening, such as Crisco
6 ounces semisweet chocolate, chopped

1. Position a rack in the middle of the oven. Preheat the oven to 325°F. Line an 8 × 8-inch pan with 1- to 2-inch sides with heavy aluminum foil, letting the foil extend over two ends of the pan. Oil the aluminum foil.

2. Warm the golden syrup in a small saucepan over low heat until it pours easily, about 5 minutes. Do not let it boil.

3. Put the miniature chocolate chips in the workbowl of a food processor fitted with the steel blade and process about 20 seconds. Some of the chocolate chips will be finely grated and some will form small crumbs.

4. Put the grated chocolate chips, currants, and cookie pieces in a medium bowl and stir together. Mix in the warm golden syrup, stirring until all of the ingredients are coated with syrup. Transfer the mixture to the prepared pan. Use the back of the mixing spoon to press the mixture into an even layer.

5. Bake for about 17 minutes, or until the edges are bubbling. Remove the pan from the oven. Set aside to cool for 20 minutes.

6. Put the vegetable shortening and chopped chocolate in a heatproof container and place it over, but not touching, a saucepan of barely simmering water. Stir the mixture over the hot water until the chocolate is melted and the mixture is smooth. Pour the chocolate mixture over the slightly cooled bars. Use a metal spatula to spread the chocolate evenly over the top. Cool until the chocolate topping is firm. Use the overhanging ends of aluminum foil to lift the cooled bars out of the pan. Loosen the foil from the sides. Cut into 20 rectangular pieces, 5 rows in one direction and 4 rows across. Use a wide metal spatula to slide each bar off the foil.

Good Advice: I find it tiring and difficult to grate a large amount of chocolate, so I produce grated chocolate by processing miniature chocolate chips in a food processor. ✿ Lyle's Golden Syrup is a pure cane syrup that is made in England. Dark corn syrup could be substituted. Social Tea cookies make a good substitute for the biscuits (cookies) that they use in England. *To Freeze:* Wrap individual bars in plastic wrap. Place them in a metal or plastic freezer container and cover tightly. Label with the date and contents. Freeze up to 1 month. *To Serve:* Remove as many bars from the freezer as you need. Defrost the wrapped bars in the refrigerator for 4 hours or overnight. Let the bars sit at room temperature about 1 hour before serving to soften them and bring out the flavor of the chocolate topping. Leftover bars can be covered with plastic wrap and stored for up to 3 days at room temperature.

Super S'mores

 was in college before I ever tasted a s'more with toasted marshmallows and melted chocolate squishing out between two graham cracker cookies. I've created a super s'more by adding pecans to the graham cracker, marshmallow, and milk chocolate combination. The pecans add crunch and make a less sweet, more grown-up version. 🏃 These s'mores are as simple as layering store-bought ingredients in a pan—you don't even need a mixing bowl—and baking them briefly to melt the marshmallows. Even the chocolate chips for the topping melt by themselves when sprinkled over the hot marshmallows.

MAKES 24 COOKIES

> 10 whole graham crackers ($4^3/4 \times 2^1/4$ inches)
> 3 cups miniature marshmallows
> $1^1/4$ cups coarsely chopped pecans
> 2 cups (11.5 ounces) milk chocolate chips

1. Position a rack in the center of the oven. Preheat the oven to 375°F. Line a $13 \times 9 \times 2$-inch pan with heavy foil, letting the foil extend over the ends of the pan.

2. Line the bottom of the pan with the graham crackers. There will be 1 row across of 5 graham crackers and 1 row across of 5 graham crackers trimmed slightly at their ends to fit the pan. Use the trimmings to fill in any spaces at the ends. Place the marshmallows evenly over the graham crackers and sprinkle the pecans evenly over the marshmallows.

3. Bake about 9 minutes, or until the marshmallows become light brown on top. They will puff and look perfectly toasted. Remove the pan from the oven and immediately sprinkle the milk chocolate chips over the hot marshmallows. (The marshmallows will deflate as they cool.) Let sit at room temperature for 5 minutes, or until the chocolate chips melt. Use a thin metal spatula to spread the melted chocolate chips evenly over the marshmallows.

4. Let sit until the chocolate is firm, about 3 hours, or refrigerate just until the chocolate is firm, about 40 minutes. Use the overhanging ends of aluminum foil to lift the bars out of the pan. Peel the foil away from the edges. Use a large, sharp knife to cut 24 bars, 4 rows lengthwise and 6 rows across. They will measure about 2 inches by a scant $1^1/2$ inches. Slide the bars off the foil.

Good Advice: You will need to trim 5 of the graham crackers so that they all fit into the bottom of the pan. 🏃 Watch the cookies carefully and remove them from the oven as soon as the marshmallows turn evenly light brown. Let the chocolate firm before cutting the bars. **To Freeze:** Place the bottoms of 2 bars together and wrap them in plastic wrap. Put the wrapped bars in a metal or plastic freezer container and cover tightly. Label with the date and contents. Freeze up to 3 months. **To Serve:** Defrost the wrapped bars for about 3 hours at room temperature. Serve within 2 days.

Mistake Shortbread

ne day I was making a cookie base for some bars and I accidentally mixed in twice as much butter as the recipe called for, but couldn't bear to throw away the dough. I spread the dough in a square pan, baked it, and produced this delicate shortbread that melts in your mouth.

MAKES 25 COOKIES

1 cup unbleached all-purpose flour
$^1/_2$ cup cornstarch
$^1/_2$ teaspoon baking powder
$^1/_2$ pound (2 sticks) soft unsalted butter
$^1/_3$ cup sugar
1 teaspoon vanilla extract

1. Position a rack in the middle of the oven. Preheat the oven to 300°F. Have ready a 9 × 9 pan with 1- to 2-inch sides.

2. Sift the flour, cornstarch, and baking powder together and set aside. Put the butter in a large mixing bowl and mix with an electric mixer on low speed for 15 seconds. Add the sugar and beat on medium speed for 2 minutes, until the mixture lightens slightly in color and looks fluffy, stopping the mixer and scraping the sides of the bowl once during the mixing. Decrease the speed to low and mix in the vanilla. Add the flour mixture, mixing until a smooth, sticky dough forms. Use a thin metal spatula to spread the dough evenly in the prepared pan.

3. Bake about 30 minutes, or until the top is evenly golden. Use a small, sharp knife to cut the warm shortbread in 5 rows lengthwise and 5 rows across, cutting through to the bottom. Cool thoroughly in the pan on a wire rack.

To Freeze: Place the bottoms of 2 cookies together and wrap them in plastic wrap. Put the wrapped cookies in a metal or plastic freezer container and cover tightly. Label with the date and contents. Freeze up to 3 months. **To Serve:** Defrost the wrapped cookies at room temperature. Store leftover cookies, wrapped in plastic wrap, up to 3 days at room temperature.

Peanut Thinsies

I f you live in Maine, the winter solstice is a time for celebration. It means we've turned the darkness corner and our days of four o'clock sunsets are over for another year. It also means that my friend Anne Jenkins will be welcoming the coming light with her annual winter solstice tea, actually a cookie feast. When I asked this expert cookie baker to contribute a recipe to my book, she immediately suggested these Peanut Thinsies, thin crisp wafers composed mostly of crushed peanuts.

MAKES ABOUT 54 COOKIES

> 1 pound lightly salted peanuts
> 2 tablespoons unbleached all-purpose flour
> 2 large eggs
> 1 cup sugar
> 1 teaspoon vanilla extract

1. Position 2 oven racks in the middle and upper third of the oven. Preheat the oven to 350°F. Line 2 baking sheets with nonstick baking liners or parchment paper.

2. Put half of the peanuts in a resealable plastic bag. Crush them into small pieces with a rolling pin or the flat side of a meat pounder. The crushed nuts should vary in size from halves and quarters to small pieces. Repeat with the remaining peanuts. Put the peanuts in a bowl and stir in the flour.

3. Put the eggs and sugar in the large bowl of an electric mixer. Beat on medium speed until the mixture lightens in color and is fluffy, about 1 minute. On low speed add the peanut mixture and vanilla, mixing just until the ingredients are blended. The batter will be thick and wet. Drop teaspoons of batter $2^1/_2$ inches apart on the prepared baking sheets. The batter will form 1-inch mounds. Set aside the remaining batter.

4. Bake for about 6 minutes, or until the edges of the cookies brown lightly and the tops are golden. Cool the cookies on the baking sheet for 5 minutes, until the bottoms are firm enough to slide off. Use a thin metal spatula to transfer the cookies to wire racks to cool thoroughly. If any cookies stick to the pan, loosen them with the metal spatula.

5. When the lined baking sheets are cool, stir the remaining batter to blend it together and drop by teaspoons $2^1/_2$ inches apart on the baking sheets. Bake and cool the cookies as before.

Good Advice: Anne recommends that these cookies be made on a dry, clear day so that they crisp properly. ❀ Buy lightly salted canned peanuts. If you can't find lightly salted peanuts, rub salted peanuts in a clean dish towel to remove some of the salt. ❀ You will need to bake the cookies on 4 baking sheets, so some of the batter must wait while the first batch of cookies bakes. Stir the batter before dropping the final sheets of cookies. **To Freeze:** Place the bottoms of 2 cookies together and wrap in plastic wrap. Put the wrapped cookies in a metal or plastic freezer container and cover tightly. Label with the date and contents. Freeze up to 3 months. **To Serve:** Defrost the wrapped cookies at room temperature. Serve within 5 days.

Rafiki Oatmeal Cookies

These cookies keep well in the jungle. Maybe you don't think that's relevant, but Chris McLarty, who owns Rafiki Safaris, always carries them on her jungle expeditions. *Rafiki* means "friends" in Swahili, and at the end of a particularly long day, Chris surprises her tired trekker friends with cookies from home. That sounds like my kind of safari.

MAKES 72 COOKIES

1 cup unbleached all-purpose flour
$^1/_2$ teaspoon baking soda
$^1/_2$ teaspoon baking powder
$^1/_2$ teaspoon salt
8 tablespoons (1 stick) soft unsalted butter
$^1/_2$ cup granulated sugar
$^1/_2$ cup brown sugar
1 large egg
1 teaspoon vanilla extract
1 cup oatmeal (not quick-cooking)
1 cup coarsely chopped walnuts

1. Position 2 oven racks in the lower middle and upper middle of the oven. Preheat the oven to 350°F. Line 3 baking sheets with parchment paper.

2. Stir the flour, baking soda, baking powder, and salt together in a small bowl and set aside. Put the butter, granulated sugar, and brown sugar in the large bowl of an electric mixer and beat on medium speed until the mixture is blended and smooth, 1 minute. Add the egg and mix on low speed until blended thoroughly, about 15 seconds. Stop the mixer and scrape the bowl during this mixing. On low speed, mix in the flour mixture until it is incorporated. Mix in the vanilla, oatmeal, and walnuts.

3. Pinch off a rounded teaspoon of dough for each cookie and smooth it slightly to form a 1-inch piece. Place the cookies $1^1/_2$ inches apart on the baking sheets. Set aside 1 baking sheet of cookies at room temperature.

4. Bake the remaining 2 sheets for 10 to 11 minutes, or until the cookies and their bottoms are light golden. After 5 minutes, reverse the baking sheets front to back and top to bottom to ensure even browning. Watch the cookies carefully as they near the end of their baking time. Bake the third sheet of cookies on a rack set in the middle of the oven, reversing the baking sheet after 5 minutes. Cool the cookies on the baking sheets for 5 minutes. Transfer the cookies to wire racks to cool completely.

Good Advice: Chris packs the cookies in clean, empty cardboard tubes from Pringles potato crisps, which also makes a good way to pack them for shipping. **To Freeze:** Line a 2-quart metal or plastic freezer container with plastic wrap. Fill with the cooled cookies, press plastic wrap onto the cookies, and cover tightly. Label with the date and contents. Freeze up to 3 months. **To Serve:** Remove as many cookies from the freezer as needed, cover them with plastic wrap, and defrost at room temperature. Serve within 5 days.

Graham Cracker Chocolate Chip Bars

M y fondness for graham cracker crumb crusts with chocolate chips was the spark that kindled the idea for these bars. Although my friends and family indulge me in my dessert experiments, I felt that serving them a graham cracker crust was asking a bit much. I solved my dilemma by using condensed milk to bind the basic crust ingredients together and baking the mixture in a square pan, which transformed the crust into bars.

MAKES 8 TO 9 LARGE BARS

> 2 cups graham cracker crumbs
> $1/2$ teaspoon ground cinnamon
> 4 tablespoons ($1/2$ stick) unsalted butter, melted
> 1 teaspoon vanilla extract
> $3/4$ cup sweetened condensed milk
> 1 cup (6 ounces) semisweet chocolate chips

1. Position a rack in the middle of the oven. Preheat the oven to 325°F. Line an 8 × 8-inch pan with heavy aluminum foil, letting the foil extend over the ends of the pan. Butter the bottom and sides of the aluminum foil.

2. Put the graham cracker crumbs and cinnamon in a large bowl and mix together. Add the melted butter and stir until the crumbs are evenly moistened. Stir the vanilla into the condensed milk; add to the crumbs. Mix in the chocolate chips. The mixture will be thick. Spread it evenly in the prepared pan.

3. Bake for about 30 minutes, or until a toothpick inserted in the center no longer has liquid clinging to it. The bars will be soft, but will firm as they cool.

4. Cool the bars in the pan. Use the overhanging ends of aluminum foil to lift them out and cut them into 8 or 9 pieces. Peel the foil from the sides of the bars; use a wide spatula to slide each bar off the foil.

To Freeze: Wrap individual bars in plastic wrap. Place in a metal or plastic freezer container and cover tightly. Label with the date and contents. Freeze up to 1 month. **To Serve:** Defrost the wrapped bars at room temperature. Serve within 4 days.

Uncle Howie's Extraordinary Butterscotch Chip Bars

t's an official tradition. Every time I write a new dessert book, my Uncle Howie concocts a new variation of my mom's famous Extraordinary Chocolate Chip Cake that appeared in *Bake and Freeze Desserts*. In this version, Uncle Howie uses butterscotch chips to change the texture from a cake to a dense, fudgy bar. After telling me about the recipe, my uncle called to see if I had baked it yet, but I hadn't. "You haven't tried this? Make it right away," he urged. I did and chalked up another success for my uncle.

MAKES 16 TO 20 BARS

> 2 cups unbleached all-purpose flour
> 2 cups packed light brown sugar
> 8 tablespoons (1 stick) cold unsalted butter, cut into 6 pieces
> 1 large egg
> 2 teaspoons baking soda
> 1 cup sour cream
> 2 tablespoons milk
> 2 cups (12 ounces) butterscotch chips

1. Position the oven rack in the middle of the oven and preheat to 325°F. Butter a 13 × 9 × 2-inch baking pan.

2. Put the flour and brown sugar in the large bowl of an electric mixer and mix on low speed for 15 seconds. Add the butter and mix until the butter pieces are the size of peas, about 1 minute. You will still see loose flour. Mix in the egg. The mixture will look dry. Rub any lumps out of the baking soda and gently mix it into the sour cream. Stir in the sour cream mixture and the milk just until the batter is evenly moistened. Stir in the butterscotch chips. The batter will be thick. Spread it evenly in the prepared baking pan.

3. Bake for about 50 minutes. To test for doneness, gently press your fingers on the top. The middle should feel slightly soft and the edges firm. Insert a toothpick in the center. When the toothpick comes out with a few crumbs clinging to it, the bars are done. Cool them thoroughly in the baking pan on a wire rack.

Good Advice: These bars have a firm butterscotch-fudge consistency if served cold. At room temperature, they are soft and more like a cake. 🏃 If the bars bake just until a toothpick comes out sticky, they have a moist, dense texture and deflate slightly as they cool. If baked until a toothpick comes out with a few crumbs clinging to it, they have a texture similar to that of a brownie. **To Freeze:** Cut either into 2 or 3 large pieces or 16 to 20 individual pieces. Slide a thin metal spatula under the bars to loosen any of the sticky butterscotch layer from the bottom of the pan, then remove them from the baking pan. Wrap large pieces in plastic wrap, then in heavy aluminum foil. Wrap individual bars in plastic wrap, place in a metal or plastic freezer container, and cover tightly. Label with the date and contents. Freeze up to 3 months. **To Serve:** Defrost the wrapped bars in the refrigerator. Unwrap and serve cold or bring the wrapped bars to room temperature for about 1 hour before serving. Leftover bars can be covered with plastic wrap and refrigerated up to 5 days.

Chocolate Truffle Squares

aking sophisticated truffles into bar cookies completely reverses any idea that bars should be humble. These all-chocolate bars have a chocolate cookie crumb crust filled with chocolate-glazed whipped truffle. The finished squares are part cookie bar, part candy truffle, all totally impressive.

MAKES TWENTY-FIVE 1½-INCH SQUARES

2 cups warm Chocolate Truffle Sauce (page 20)
1 Chocolate Wafer Cookie Crumb Crust (page 22), cooled or frozen,
    baked in a 8 × 8-inch pan with 1- to 2-inch sides, lined with heavy
    aluminum foil that extends over the ends of the pan

1. Pour ⅔ cup of the warm truffle sauce into a small bowl and set aside at room temperature. Pour the remaining 1⅓ cups truffle sauce into a large mixing bowl and press plastic wrap onto the surface. Refrigerate the sauce until it is cold to the touch, thick, and just beginning to harden around the edges, about 45 minutes. Stir once to ensure the mixture chills throughout. It should not be hard.

2. Remove the cold, but still soft, truffle sauce from the refrigerator. Whisk it with a large whisk until the chocolate lightens slightly from dark to medium brown, about 1 minute. Immediately spread the whipped truffle over the crumb crust to form a smooth layer of filling. Refrigerate until the filling is firm, about 30 minutes.

3. Pour the reserved ⅔ cup sauce over the filling and spread it evenly with a thin metal spatula. (If it has cooled and thickened too much to pour, warm it for about 1 minute over low heat until pourable but still thick.) Refrigerate the pan, uncovered, until the topping is firm.

4. Use the overhanging ends of aluminum foil to lift the cold confection out of the pan; then loosen the foil from the sides. Cut into 25 bars, 5 rows in each direction. Use a wide spatula to slide the bars off the aluminum foil.

Good Advice: You will need a double recipe of Chocolate Truffle Sauce (page 20). *To Freeze:* Wrap each bar in plastic wrap, place in a metal or plastic freezer container, and cover tightly. Label with the date and contents. Freeze up to 3 months. *To Serve:* Defrost the wrapped bars in the refrigerator for at least 3 hours or overnight. Serve them cold or softened slightly for 30 minutes. Leftover bars can be covered with plastic wrap and stored in the refrigerator up to 5 days.

My Sister's Oatmeal Bars

When my sister, Susan, sent me this recipe, she wrote; "You can't believe something this simple is so good." After trying them, I knew exactly what she meant. With only three ingredients that take about two minutes to mix together, these crisp, buttery bars are a recipe to treasure. 🏃 My sister and her family are farmers in Vermont. Whatever they don't grow themselves, they buy from their local food cooperative. That's where she received this recipe from Edna Conrad, who brought the bars to a potluck dinner.

MAKES 16 BARS

> 8 tablespoons (1 stick) soft unsalted butter
> $^1/_2$ cup plus 2 tablespoons sugar
> 1 cup oatmeal (not quick-cooking)

1. Position a rack in the middle of the oven. Preheat the oven to 325°F. Butter an 8 × 8 × 2-inch pan.

2. Put the butter and sugar in the large bowl of an electric mixer and beat on medium speed for 1 minute, until blended and smooth. Mix in the oatmeal until it is incorporated. Press the mixture evenly in the prepared pan.

3. Bake for about 30 minutes, or until the edges are light brown and the top is golden. Remove from the oven and immediately cut into 16 pieces. Cool the bars in the pan. They will crisp as they cool.

Good Advice: Cut the bars while they're hot, then let them cool in the pan. The bars will break and crumble if you try to cut them after they cool and crisp up. **To Freeze:** Wrap individual bars tightly in plastic wrap. Put the wrapped bars in a metal or plastic freezer container and cover tightly. Label with the date and contents. Freeze up to 3 months. **To Serve:** Defrost the wrapped bars at room temperature for about 2 hours. Leftover bars can be covered with plastic wrap and stored at room temperature up to 3 days.

Slice and Bake Cookies from the Freezer

lice and bake cookies. I'll bet you're thinking of the tubes of dough sealed in plastic found in the refrigerator case at your grocery. Well, these cookies do have some good things in common with those, but these are not your grocery store cookies. You'll have homemade cookie dough available whenever you want it; it only needs to be sliced and popped in the oven. They'll be interesting—cookies with black and white checkerboard patterns, flaky spirals glazed with cinnamon sugar, plump date and nut cookies, and even an almond-filled strudel.

The dough for these cookies is formed into long rolls (logs), then either sliced and baked or frozen for later baking. As long as the logs of dough are rolled smooth, you're guaranteed perfectly shaped cookies. With the exception of the strudel, there are two opportunities for freezing, as unbaked logs of dough or as baked cookies. Usually, I bake part of a recipe of dough and freeze the remainder for baking as I need it.

If the rolls of dough are cold, they cut into neat, even slices. Warm, soft dough has a tendency to squash and flatten when you cut it, while frozen dough is difficult to cut and may even break apart.

By using two or more colors of dough for one cookie, you can create patterned cookies. Both of the patterned cookie recipes give two options. In Mocha Checkerboards and Stripes, the chocolate and coffee doughs can be formed into checkerboards or stacked in a striped design. For Raspberry and Lemon Pinwheels and Whirlybirds, the two flavors of dough can form either of the spiral motifs.

Mocha Checkerboards and Stripes

hings that look complicated usually become simple when you take them one step at a time. I used to marvel at the intricate multicolored checkerboard-patterned cookies that I bought from bakeries until I tried baking some of my own and discovered that the checked pattern was made by stacking alternating colors of ropes of dough. For my checkerboards, I divide one batch of dough into thirds and flavor it with chocolate, coffee, or vanilla. Two colors make the checked pattern and the third one wraps around the stacked dough to enclose it in a contrasting border. For three-colored striped cookies, stack the three colors on top of each other and slice them. It sounds as simple as it is.

MAKES ABOUT 60 CHECKERBOARDS, OR 44 STRIPED COOKIES 3 × 2 INCHES,
OR 88 HALF SLICES 2 × 1$^1/_2$ INCHES

2 ounces semisweet chocolate, chopped
2 cups unbleached all-purpose flour
$^1/_2$ teaspoon baking powder
$^1/_4$ teaspoon salt
$^1/_2$ pound (2 sticks) soft unsalted butter
1 cup sugar
2 large eggs, separated
1 teaspoon vanilla extract
2 teaspoons instant decaffeinated coffee dissolved in 1 teaspoon hot water
1 tablespoon sifted unsweetened Dutch process cocoa powder,
    such as Droste or Hershey's European

MAKE THE COOKIE DOUGH

1. Preheat the oven to 175°F.

2. Put the semisweet chocolate in a small heatproof container and melt it in the oven, 8 to 10 minutes. Remove as soon as it is melted and stir until smooth. Set aside to cool slightly.

3. Sift the flour, baking powder, and salt together. Set aside.

4. Put the butter in a large mixing bowl and mix with an electric mixer on medium speed for 15 seconds. Add the sugar and beat until the butter and sugar are blended, 1 minute. Mix in the egg yolks and vanilla. Decrease the speed to low and add the flour mixture, mixing until a smooth dough forms. You will have about 3 cups of dough.

5. Put a generous cup of dough in a medium bowl and stir in the dissolved coffee until it is incorporated. Form a generous cup of dough into a 6-inch square. This leaves a scant cup of dough in the mixing bowl. On low speed add the cooled melted chocolate and

the cocoa powder to the dough in the mixing bowl and mix until they are incorporated completely. Form the coffee and chocolate portions into 6-inch squares. Wrap each square of dough in plastic wrap and refrigerate until firm, about 1 hour.

FOR THE CHECKERBOARD COOKIES

1. Remove the chocolate and coffee doughs from the refrigerator. Divide each into 6 parts. Roll each part into 7$\frac{1}{2}$-inch-long ropes about $\frac{1}{2}$ inch in diameter. To make 2 stacks of dough, place alternating colors of three ropes together in a row; chocolate-coffee-chocolate. Beat the egg whites with a fork until foamy and use a pastry brush to brush the top of the stack lightly with egg white. Place a second row of alternating colors on top; coffee-chocolate-coffee. Press the ropes gently together. Make a second, separate stack with the remaining dough ropes.

2. Remove the vanilla dough from the refrigerator and divide it in half. Roll one piece of dough between 2 sheets of wax paper into a sheet as long as the dough stack and four times as wide, about 7$\frac{1}{2}$ × 5$\frac{1}{2}$ inches. Discard the top piece of wax paper. Brush the dough lightly with egg white. Wrap this vanilla dough around one stack of dough ropes, removing the wax paper as you wrap. Gently press the seam along the length of the roll to seal it, and trim any ragged edges. Roll out the second piece of vanilla dough and wrap it around the remaining stack of dough. Freeze the rolls unbaked, or wrap and refrigerate for about 1 hour until cold and firm, then slice and bake the cookies.

FOR THE STRIPED COOKIES

1. Line 2 disposable aluminum mini-loaf pans 5$\frac{3}{4}$ × 3$\frac{1}{4}$ × 2 with plastic wrap, letting the plastic wrap extend over the ends of the pan.

2. Remove the 3 colors of dough from the refrigerator and cut each in 2 pieces. Press a piece of vanilla dough evenly into each pan, using the back of a spoon to press it smooth. Beat the egg whites with a fork until foamy and use a pastry brush to brush the vanilla dough lightly with egg white. Press a piece of chocolate dough evenly over each piece of the vanilla dough, smooth with a spoon, and brush lightly with egg white. Press a piece of coffee dough evenly over each piece of the chocolate dough. Refrigerate until firm. Once the dough is cold and firm, you can slice and bake the cookies.

Good Advice: The quantity of chocolate dough increases when the chocolate is added, so make the divisions for the coffee and vanilla doughs slightly larger than the one for the chocolate dough. If you end up with more chocolate dough than you want, pat the leftover dough into several wafers and bake them as chocolate cookies. ❦ To make larger cookies, stack more ropes of dough together. ❦ The colors remain distinct if the cookies bake just until the edges turn golden. When the cookies turn brown, they taste fine, but the pattern is lost. ❦ You can divide the dough in half and use half for checkerboards and half for stripes. **To Freeze the Cookie Roll Unbaked:** Wrap the roll tightly in plastic wrap, then heavy aluminum foil. Label with the date and contents. Freeze up to 3 months. **To Freeze the Striped Cookies Unbaked:** Lift the dough and plastic wrap from the pan. Wrap tightly in the plastic wrap, then heavy aluminum foil. Label with the date and contents. Freeze up to 3 months. **To Bake and Serve Checkerboards or Stripes:** Defrost the prepared dough in the refrigerator until it is firm but slices easily, at least 3 hours or overnight. ❄ Preheat the oven to 350°F. Position the oven racks in the upper middle and lower middle of the oven. Line 2 baking sheets with parchment paper. ❄ Unwrap the defrosted dough. Use a large, sharp knife to cut the dough into ¼-inch slices. The pattern on each cookie will be checkerboards or stripes. The unbaked striped cookies can be cut in half to make smaller cookies. Place the cookies ¾ inch apart on the prepared baking sheets. ❄ Bake until the edges of the cookies just begin to turn golden, or about 10 minutes. Reverse the baking sheets top to bottom and front to back after 6 minutes to ensure that the cookies bake evenly. They do not spread much. Cool the cookies for 5 minutes on the baking sheets, then transfer them to wire racks to cool completely. Serve within 5 days. **To Freeze and Serve Baked Cookies:** Stack 6 cookies together and wrap them in plastic wrap. Put them in a metal or plastic freezer container and cover tightly. Label with the date and contents. Freeze up to 3 months. Remove as many cookies from the freezer as needed and defrost the wrapped cookies at room temperature. Serve within 3 days.

Raspberry and Lemon Pinwheels and Whirlybirds

piral-patterned cookies are formed when two colors of dough are rolled up together jelly-roll style and sliced. Raspberry purée tints half of this dough a soft pink and creates pastel cookies just right for a spring graduation, baby shower, Mother's Day, or wedding cookie table. Single rolls make pinwheels, and a roll with two pinwheels makes whirlybirds.

MAKES ABOUT 36 COOKIES

1 cup fresh or previously frozen and defrosted unsweetened raspberries
1 cup plus 3 tablespoons unbleached all-purpose flour
$1/4$ teaspoon baking powder
$1/8$ teaspoon salt
8 tablespoons (1 stick) soft unsalted butter
$1/2$ cup granulated sugar
1 large egg, separated
$1/2$ teaspoon vanilla extract
$3/4$ teaspoon almond extract
1 teaspoon grated lemon zest

1. Purée the raspberries in a food processor. Use the back of a spoon to press them through a strainer to remove the seeds. Measure and set aside 2 tablespoons of strained purée. Save any additional purée for another use.

2. Sift together 1 cup of the flour, the baking powder, and salt. Set aside.

3. Put the butter in a large mixing bowl and beat with an electric mixer on medium speed for 15 seconds. Add the sugar and beat until the butter and sugar are blended together, 1 minute. Mix in the egg yolk, vanilla, and almond extract. Decrease the speed to low and add the flour mixture, mixing until a smooth dough forms. You will have about $1^{1}/2$ cups of dough.

4. Remove half the dough to a medium bowl and stir in the lemon zest. On low speed mix 2 tablespoons of raspberry purée and the remaining 3 tablespoons of flour into the dough in the mixing bowl. Form each piece of dough into a 5-inch disk. Wrap each in plastic wrap and refrigerate until firm, about 1 hour.

5. Roll each piece of dough out between 2 sheets of wax paper into a rectangle 9 × 6 inches, about $3/16$ inch thick. Remove the top piece of wax paper from each. Beat the egg white with a fork until foamy. Use a pastry brush to brush egg white lightly on the lemon dough. Wax paper side up, press the raspberry dough on top. Discard the top piece of wax paper. Trim the dough edges evenly.

6. To form pinwheels, roll the two layers of dough into a tight cylinder, starting on a long side and removing the remaining piece of wax paper as you roll. Gently press the seam along the length of the roll to seal it and trim any ragged edges. You will have a roll about 9 inches long. To form whirlybirds, roll the stacked dough (from the long sides) from each end to the center, forming 2 thin rolls that are attached. Remove the wax paper as you roll. Gently press the seam along the length of the roll to seal it, and trim any ragged edges. The roll will be about 9 inches long. Freeze either roll unbaked or refrigerate for about 1 hour until cold and firm, then slice and bake the cookies.

Good Advice: Since the lemon dough is firmer and holds it shape better than the raspberry dough, it should always be placed on the bottom of the stack so it forms the outside of the cookie. *To Freeze the Cookie Roll Unbaked:* Wrap the roll tightly in plastic wrap, then in heavy aluminum foil. Label with the date and contents. Freeze up to 3 months. *To Bake and Serve Pinwheels or Whirlybirds:* Defrost the prepared dough in the refrigerator until it is firm but slices easily, at least 3 hours or overnight. ❀ Preheat the oven to 350°F. Position the oven racks in the upper middle and lower middle of the oven. Line 2 baking sheets with parchment paper. ❀ Unwrap the defrosted dough. Use a large, sharp knife to cut it into $1/4$-inch slices. Place the cookies 1 inch apart on the prepared baking sheets. ❀ Bake until the edges of the cookies just begin to turn golden, or about 10 minutes. Reverse the baking sheets top to bottom and front to back after 6 minutes to ensure that the cookies bake evenly. They do not spread much. Cool 5 minutes on the baking sheets, then transfer to wire racks to cool completely. Serve within 5 days. *To Freeze and Serve Baked Cookies:* Stack 6 cookies together and wrap them in plastic wrap. Put them in a metal or plastic freezer container and cover tightly. Label with the date and contents. Freeze up to 3 months. Remove as many cookies from the freezer as needed and defrost the wrapped cookies at room temperature. Serve within 5 days.

Cinnamon Spiral Crisps

 These crunchy, sweet cookie spirals are simply thin sheets of flaky pastry rolled with cinnamon sugar. When the rolls are sliced into thin disks, they bake into crisp sugar-glazed wafers.

MAKES ABOUT 32 COOKIES

1/4 cup sugar
1 teaspoon ground cinnamon
1 cup unbleached all-purpose flour
1/8 teaspoon salt
8 tablespoons (1 stick) cold unsalted butter, cut into 8 pieces

1. Put the sugar and cinnamon in a small bowl and stir to blend. Set aside.

2. Put the flour and salt in the large bowl of an electric mixer. On low speed add the butter pieces. Mix just until they are the size of small lima beans, about 45 seconds. They will not all be the same size, and you will still see loose flour. Slowly add 3 tablespoons ice water, a tablespoon at a time. Stop beating as soon as the mixture begins to hold together and comes away from the sides of the bowl, about 30 seconds. Turn the dough out onto a lightly floured rolling surface and form it into a square disk about 1 inch thick. Refrigerate for 15 minutes, until the dough is cold and firm.

3. On a lightly floured surface with a lightly floured rolling pin, roll the dough into a 12 × 9-inch rectangle about 1/8 inch thick. The short end of the dough should be facing you and parallel to the edge of the counter. Sprinkle the cinnamon-sugar mixture evenly over the dough. Beginning with the short end, roll the dough into a tight roll about 1 1/2 inches in diameter and 9 inches long. Pinch the edges to seal them. Press the seam along the length of the roll to seal it tightly. Freeze the roll unbaked, or refrigerate for about 1 hour until it is cold and firm, then slice and bake the cookies.

Good Advice: As the end of the baking time nears, watch these cookies closely. If they overbake, the glaze can quickly burn. Use shiny rather than dark-colored baking sheets to prevent burned cookie bottoms. These cookies bake best in the middle of the oven, so bake one baking sheet at a time. When they are properly baked, the sugar melts and forms a golden glaze on the bottoms of the cookies. The sugar glaze melts more evenly if the baking sheets are lined with aluminum foil rather than parchment paper. **Doubling the Recipe:** Double the ingredients and form the dough into 2 rolls. **To Freeze the Cookie Roll Unbaked:** Wrap the roll tightly in plastic wrap, then in heavy aluminum foil. Label with the date and contents. Freeze up to 3 months. **To Bake and Serve:** Defrost the roll in the refrigerator until it is firm but slices easily, at least 3 hours or overnight. Preheat the oven to 375°F. Position the oven rack in the middle of the oven. Line 2 shiny baking sheets with heavy aluminum foil. Unwrap the defrosted roll and use a large, sharp knife to cut it into 1/4-inch rounds. Place the cookies 3/4 inch apart on the prepared baking sheets. Bake 1 sheet of cookies at a time for about 12 minutes, or until the tops are golden and the bottoms are light brown and glazed with sugar. Reverse the baking sheet after 7 minutes to ensure that the cookies bake evenly. Use a metal spatula to lift a cookie to check the bottom. The cookies will puff slightly as they bake but will not spread. Immediately transfer the cookies to a wire rack to cool completely. Bake the second pan of cookies. Serve within 3 days. **To Freeze and Serve Baked Cookies:** Stack 6 cookies together and wrap them in plastic wrap. Put them in a metal or plastic freezer container and cover tightly. Label with the date and contents. Freeze up to 3 months. Remove as many cookies from the freezer as needed and defrost the wrapped cookies at room temperature. Serve within 3 days.

Swahili Shortbread

everal years ago, I invited some friends and neighbors to a holiday cookie exchange. I asked each person to bring several dozen cookies to exchange, the story of the cookie they made, and an empty container to take home an assortment of cookies. When my friend Joanne Scott walked in with her Swahili Shortbread, you could smell the butter, and I knew that it was a recipe I would want to make. The cookies were snowy white from a thick dusting of powdered sugar, and filled with shredded coconut that baked crisp and golden on the bottom of the cookies but remained soft on the inside. 🏃 Joanne received the recipe from Chris McLarty, who leads safaris to Africa. Chris named the cookies for the Swahili village of Lamu in Kenya, where coconuts grow abundantly.

MAKES ABOUT 40 COOKIES

> 2 cups unbleached all-purpose flour
> $^1/_4$ teaspoon salt
> $^1/_2$ pound (2 sticks) soft unsalted butter
> $^1/_4$ cup sugar
> 1 teaspoon vanilla extract
> 2 cups shredded sweetened coconut
> Powdered sugar for dusting baked cookies

1. Stir the flour and salt together in a small bowl and set aside.

2. Put the butter, sugar, and vanilla in the large bowl of an electric mixer and beat on medium speed until smooth and fluffy, about 1 minute. On low speed, add the flour mixture, mixing until the flour is incorporated and a smooth dough forms. Mix in the coconut.

3. Divide the dough into 2 pieces and form each piece into a log about 6 inches long and $1^1/_2$ inches in diameter. Wrap each log in plastic wrap. Freeze the rolls unbaked, or refrigerate them for about 2 hours until cold and firm, then slice and bake the cookies.

Good Advice: Joanne advised that these cookies not be baked on an insulated baking sheet. The bottoms do not brown and the coconut doesn't become crisp on these thick double-layered pans. 🏃 The cookies bake to the desired crisp texture if you slice them as close to $^1/_4$ inch thick as possible. 🏃 As long as the weather isn't humid and they are stored in a dry place, these can be kept for 5 days at room temperature. I once put them in a tin with moist brownies and the cookies softened in a few hours. To Freeze the Cookie Rolls Unbaked: Wrap each plastic-wrapped log in heavy aluminum foil. Label with the date and contents. Freeze up to 3 months. To Bake and Serve: Defrost one or both logs in the refrigerator until the dough is firm but slices easily, at least 3 hours or overnight. 🏃 Preheat the oven to 300°F. Position the oven racks in the lower third and upper third of the oven. Line 2 baking sheets with parchment paper. 🏃 Unwrap the defrosted rolls. Using a large, sharp knife and a slight sawing motion, cut them into rounds about $^1/_4$ inch thick. Place the cookies 1 inch apart on the prepared baking sheets.  Bake 2 sheets at a time for about 20 minutes, or until the edges and bottoms of the cookies are golden. Use a metal spatula to lift a cookie to check the bottom. Cool the cookies for 5 minutes on the baking sheet, then transfer them to a wire rack to cool completely. Dust generously with powdered sugar. Store in a clean metal container and serve within 5 days. **To Freeze and Serve Baked Cookies:** Place the bottoms of 2 cookies together and wrap them carefully in plastic wrap. Put the wrapped cookies in a metal or plastic freezer container and cover tightly. Label with the date and contents. Freeze up to 3 months. Defrost the wrapped cookies at room temperature. Serve within 5 days.

Avenue "J" Butter Cookies

When I was a child, we spent summers in Brooklyn at my grandfather's house on Avenue "J." That's where I first began to notice food. My parents had grown up in Brooklyn, and I tagged along with them on their shopping expeditions as they bought all of the big-city specialties that weren't available in the small Florida town where we lived. We shopped daily, filling our shopping bags with fresh whitefish from the fish market, hand-picked vegetables from the produce stand, potato knishes from the delicatessen, and butter cookies from Stern's bakery. ✿ I haven't had a Stern's butter cookie for at least thirty-five years, but I remember every detail. They were small rounds about ⅓ inch thick. Their straight sides were coated with sugar and the center had a golden dot of glaze that I've since realized was beaten egg. Although the cookies were exceptionally light, they kept their rich taste of butter. I used to eat around the edge and save the golden dot in the center for last, just as I do now with these cookies that reproduce the originals.

MAKES 72 COOKIES

> 1¼ cups unbleached all-purpose flour
> ¼ cup cake flour
> ½ teaspoon baking powder
> 1 cup slivered or sliced blanched almonds
> 1 cup powdered sugar
> ½ pound plus 2 tablespoons (2¼ sticks) soft unsalted butter
> 1 teaspoon vanilla extract
> 2 tablespoons granulated sugar
> 1 large egg, lightly beaten, for glazing the cookie centers

1. Sift the flours and baking powder together and set aside.

2. Put the almonds and powdered sugar in the work bowl of a food processor fitted with the steel blade and process with a few short bursts to combine the ingredients. Process about 30 seconds until the almonds are finely ground.

3. Put the butter and almond mixture in the large bowl of an electric mixer and beat on low speed to combine them. Increase the speed to medium and beat until fluffy and the color lightens, 1 minute. Mix in the vanilla. Decrease the speed to low and add the flour mixture in 2 additions, mixing until the flour is incorporated and a soft dough forms. Stop the mixer and scrape the bowl. Leave the dough in the bowl, cover, and refrigerate until it is firm enough to roll into logs, about 20 minutes.

4. Divide the dough into 3 pieces. Form each piece of dough into a log about 8 inches long and 1 inch in diameter. Wrap each log in plastic wrap. Freeze the rolls unbaked or refrigerate them for about 1 hour until cold and firm, then slice and bake the cookies.

Good Advice: The granulated sugar and egg are added when the cookies bake. Bake these cookies until the bottoms and edges are light brown so they have a rich browned butter taste. **To Freeze the Cookie Rolls Unbaked:** Wrap each plastic-wrapped log in heavy aluminum foil. Label with the date and contents. Freeze up to 3 months. **To Bake:** Defrost as many logs as you need in the refrigerator at least 5 hours or overnight. 🏃 Preheat the oven to 350°F. Position the oven racks in the lower third and upper third of the oven. Line 3 baking sheets with parchment paper. 🏃 Unwrap the defrosted logs, leaving them on the plastic wrap. Brush the dough with the beaten egg. Sprinkle a strip of 2 tablespoons granulated sugar on each piece of plastic wrap, then roll each log back and forth over the sugar to coat it. Use a large, sharp knife to cut each roll into $1/3$-inch-thick rounds. Place the cookies 1 inch apart on the prepared baking sheets. Brush a dab of beaten egg in the center of each cookie. Set aside 1 baking sheet at room temperature. 🏃 Bake 2 sheets for about 12 minutes, or until the edges and bottoms of the cookies are light brown, reversing the baking sheets after 7 minutes front to back and top to bottom to ensure that the cookies bake evenly. Bake the remaining sheet of cookies on the middle rack of the oven, reversing the baking sheet after 7 minutes. Cool the cookies for 5 minutes on the baking sheet. Transfer them to a wire rack to cool completely. Store at room temperature up to 3 days. **To Freeze Baked Cookies:** Line a metal or plastic freezer container with plastic wrap. A 2-quart container or the equivalent will hold all of the cookies. Fill the container with the cooled cookies, press plastic wrap firmly but gently onto the cookies, and cover tightly. Label with the date and contents. Freeze up to 3 months. **To Serve:** Defrost the wrapped cookies at room temperature. Serve within 4 days.

Maple, Date, and Walnut Chews

ew Englanders have a reputation for plain talk, even when naming cookies. So of course any soft cookie that has lots of fruit and nuts to munch on would be called a "chew." The scent of maple syrup and spices drifts up from the mixing bowl, and you know that you're on to one of those good old-fashioned New England cookie recipes that built a baking tradition.

MAKES 28 COOKIES

1¼ cups unbleached all-purpose flour
½ teaspoon baking soda
¼ teaspoon salt
1 teaspoon ground cinnamon
¼ teaspoon ground allspice
12 tablespoons (1½ sticks) soft unsalted butter
¾ cup packed dark brown sugar
1 large egg
1 teaspoon vanilla extract
¼ cup pure maple syrup
1 cup coarsely chopped walnuts
8 ounces pitted dates, cut in ½-inch pieces

1. Sift the flour, baking soda, salt, cinnamon, and allspice together and set aside.

2. Put the butter and brown sugar in the large bowl of an electric mixer and beat on medium speed for about 1 minute until smooth. Add the egg and vanilla and mix on low speed for about 15 seconds, until thoroughly blended in. Stop the mixer and scrape the bowl. Beat in the syrup. Add the flour mixture, mixing just until the flour is incorporated. Stir in the walnuts and dates.

3. Divide the dough into 2 pieces. Form each piece into a log about 7½ inches long and 1¾ inches in diameter. Wrap each log in plastic wrap and freeze them unbaked, or refrigerate the rolls for at least 3 hours or overnight until cold and firm, then slice and bake the cookies.

Good Advice: Coat the knife used to chop the dates with oil to prevent the dates from sticking to the knife. **To Freeze the Cookie Rolls Unbaked:** Wrap each plastic-wrapped log in heavy aluminum foil. Label with the date and contents. Freeze up to 3 months. **To Bake and Serve:** Defrost one or both logs in the refrigerator at least 5 hours or overnight. 🏃 Preheat the oven to 350°F. Position the oven racks in the middle and upper third of the oven. Line 2 heavy baking sheets with parchment paper. 🏃 Unwrap the defrosted rolls. Use a large, sharp knife to cut them into ½-inch-thick rounds. Place the cookies 1 inch apart on the prepared baking sheets. (If the dough crumbles when sliced, press it back together.) 🏃 Bake for about 11 minutes, reversing the sheets top to bottom and back to front after 6 minutes of baking. The edges and bottoms of the cookies will be golden. Cool them for 5 minutes on the baking sheets, then transfer them to wire racks to cool completely. Serve within 3 days. **To Freeze and Serve Baked Cookies:** Put 2 cookie bottoms together and wrap them in plastic wrap. Put the wrapped cookies in a metal or plastic freezer container and cover tightly. Label with the date and contents. Freeze up to 3 months. Defrost the wrapped cookies at room temperature. Serve within 3 days.

Shortbread

emories of our walking trip to England's Lake District with our English cousins, Gillian and Illtyd Lewis inspired this buttery chapter. Since Illtyd is director of the Tea Council in Great Britain, he's an authority on British tearooms and was able to lead us to cozy tearooms, historical ones, and famous ones. Every one we visited had its own shortbread specialty. There were thick and thin plain butter shortbreads; shortbreads layered with toffee, lemon, or jam; and shortbreads flavored with brown sugar or ginger. One tearoom even had a case of shortbread with ten different toppings. The trip became a shortbread odyssey as we sampled each tearoom's specialty.

Shortbread dough contains little or no liquid and the butter flavor prevails. The term *short* refers to a dough that has a large proportion of fat to flour, fat in this case being synonymous with butter. Adding other ingredients simply turns the cookies into hazelnut butter, lemon butter, or butter pecan shortbread, for example. Replacing some of the flour with cornstarch or white rice flour lowers the gluten content and tenderizes the cookies.

There are two basic methods for mixing the dough. For crumbly-textured Thick Scottish Shortbread, you blend butter pieces with the dry ingredients until crumbs form and gently press the crumbs into a pan so the shortbread retains its light texture. Or for a smooth, fine texture, as found in Shortbread Rounds, you beat the butter and sugar to a smooth mixture before adding the dry ingredients.

Shortbread dough can be pressed into a baking pan, rolled and cut into shapes, or pressed into ceramic molds that produce raised patterns when the cookies are removed. Any shortbread that bakes in one large piece should be cut into pieces with a sharp knife while it's warm and soft so it doesn't crumble and break.

English Shortbread Batons

Every year on the Monday before Thanksgiving the Camden Garden Club meets to decorate the Christmas wreaths that hang from the lampposts along the village main street. One year as I was winding tiny lights around a balsam wreath, I heard my neighbor Bess Reid complimenting Hilly Cheney on her shortbread recipe. I asked if Bess and Hilly would share the recipe with me, and promptly received it with assurances from Bess that it had an especially tender texture and was "a cinch cookie." 🧍 A hefty portion of cornstarch replaces some of the flour and gives this shortbread its delicate quality.

MAKES ABOUT 144 COOKIES

> 1 pound (4 sticks) soft unsalted butter
> 1 cup minus 2 tablespoons sugar
> 3^1/$_3$ cups unbleached all-purpose flour
> 1^2/$_3$ cups cornstarch
> Pinch salt
> ^{1}/$_2$ teaspoon vanilla extract
> ^{1}/$_2$ teaspoon almond extract

1. Position 2 oven racks in the middle and upper third of the oven. Preheat the oven to 350°F. Line 3 baking sheets with parchment paper or regular weight aluminum foil for easier cleanup.

2. Put the butter in the large bowl of an electric mixer and mix on low speed for 15 seconds. Add the sugar and beat on medium speed for 2 minutes, until the mixture lightens in color and looks fluffy. Stop the mixer and scrape the sides of the bowl once during the mixing. Decrease the speed to low and mix in the flour, cornstarch, and salt until the dough holds together and all of the flour is incorporated, about 2 minutes. The dough will look crumbly. Stop the mixer and scrape the bowl during the mixing. Add the vanilla and almond extracts and continue mixing until you get a smooth dough that comes away from the sides of the bowl.

3. Divide the dough into 4 pieces. Pat each piece into a square about 4^1/$_2$ inches. Roll out 1 piece at a time ^{1}/$_2$ inch thick and about 6^1/$_2$ inches square. Trim the edges evenly. Using a ruler to measure, cut the dough with a large, sharp knife into 2 × ^{1}/$_2$-inch strips. Place the cookies ^{3}/$_4$ inch apart on the prepared baking sheets. Repeat with the remaining dough. Any scraps can be rolled with the last portion of dough. Set aside 1 sheet of cookies at room temperature.

4. Bake 2 sheets of cookies for about 25 minutes, or until the edges and bottoms are golden, reversing the sheets after 13 minutes front to back and top to bottom to ensure that the cookies bake evenly. Bake the remaining sheet of cookies on the middle rack of the oven, reversing the baking sheet after 13 minutes. Cool the cookies on the baking sheets for 5 minutes, then transfer them to wire racks to cool thoroughly.

Good Advice: Bess advised me that the cookie would have its proper texture only if the butter and sugar were creamed thoroughly. The butter must be softened well and the creamed mixture should have a light color and a fluffy consistency. ✻ The dough will not stick to the rolling surface, and it is not necessary to dust the rolling pin or rolling surface with flour. ✻ This large recipe requires 3 baking sheets. Bake 2 sheets and let the third pan wait at room temperature until the oven is free.

Doubling the Recipe: This is a large recipe, so it is easier to mix separate batches of dough.

To Freeze: Stack 4 cookies together and wrap them in plastic wrap. Put the wrapped cookies in a metal or plastic freezer container and cover tightly. Label and date. Freeze up to 3 months.

To Serve: Defrost the wrapped cookies at room temperature. Leftover cookies can be covered with plastic wrap and stored at room temperature up to 4 days.

Thick Scottish Shortbread/Shortcake

efore our first visit to Edinburgh, we were told not to miss the fairy-tale castle that dominates the city or the magnificent Botanical Gardens and glass houses, but nobody mentioned this inch-thick, tender shortbread that is a Scottish specialty. Luckily, I spotted it displayed in the first tea shop we tried. I guess it's so prevalent that people take it for granted. The especially soft crumbly texture makes it something between a cake and a cookie, and I serve it as a shortcake topped with strawberries, raspberries, or blackberries and lots of softly whipped cream.

MAKES TWELVE $2^{1}/_{2} \times 2$-INCH PIECES

$1^{1}/_{2}$ cups unbleached all-purpose flour
$^{3}/_{4}$ cup cornstarch
$^{1}/_{8}$ teaspoon salt
$^{1}/_{2}$ cup plus 2 tablespoons superfine granulated sugar
$^{1}/_{2}$ pound (2 sticks) unsalted butter cut into 16 pieces, slightly softened for about 1 hour
1 teaspoon vanilla extract

1. Position a rack in the middle of the oven. Preheat the oven to 300°F. Line an $8 \times 8 \times 2$-inch pan with heavy aluminum foil, letting the foil extend over two sides of the pan.

2. Sift the flour, cornstarch, and salt into the large bowl of an electric mixer. Add $^{1}/_{2}$ cup of the superfine sugar and mix on low speed just to blend. Drape a clean dish towel over the mixer to prevent the flour from splashing when the butter is added. Add the butter pieces and mix until fine crumbs form, 1 minute. Add the vanilla and continue mixing until large crumbs form, $^{1}/_{4}$ to $^{1}/_{2}$ inch in size, about 45 seconds.

3. Gently press the dough evenly into the prepared pan; do not pack it.

4. Bake for about 1 hour and 10 minutes, or until the edges and top of the shortbread just begin to turn golden. Remove from the oven and immediately sprinkle the remaining 2 tablespoons superfine sugar over the top. Cut 4 rows lengthwise and 3 rows across, cutting through to the bottom. Cool thoroughly. Lift the aluminum foil and shortbread from pan.

Good Advice: Sprinkle the sugar over the shortbread while it is warm so it clings. The baked shortbread cuts into squares easily when it is warm, but they should be left in the pan until cool so they don't crack. Line the pan with heavy aluminum foil and the cooled cookies will lift easily from the pan. *To Freeze:* Wrap individual pieces of shortbread in plastic wrap. Place in a metal or plastic freezer container and cover tightly. Label with the date and contents. Freeze up to 3 months. *To Serve:* Defrost the wrapped shortbread at room temperature and serve at room temperature. If desired, top each shortbread with sweetened berries and whipped cream. Leftover shortbread can be covered with plastic wrap and stored at room temperature up to 3 days.

A Scot's Favorite Shortbread

I'm fortunate to have a Scotsman for a neighbor, so when I was testing Scottish short-bread recipes I marched up to their house after every baking session with samples. Graham and his wife, Joan, took their shortbread tasting seriously, and the next morning she would ring my doorbell with the written results of their tasting. This was the one that won Graham's highest accolade: "It took me back to my youth. This is shortbread!"

MAKES 16 PIECES

1½ cups unbleached all-purpose flour
¾ cup cornstarch
⅛ teaspoon salt
¾ cup superfine sugar
½ pound (2 sticks) cold unsalted butter, cut into 16 pieces
1 teaspoon vanilla extract

1. Position a rack in the middle of the oven. Preheat the oven to 300°F. Line a 9 × 9 × 2-inch pan with heavy aluminum foil, letting the foil extend over two sides of the pan.

2. Sift the flour, cornstarch, and salt into the large bowl of an electric mixer. Add ½ cup of the superfine sugar and mix on low speed just to blend. Drape a clean dish towel over the bowl to prevent the flour from splashing when the butter is added. Add half of the butter pieces and mix until they are the size of peas, 1 minute. Add the remaining butter pieces and beat until the mixture forms fine crumbs, about 1 minute. With the machine running, add the vanilla. Continue mixing until large crumbs form, ¼ to ½ inch in size, about 45 seconds, and the dough holds together.

3. Press the dough evenly into the prepared pan and sprinkle 2 tablespoons of the superfine sugar over the top. Use a fork to prick the dough at 1-inch intervals, pressing the fork to the bottom of the pan.

4. Bake for about 1 hour, until the edges of the shortbread just begin to turn golden. The top will be a pale, slightly golden color. Remove from the oven and immediately sprinkle the remaining 2 tablespoons of superfine sugar over the top. Cut 4 rows lengthwise and 4 rows across, cutting through to the bottom. Cool thoroughly in the pan. Lift the aluminum foil and shortbread from pan. The shortbread will separate into pieces.

Good Advice: Although the ingredients are similar to those in Thick Scottish Shortbread, this is baked in a larger pan and mixed another way, so the result is completely different. The baked shortbread will be about ¾ inch thick. **Doubling the Recipe:** Mix the shortbread in 2 batches and bake it in 2 pans. **To Freeze:** Wrap individual pieces of shortbread in plastic wrap. Place in a metal or plastic freezer container and cover tightly. Label with the date and contents. Freeze up to 3 months. **To Serve:** Defrost the wrapped cookies at room temperature and serve at room temperature. Left-over shortbread can be covered with plastic wrap and stored at room temperature up to 3 days.

Grasmere Crisp Ginger Shortbread

rasmere is a tiny, picturesque village in England's Lake District. If you look for a long line of people outside a tiny cottage in the village center, you will find Sarah Nelson's famous gingerbread shop. The shop consists of a four-foot counter and sells nothing but thin crisp squares of spicy gingerbread that has so much ginger it tastes hot. The recipe is a closely guarded secret, and though you can smell the gingerbread baking, the bakers are hidden behind a floor-to-ceiling solid wood wall. 🏃 When we returned home from England, laden with several pounds of the gingerbread, I baked batch after batch of gingerbread and compared each with a piece from Grasmere. I discovered that stem ginger in syrup gave the cookie its spicy hot, soft center, and a combination of whole wheat flour, white flour, and oat bran supplied the right texture for the dough. Since the dough is soft, it can be pressed into a thin layer that makes a 3/8-inch-thick cookie. I can't say it looks exactly like Sarah Nelson's gingerbread, but it sure tastes like it.

MAKES 12 PIECES

> 1/4 cup whole wheat flour
> 1/4 cup unbleached all-purpose flour
> 1/4 teaspoon baking soda
> 1/4 teaspoon cream of tartar
> 1/2 teaspoon ground ginger
> 1/4 teaspoon ground cinnamon
> 1/2 cup oat bran
> 4 tablespoons (1/2 stick) unsalted butter
> 1/3 cup packed light brown sugar
> 2 teaspoons molasses
> 1/4 cup puréed preserved ginger in syrup, about 9 pieces, mixed with 1 teaspoon of the syrup

1. Position a rack in the middle of the oven. Preheat the oven to 325°F. Butter an 8 × 8 × 1 1/2- or 2-inch pan.

2. Sift the whole wheat flour, all-purpose flour, baking soda, cream of tartar, ground ginger, and cinnamon into a large mixing bowl. Stir in the oat bran. Remove 2 tablespoons of the mixture to a small bowl and set aside.

3. Heat the butter, brown sugar, and molasses in a small saucepan until the butter and brown sugar melt, stirring occasionally to keep smooth. Stir the butter mixture into the flour mixture. It will form a soft, wet dough. Stir 1 tablespoon of this into the reserved dry ingredients to form crumbs.

4. Spread the soft dough in a thin layer in the bottom of the prepared pan. Use your fingertips to spread the preserved ginger and syrup evenly over the dough. Sprinkle the reserved crumb mixture evenly over the ginger.

5. Bake for about 35 minutes, or until the mixture browns lightly. While it is warm, cut the gingerbread into 12 pieces, 4 rows across and 3 rows down. Cool in the pan. The gingerbread will crisp as it cools, but the stemmed ginger in the center will remain slightly soft.

Good Advice: Rafetto stem ginger in syrup is the preserved ginger I buy in my supermarket. Use a food processor to purée it. Finely chopped pieces of crystallized ginger can be substituted for the preserved ginger, but they are not as moist and don't duplicate the Grasmere version as accurately. *To Freeze:* Place the bottoms of 2 cookies together and wrap them in plastic wrap. Put the wrapped cookies in a metal or plastic freezer container and cover tightly. Label with the date and contents. Freeze up to 3 months. *To Serve:* Defrost the wrapped cookies at room temperature. Leftover cookies can be covered with plastic wrap and stored at room temperature up to 3 days.

Petticoat Tails

raham Phaup, my Scottish neighbor, has often told me that if I wanted to taste true Scottish shortbread, I must taste his mother's version. Not so easy, since she lives about four thousand miles away, until recently when his parents came for one of their rare visits. I gave them a few minutes to unpack before making arrangements to bake shortbread with Ella Phaup. It was the chance of a lifetime for a shortbread lover to be taught by a shortbread expert, and I wasn't going to miss it. We spent a whole morning baking these fine-grained buttery disks, which we cut into traditional, triangular-shaped petticoat tails. As we baked, Ella explained the important steps. Beat the butter and sugar until white, taste the creamed butter and sugar to see if it is too gritty, push and pull the dough until it feels smooth and soft, and bake the shortbread until it colors slightly and the center is firm. Then we tasted, and I knew true shortbread.

MAKES 16 PIECES FROM TWO 7-INCH ROUNDS

> 2¼ cups unbleached all-purpose flour
> 3 tablespoons plus 2 teaspoons white rice flour
> 2 tablespoons cornstarch
> Pinch salt
> ½ pound (2 sticks) soft unsalted butter
> ½ cup sugar

1. Position a rack in the middle of the oven. Preheat the oven to 300°F. Have ready two 9-inch pie tins with 7-inch bottoms.

2. Sift the flour, rice flour, cornstarch, and salt together. Set aside.

3. Put the butter and sugar in the large bowl of an electric mixer and beat on medium speed for 1 minute. Taste the mixture and note the gritty sugar texture. Beat 4 minutes more, until the color whitens and the beating mixture makes a faint slapping sound against the sides of the bowl. Taste again and the texture will be almost smooth, with just a slight grittiness. Stop the mixer and scrape the sides of the bowl during the mixing. Decrease the speed to low and add the dry ingredients a tablespoon at a time. Mix until large smooth crumbs form and all of the flour is incorporated. Remove the bowl from the mixer and use your hands to push and pull the dough against the sides of the bowl until it feels smooth and soft, about 3 minutes.

4. Divide the dough in half and press one portion firmly into each of the pans. There will be a ½-inch-thick even layer of dough in each pan. Use your thumb and forefinger to pinch a scalloped design around the edge. Use a fork to prick the dough in the bottom of the pan at 1-inch intervals.

5. Bake for about 55 minutes, until the center is firm to the touch and the top light golden. Cool for 5 minutes in the pan. Use a sharp knife to mark 8 wedge-shaped cookies in each pan, cutting about halfway through to the bottom of the pan. Cool 10 minutes longer.

Transfer the shortbread to a wire rack to cool thoroughly. Break or cut apart any cookies that are not separated.

Good Advice: After beating the butter and sugar for 1 minute, take a tiny taste of the mixture and notice the grittiness of the sugar. After about 5 minutes of beating, taste the mixture again and notice that the sugar is almost completely dissolved and the sugar crystals feel quite small in your mouth. Listen to the butter. As it approaches the correct texture, it will begin to make a faint slapping sound against the side of the bowl. ❧ Replacing some of the flour with white rice flour, which has no gluten, lowers the total gluten content and makes the shortbread especially tender. **Doubling the Recipe:** Mix the dough in 2 batches and bake in 4 pans. **To Freeze:** Place the bottoms of 2 pieces of shortbread together and wrap them in plastic wrap. Put the wrapped shortbread in a metal or plastic freezer container and cover tightly. Label with the date and contents. Freeze up to 3 months. **To Serve:** Defrost the wrapped cookies at room temperature. Leftover cookies can be covered with plastic wrap and stored at room temperature up to 3 days.

Millionaire's Shortbread

his popular English shortbread is triple-layered. The shortbread base is topped with a soft toffee filling and then coated with dark chocolate. I imagine the name came from the fact that even if you had a million dollars you couldn't buy a richer shortbread.

MAKES 36 COOKIES ABOUT 1 1/2 INCHES SQUARE

Shortbread Layer

1 cup unbleached all-purpose flour
1/2 cup cornstarch
1/2 teaspoon baking powder
12 tablespoons (1 1/2 sticks) soft unsalted butter
1/3 cup sugar

Toffee Filling

1/2 cup sugar
12 tablespoons (1 1/2 sticks) unsalted butter, cut in 6 pieces
One 14-ounce can sweetened condensed milk
1/4 cup Lyle's Golden Syrup
4 ounces (2/3 cup) semisweet chocolate chips

Position a rack in the middle of the oven. Preheat the oven to 350°F. Line a 9 × 9 × 2-inch pan with heavy aluminum foil, letting the foil extend over two ends of the pan. Butter the foil.

MAKE THE SHORTBREAD BASE

1. Sift the flour, cornstarch, and baking powder together and set aside.

2. Put the butter in a large bowl and beat with an electric mixer on low speed for 15 seconds. Add the sugar and beat on medium speed for 2 minutes, until the mixture lightens slightly in color and looks fluffy. Stop the mixer and scrape the sides of the bowl once during the mixing. Decrease the speed to low and mix in the dry ingredients until a smooth dough forms that holds together and comes away from the sides of the bowl in large clumps, about 1 minute. Stop the mixer and scrape the bowl and the beaters during the mixing. Press the dough evenly into the prepared pan.

3. Bake 25 minutes. Remove from the oven and set aside on a rack. Reduce the oven temperature to 325°F.

COOK THE FILLING

1. Put the sugar, butter, condensed milk, and golden syrup in a large saucepan. Cook over medium-low heat, stirring constantly, until the sugar dissolves and the butter melts. Increase the heat to medium-high and bring the mixture to a boil. Stand away from the mixture when it boils; it can splatter. Boil gently for 5 minutes, stirring constantly. The

mixture will become a light caramel color. You may see small brown specks of caramelized sugar, but these will disappear when the filling bakes. Pour the warm filling over the shortbread base.

2. Bake for about 10 minutes, just until the filling bubbles gently. Remove from the oven and let sit for 5 minutes. Sprinkle the chocolate chips evenly over the warm toffee and let sit for 10 minutes to melt the chocolate. Use a thin metal spatula to spread the chocolate in a thin layer over the toffee. Leave at room temperature until the chocolate is firm. (To speed the cooling, refrigerate the shortbread just until the chocolate is firm, about 1 hour. Do not let the shortbread and filling become cold as the shortbread will crumble when cut.)

3. When the chocolate is firm enough to hold its shape when cut, lift the shortbread and aluminum foil out of the pan. Use a sharp knife to cut the shortbread into 36 squares, 6 rows across and 6 rows down. Cool the shortbread thoroughly on the aluminum foil at room temperature or in the refrigerator before removing it.

Good Advice: Since the toffee mixture splatters as it cooks, prepare it in a large saucepan to prevent it from splashing out of the pan and burning you. ✿ I have tried full-fat, low-fat, and no-fat condensed milk for these cookies, but notice no difference in the result. Light corn syrup can be substituted for the Lyle's Golden Syrup, but I prefer the taste of the golden syrup. **To Freeze:** Place the bottoms of 2 pieces of shortbread together and wrap them in plastic wrap. Put the wrapped shortbread in a metal or plastic freezer container and cover tightly. Label with the date and contents. Freeze up to 3 months. **To Serve:** Defrost the wrapped shortbread at room temperature. Leftovers can be covered with plastic wrap and stored at room temperature up to 3 days.

Lemon-Glazed Shortbread Wedges

 easpoon for teaspoon, lemon zest adds a stronger lemon flavor to foods than lemon juice. Since shortbread traditionally contains little or no liquid, I use lemon zest in the dough and lemon juice and zest in the glaze to pack the lemon punch in these sweet and tart cookies.

MAKES 12 WEDGE-SHAPED COOKIES

Shortbread

> 1 cup unbleached all-purpose flour
> 1/2 cup white rice flour
> 12 tablespoons (1 1/2 sticks) soft unsalted butter
> 1/3 cup sugar
> 1 teaspoon grated lemon zest
> 1/2 teaspoon vanilla extract
> 1/4 teaspoon almond extract

Lemon Glaze

> 1/2 cup powdered sugar
> 2 tablespoons fresh lemon juice
> 3/4 teaspoon grated lemon zest

PREPARE THE COOKIES

1. Position a rack in the middle of the oven. Preheat the oven to 325°F. Butter a 10-inch pie tin 1 1/2 inches deep.

2. Sift the flours together. Set aside.

3. Put the butter in a large bowl and beat with an electric mixer on low speed for 15 seconds. Add the sugar and lemon zest and beat on medium speed for 2 minutes, until the mixture lightens in color and looks fluffy. Stop the mixer and scrape the sides of the bowl once during the mixing. Add the vanilla and almond extracts. Decrease the speed to low and blend in the flour mixture until you have a smooth dough that holds together and comes away from the sides of the bowl, about 1 minute. Stop the mixer and scrape the bowl and the beaters during the mixing. Press the dough evenly into the prepared pan.

4. Bake for about 35 minutes, or until the top is pale golden and the edges light brown. Glaze and cut the shortbread while it is warm.

PREPARE THE LEMON GLAZE

1. Put the powdered sugar in a small bowl. Stir in the lemon juice and lemon zest until the mixture is smooth. The glaze will be syrupy. Immediately pour the glaze over the warm shortbread and spread it evenly with the back of a spoon.

2. Working from the center to the edge, use a sharp knife to cut the warm shortbread into 12 wedges. Cool the shortbread in the pan until the glaze is firm.

Good Advice: Wash and dry the lemons before grating the zest from them. Be sure to use only the yellow zest; the white pith is bitter. One lemon produces about 1 teaspoon of zest. ✴ Baking this shortbread in a pie tin with sloping sides makes the wedge-shaped cookies easy to remove. Use a 10-inch pie pan that has a 9-inch bottom. ✴ Cut the wedges from the center to the edge to prevent the point of the triangle from crumbling. *To Freeze:* Place the bottoms of 2 shortbread wedges together and wrap them in plastic wrap. Put the wrapped shortbread in a metal or plastic freezer container and cover tightly. Label with the date and contents. Freeze up to 3 months. *To Serve:* Defrost the wrapped cookies at room temperature. Leftover shortbread can be covered with plastic wrap and stored at room temperature up to 3 days.

Shortbread Rounds

very Christmas, I look forward to the holiday cookies that my friend Rosalee Glass bakes. Her cookie tins hold the classics that I remember from my childhood—nut cookies coated with powdered sugar, chocolate-covered bars, and these thick, buttery shortbread rounds. Rosalee thinks she adapted her recipe from an out-of-print edition of the *Joy of Cooking*.

MAKES 24 COOKIES

> 1½ cups plus 2 tablespoons unbleached all-purpose flour
> ¼ teaspoon baking powder
> ¼ teaspoon salt
> ½ pound (2 sticks) cold unsalted butter
> ½ cup powdered sugar, sifted
> 1 teaspoon vanilla extract

1. Position the oven racks in the middle and lower middle of the oven. Preheat the oven to 325°F. Line 2 baking sheets with parchment paper.

2. Sift the flour, baking powder, and salt together. Set aside.

3. Put the butter in a large bowl and beat with an electric mixer on low speed for 15 seconds. Add the powdered sugar and beat on medium speed until the butter and sugar are blended together. Add the vanilla. Decrease the speed to low and mix in the flour mixture until the dough looks smooth and holds together.

4. On a lightly floured surface with a lightly floured rolling pin, roll the dough out to ⅓-inch thickness. Using a round pastry cutter 2 inches in diameter, cut out circles and place them on the prepared baking sheet about 1 inch apart. Gather together the dough scraps, roll them, and cut out more circles.

5. Bake for about 18 minutes, or until the edges and bottoms of the cookies are golden. Reverse the baking sheets after 10 minutes, front to back and top to bottom, to ensure that the cookies bake evenly. Cool them on the baking sheets for 5 minutes, then transfer them to wire racks to cool completely.

Good Advice: Use cold butter so a firm dough forms. The first time I prepared these cookies, I used very soft butter. The resulting dough was so soft the cookies spread over the sheet and baked into one giant wafer. ✿ Use a ruler to measure the ⅓-inch thickness. The cookies actually taste different if they are rolled thinner; it's not a bad taste, but not as good as Rosalee's cookies. **To Freeze:** Place the bottoms of 2 cookies together and wrap them in plastic wrap. Put the wrapped cookies in a metal or plastic freezer container and cover tightly. Label with the date and contents. Freeze up to 3 months. **To Serve:** Defrost the wrapped cookies at room temperature. Leftover cookies can be covered with plastic wrap and stored at room temperature up to 4 days.

Brown Sugar Pecan Shortbread

 h, what that brown sugar and butter combination can do! Imagine the aroma when they cook together. Then you will understand what happens when they're paired to produce these golden brown, thick rounds studded with chopped pecans.

MAKES FIFTEEN 2³/₄-INCH COOKIES

³/₄ cup unbleached all-purpose flour
¹/₂ cup cake flour
¹/₄ teaspoon salt
³/₄ teaspoon ground cinnamon
12 tablespoons (1¹/₂ sticks) soft unsalted butter
¹/₂ cup plus 2 tablespoons packed light brown sugar
³/₄ cup coarsely chopped pecans
15 pecan halves

1. Position a rack in the middle of the oven. Preheat the oven to 325°F. Line a baking sheet with parchment paper.

2. Sift the flours, salt, and cinnamon together. Set aside.

3. Put the butter and brown sugar in the large bowl of an electric mixer and beat on medium speed for 2 minutes, until the color lightens and the mixture looks smooth. Stop the mixer and scrape the sides of the bowl and the beaters during the mixing. Decrease the speed to low and slowly add the flour mixture. Mix until all of the flour is incorporated and a smooth dough forms. Stir in the chopped pecans.

4. Using about 1¹/₂ tablespoons of dough for each cookie, roll into 15 smooth balls. Place the balls 2 inches apart on the prepared baking sheet and use the palm of your hand to flatten each into a 2-inch disk. Press a pecan half into the center of each cookie.

5. Bake for about 30 minutes. Gently touch a cookie; it should feel crusty on the outside but soft underneath. Be careful not to burn yourself. The bottoms should be evenly golden. Cool the cookies for 5 minutes on the baking sheet, then transfer them to a wire cake rack to cool thoroughly. The soft cookies crisp as they cool.

Good Advice: Cake flour replaces some of the all-purpose flour and makes the cookies tender. On a hot day, the dough may become too soft to roll into smooth balls. Refrigerate the dough to firm it, then form the cookies. **To Freeze:** Place the bottoms of 2 cookies together and wrap them in plastic wrap. Put the wrapped cookies in a metal or plastic freezer container and cover tightly. Label with the date and contents. Freeze up to 3 months. **To Serve:** Defrost the wrapped cookies at room temperature. Serve within 4 days.

Toasted Hazelnut Shortbread Hearts Dipped in Milk Chocolate

he texture of this lavish chocolate-dipped shortbread is delicate. The hazelnuts add the right amount of crunch, and the cookies hold their heart shape perfectly as they bake.

MAKES ABOUT 62 COOKIES

1/2 cup cornstarch
3/4 cup peeled hazelnuts, toasted (pages 3–4)
1 3/4 cups unbleached all-purpose flour
1/2 teaspoon baking powder
1/4 teaspoon salt
1/2 pound plus 4 tablespoons (2 1/2 sticks) soft unsalted butter
2/3 cup superfine granulated sugar
2 teaspoons vanilla extract
1 tablespoon vegetable shortening, such as Crisco
6 ounces milk chocolate, chopped (preferably Callebaut or Dove Bar)

MAKE THE COOKIES

1. Position 2 oven racks in the lower middle and upper third of the oven. Preheat the oven to 400°F. Line 2 heavyweight baking sheets with parchment paper.

2. Put the cornstarch and hazelnuts in the work bowl of a food processor fitted with the steel blade and process with a few short bursts to combine. Process the mixture about 3 minutes until the hazelnuts are finely ground. Set aside.

3. Sift the flour, baking powder, and salt together. Set aside.

4. Put the butter in a large bowl and beat with an electric mixer on low speed for 15 seconds. Add the sugar slowly and beat on medium speed for 2 minutes, until the mixture lightens slightly in color and looks smooth. Stop the mixer and scrape the sides of the bowl once during the mixing. Blend in the vanilla. Decrease the speed to low and mix in the nuts. Add the flour mixture and beat just until a soft dough forms. Stop the mixer and scrape the bowl and the beaters during the mixing. Form the dough into two 6-inch disks and wrap in plastic wrap. Refrigerate until the dough is cold and just firm enough to roll, about 1 hour.

5. Remove 1 disk of dough from the refrigerator. Lightly flour the rolling surface and rolling pin and roll the dough 1/4 inch thick. Use a 2-inch heart-shaped metal cutter to cut out cookie hearts. With a metal spatula, lift and transfer the cookies to the prepared baking sheets, placing them 1 inch apart. Remove the second disk from the refrigerator and repeat. Gather the scraps together and repeat until all the dough is used.

6. Bake the cookies for about 20 minutes, or until they are golden, reversing the baking sheets after 12 minutes front to back and top to bottom to ensure that the cookies bake evenly. Cool the cookies on the baking sheets for 5 minutes, then use a wide metal spatula to transfer them to wire racks to cool completely.

PREPARE THE CHOCOLATE COATING

Put the vegetable shortening and milk chocolate in a heatproof container and place it over, but not touching, a saucepan of barely simmering water. Stir over the hot water until the chocolate is melted and the mixture is smooth. Put the melted chocolate mixture in a small, shallow bowl. Dip one side of the top of each cookie in the chocolate and place it on the wire rack until the chocolate is firm. Use a sweeping motion to pull one side of the cookie through the chocolate.

Good Advice: Cold dough will not stick to the rolling surface when it is rolled out. 🍪 The combination of milk chocolate and vegetable shortening produces a chocolate coating with an appealing satin sheen. *To Freeze:* Place the bottoms of 2 cookies together and wrap them in plastic wrap. Put the wrapped cookies in a metal or plastic freezer container and cover tightly. Label with the date and contents. Freeze up to 2 months. *To Serve:* Defrost the wrapped cookies at room temperature or in the refrigerator if the weather is warm. Serve within 3 days.

Butter Cookies and Crisps

lthough all of these butter cookies are crisp, all of these crisps are not butter cookies. Butter cookies contain a large quantity of butter beaten with sugar and eggs to produce a light, tender texture. Even when the cookies contain chocolate, dried fruit, or caramelized sugar, it's the butter flavor that shines through. Crisps, on the other hand, are crunchy throughout. Some are so thin they're almost translucent. Crisps contain a large proportion of sugar and a small proportion of flour. This produces a liquid batter that bakes into brittle cookies. Crisps taste of butter, but it's not always the main flavor. Butter Pecan Crisps are actually mounds of pecans held together by a soft butter dough. It's a butter cookie–crisp alliance.

Most of these cookies can be formed quickly by dropping mounds of batter onto a baking sheet or rolling the dough into balls and then flattening them into wafers. Cherry Orange Flaky Flats use a combination of butter and vegetable shortening to produce a tender cookie with the same flaky layers found in a pie crust.

Ultra-thin Almond Tuiles that curve like French roof tiles and crisp, lace-textured cookies like Cashew Lace Crisps always surprise me. They look difficult but are the simplest of drop cookies. Try them if you want to make an impression.

Butter Nuggets

he dictionary definition of a nugget as "a small lump of gold . . . that has great value" makes a perfect description for these edible cookie nuggets. Packed with the greatest butter flavor and most melting texture of any butter cookie that I have ever baked, they prove their "great value" with every bite.

MAKES 72 COOKIES

2^1/$_4$ cups unbleached all-purpose flour
^{1}/$_2$ cup cornstarch
^{1}/$_2$ teaspoon baking powder
^{1}/$_4$ teaspoon salt
^{3}/$_4$ pound (3 sticks) soft unsalted butter
1 cup sugar
3 large egg yolks
2 teaspoons vanilla extract
^{1}/$_2$ teaspoon almond extract

1. Sift the flour, cornstarch, baking powder, and salt together and set aside.

2. Put the butter in a large bowl and mix with an electric mixer on low speed for 15 seconds. Add the sugar and beat on medium speed for 2 minutes, until lightened in color and fluffy. Stop the mixer and scrape the sides of the bowl once during the mixing. Blend in the egg yolks, vanilla, and almond extract until smooth, 1 minute. Stop the mixer and scrape the bowl. On low speed add the flour mixture, mixing just until the flour is incorporated completely. The dough will be soft.

3. Form the dough into 3 rectangles 4^1/$_2$ × 4 inches and ^{3}/$_4$ inch thick. Wrap each piece of dough in plastic wrap and refrigerate until firm, about 1 hour or overnight, or the disks of dough can be frozen.

Good Advice: When I first baked these ^{1}/$_2$-inch-thick cookies, the bottoms kept burning before the insides were done. The low baking temperature produces crisp cookies with golden bottoms. **To Freeze Unbaked Dough:** Wrap each plastic-wrapped disk in heavy aluminum foil. Label with the date and contents. Freeze up to 3 months. To bake the cookies, defrost as many pieces of dough as needed overnight in the refrigerator. Cut and bake as directed. **To Bake:** Position 2 oven racks in the middle and upper third of the oven. Preheat the oven to 300°F. Line 3 baking sheets with parchment paper or heavy aluminum foil. ❀ Remove a disk of dough from the refrigerator and unwrap it. Cut it into six ^{3}/$_4$-inch strips. Cut each strip into four 1-inch pieces. Place the cookies 1 inch apart on the baking sheets. Repeat with the remaining dough. ❀ Bake 2 sheets of cookies for 22 to 27 minutes, until the edges and bottoms are dark golden. Reverse the baking sheets after 12 minutes front to back and top to bottom to ensure that the cookies bake evenly. Cut one in half to check if the center is moist. If it is, continue baking for several additional minutes. Bake the remaining sheet on the middle rack, reversing the baking sheet after 12 minutes. Cool the cookies on the baking sheets for 5 minutes, then transfer them to wire racks to cool completely. **To Freeze:** Line a plastic freezer container with plastic wrap. Fill it with the cooled cookies, press plastic wrap onto them, and cover tightly. Label with the date and contents. Freeze up to 3 months. **To Serve:** Cover them with plastic wrap and defrost at room temperature. Serve within 5 days.

Cherry Orange Flaky Flats

hese cookies turned me into a woman with a mission. I had noticed a picture in Linda Dannenburg's book, *Paris Boulangerie Pâtisserie*, of a flaky cookie that looked full of butter. When I tried the recipe, it wasn't what I expected, so I set out to create a cookie that tasted as good as the picture looked. I tried butter doughs, sour cream doughs, and what I thought would be flaky doughs, and baked dozens of cookies. None of them was as delicate, flaky, or buttery as I wanted. Finally I decided to begin with my basic pie crust recipe and build the recipe from there. Mission completed. Bite into a cookie and you'll see the flaky layers, taste the rich orange buttery flavor, and know why I wrote on my final page of testing notes, "Worth the testing!"

MAKES ABOUT TWENTY-FOUR 2-INCH SQUARES

1 cup unbleached all-purpose flour
$^1/_3$ cup cake flour
$^1/_4$ teaspoon salt
3 tablespoons plus 2 teaspoons sugar
6 tablespoons ($^3/_4$ stick) cold unsalted butter, cut in 4 pieces
3 tablespoons cold vegetable shortening
$^1/_2$ teaspoon grated lemon zest
$1^1/_2$ teaspoons grated orange zest
1 large egg, separated
1 teaspoon vanilla extract
$^1/_2$ cup pitted dried cherries

1. Position a rack in the middle of the oven. Preheat the oven to 350°F. Line a baking sheet with parchment paper.

2. Put the flours, salt, and 3 tablespoons of the sugar in the large bowl of an electric mixer and mix on low speed just to blend the ingredients, about 10 seconds. Stop the mixer, add the butter and shortening, and mix just until the butter and shortening pieces are the size of small lima beans, about 20 seconds. Mix in the lemon and orange zests. With the mixer running, add the egg yolk, vanilla, and 2 tablespoons ice water. Add the dried cherries. Continue mixing just until the mixture holds together and comes away from the sides of the bowl. There will be no loose flour. Press the dough into a 6-inch square about 1 inch thick. Wrap it in plastic wrap and chill it in the refrigerator for at least 2 hours or overnight.

3. Remove the dough from the refrigerator and unwrap it. If it has become cold and hard, let it sit at room temperature for 5 to 10 minutes until it is easy to roll. Put the dough between 2 pieces of wax paper and roll it into a rectangle about 12 × 8 inches and about $^1/_8$ inch thick. Remove the top piece of wax paper. Trim the edges evenly. Use a pizza cutter to cut 2-inch-wide strips along the length. Cut the strips into 2-inch squares. Turn over and peel off the other piece of wax paper. Place the squares $^1/_2$ inch apart on the prepared baking sheet, using a wide spatula. Using a pastry brush, lightly brush each

cookie with the egg white (after breaking it up with a fork) and sprinkle evenly with a pinch of the remaining 2 teaspoons sugar. (One teaspoon of sugar will cover half the cookies.)

4. Bake about 20 minutes, or until the tops are light golden and the bottoms are light brown. Transfer the cookies to wire racks to cool completely.

Good Advice: I use dried cherries in these cookies, but dried cranberries or raisins can be substituted. ✿ The cookies do not spread, so they can be placed close together on 1 baking sheet. ✿ A pizza cutter works well for cutting the cookies since it cuts smoothly through the dried cherries. ✿ Bake these cookies on a shiny, not dark, baking sheet. The cherries can burn before the cookies are ready if a dark-colored baking sheet is used; I know, I tried it. **To Freeze:** Stack 6 cookies together and wrap them in plastic wrap. Put the wrapped cookies in a metal or plastic freezer container and cover tightly. Label with the date and contents. Freeze up to 3 months. **To Serve:** Defrost the wrapped cookies at room temperature. Serve within 5 days.

Swedish Chocolate Butter Cookies

ven when they live oceans apart, people who enjoy baking find each other. These cookies came from Gulli Zilberstein, my e-pal (that's an e-mail pen pal), who lives in Sweden, where she bakes these cookies for a Stockholm café. They are flat, crisp chocolate cookies with a soft interior and crunchy almond and sugar topping.

MAKES 48 COOKIES

1½ cups unbleached all-purpose flour
2 teaspoons baking powder
7 ounces (1¾ sticks) soft unsalted butter
1 cup plus 3 tablespoons sugar
1 teaspoon vanilla extract
¼ cup unsweetened Droste Dutch process cocoa powder
1 egg white, slightly beaten with a fork
½ cup sliced almonds

1. Position 2 oven racks in the middle and upper third of the oven. Preheat the oven to 350°F. Line two 18 × 12-inch baking sheets with heavy aluminum foil.

2. Sift the flour and baking powder together and set aside.

3. Put the butter, 1 cup plus 1 tablespoon of the sugar, and the vanilla in a large mixing bowl and beat with an electric mixer on medium speed for 2 minutes, until the mixture is smooth and fluffy. Blend in the cocoa powder. Stop the mixer and scrape the sides of the bowl once during the mixing. On low speed, add the flour mixture and mix until it is incorporated completely. The dough will be soft and smooth.

4. Divide the dough into 4 pieces. Lightly flour a rolling surface. Use your hands to roll each piece of dough along the counter into a 12-inch-long sausage shape. Spacing them evenly 4 inches apart, put 2 dough sausages on each baking sheet. Press each piece of dough flat into a rectangle about 16 inches long and 2 inches wide. Brush lightly with egg white. Sprinkle each strip with 1½ teaspoons of the remaining sugar. Gently press 2 tablespoons of almonds evenly over the top of each strip.

5. Bake about 11 minutes, reversing the baking sheets after 6 minutes, front to back and top to bottom, to ensure that the cookies bake evenly. The tops should crack and the almonds will toast to a golden color. Each strip becomes 4 to 5 inches wide as it bakes. Remove the cookies from the oven and let cool 5 minutes on the baking sheets. Use a sharp knife to cut each strip at an angle into 12 diagonal strips about 1 inch wide. Cool on the sheets 5 more minutes, then transfer the cookies to wire racks to cool thoroughly.

VARIATION   Brush each strip of dough lightly with egg white. Mix 2 tablespoons sugar with 1½ teaspoons ground cinnamon. Sprinkle the cinnamon sugar mixture evenly over each strip and bake.

Good Advice: After baking, there will be 4 large strips about 14 inches long and 5 inches wide. While the cookie strips are warm and soft, cut diagonal slices to form individual cookies. Blanched or unblanched sliced almonds work equally well for the topping. **Doubling the Recipe:** Use 1 tablespoon of baking powder and double the remaining ingredients. You will have 8 strips. **To Freeze:** Stack 4 cookies together and wrap in plastic wrap. Put the wrapped cookies in a metal or plastic freezer container and cover tightly. Label with the date and contents. Freeze up to 3 months. **To Serve:** Defrost the wrapped cookies at room temperature. Serve within 3 days.

Triple-Chocolate-Topped Chocolate Butter Cookies

hese are dark chocolate buttery wafers decorated with thin lines of milk, dark, and white chocolate. The decoration is simple to add, but makes a big impression. When my son, Peter, brought twelve of his visiting Japanese friends to dinner, I knew that even though they didn't like rich desserts, they expected a grand dessert from Peter's baker mother. Peter's suggestion to serve big platters of cookies was the perfect solution. I served fifteen kinds of cookies, but they singled out these chocolate ones and kept asking Peter if I had really made them. Everyone thought they looked too fancy to be homemade.

MAKES 54 COOKIES

2^{1}/$_{2}$ cups unbleached all-purpose flour
^{1}/$_{2}$ cup unsweetened Dutch process cocoa powder, such as Droste or Hershey's European
^{3}/$_{4}$ pound (3 sticks) soft unsalted butter
^{1}/$_{4}$ teaspoon salt
1^{1}/$_{4}$ cups sugar
^{3}/$_{4}$ teaspoon instant decaffeinated coffee granules
3 large egg yolks
2 teaspoons vanilla extract
^{1}/$_{2}$ teaspoon almond extract
2 ounces milk chocolate, chopped
2 ounces white chocolate, chopped (preferably Callebaut, Lindt, or Baker's Premium)
2 ounces semisweet chocolate, chopped

1. Position 2 oven racks in the middle and upper third of the oven. Preheat the oven to 300°F. Line 3 baking sheets with parchment paper.

2. Sift the flour and cocoa powder together and set aside.

3. Put the butter and salt in a large bowl and mix with an electric mixer on low speed for 15 seconds. Increase the speed to medium, add the sugar and instant coffee, and beat on medium speed for 1 minute until smooth. Mix in the egg yolks, vanilla, and almond extract until the egg yolks are incorporated. On low speed slowly add the flour mixture. Beat just until the flour mixture is blended in completely and a soft dough forms that holds together, about 45 seconds.

4. Form the cookies by rolling 1 tablespoon of dough between the palms of your hands into a 1-inch ball; then flatten the ball into a 1^{3}/$_{4}$-inch circle. Repeat to use all the dough. Place the cookies 1 inch apart on the baking sheets. Set aside 1 baking sheet of cookies at room temperature.

5. Bake 2 sheets of cookies about 16 to 18 minutes, until they change from shiny to dull and the tops feel firm. Check to see that the bottoms of the cookies look dry. Reverse the baking sheets after 8 minutes, front to back and top to bottom, to ensure that the cookies

bake evenly. Bake the remaining sheet of cookies on the middle rack of the oven, reversing it after 8 minutes. Cool the cookies on the baking sheet for 5 minutes, then transfer them to wire racks to cool completely. Place the cookies so they are touching each other so you don't lose any chocolate when you drizzle it on.

6. Preheat the oven to 175°F. Place each type of chocolate in a separate small nonreactive ovenproof container and melt them in the oven, about 5 minutes. Remove from the oven as soon as they are melted and stir them smooth. Using a clean fork for each flavor of chocolate, dip a fork into the melted milk chocolate and wave it over the cookies to form thin lines of chocolate crisscrossing back and forth over the top. Do the same with the white chocolate and then the semisweet chocolate. Let the cookies sit until the chocolate is firm.

Good Advice: Baking these cookies at a low 300°F prevents the bottoms from overbaking before the insides of the cookies are baked. ❧ The melted chocolates for the topping should be warm so that they are liquid enough to drizzle in thin lines. **To Freeze:** Place the bottoms of 2 cookies together and wrap them in plastic wrap. Put the wrapped cookies in a metal or plastic freezer container and cover tightly. Label with the date and contents. Freeze up to 3 months. **To Serve:** Defrost the wrapped cookies at room temperature. Serve within 3 days.

Caramel Crunch Butter Cookies

hese were among the first cookies that I made as a young bride. I bravely melted sugar to a caramel and discovered it was easy; and I dared to bake a cookie without my mother standing by, and succeeded.

MAKES 24 COOKIES

1 cup sugar
1¼ cups unbleached all-purpose flour
½ teaspoon baking powder
12 tablespoons (1½ sticks) soft unsalted butter
½ teaspoon vanilla extract

1. Lightly oil a metal baking sheet with 1-inch-high sides.

2. Put ½ cup of the sugar in a large, heavy frying pan or medium saucepan, preferably with a nonstick finish, and cook over low heat. Stir occasionally with a wooden spoon to ensure that the sugar melts evenly. When it begins to melt, increase the heat to medium and cook to a golden color. Immediately pour the caramelized sugar onto the prepared baking sheet. It will spread into a smooth layer. Be careful, as the mixture is very hot. Cool until it hardens and is cool to the touch, about 30 minutes. Break the caramelized sugar into several pieces, wrap it in heavy aluminum foil, and crush it with a clean mallet, rolling pin, or meat pounder into pieces approximately ¼ to ½ inch in size. You will have ½ cup of crushed caramelized sugar. As long as the weather isn't humid, it can be tightly sealed in a tin and stored at room temperature up to 3 days.

3. Position 2 racks in the lower middle and upper middle of the oven. Preheat the oven to 325°F. Line 2 baking sheets with nonstick liners or parchment paper.

4. Sift the flour and baking powder together and set aside.

5. Put the butter, the remaining ½ cup sugar, and the vanilla in the large bowl of an electric mixer and beat on medium speed until lightened in color and fluffy, about 1 minute. Decrease the speed to low and add half the flour mixture, mixing just until it is incorporated completely. Add 2 tablespoons water, mixing until it is blended into the dough. Mix in the remaining flour mixture just until it is incorporated. Stir in the crushed caramelized sugar. Using a level tablespoon of batter for each cookie, place mounds of batter 2½ inches apart on the prepared baking sheets.

6. Bake until the edges and bottoms are golden and the cookies flatten, 14 to 16 minutes. Reverse the baking sheets after 7 minutes, front to back and top to bottom, to ensure that the cookies bake evenly. Cool them on the baking sheets for 5 minutes, then transfer them to a wire rack to cool completely. The cookies and caramelized sugar become crisp as they cool.

To Freeze: Place the bottoms of 2 cookies together and wrap them in plastic wrap. Put the wrapped cookies in a metal or plastic freezer container and cover tightly. Label with the date and contents. Freeze up to 3 months. **To Serve:** Defrost the wrapped cookies at room temperature. Serve within 2 days. These cookies soften when the weather is humid.

Cashew Lace Crisps

ace cookies are made from a cooked mixture of butter, sugar, nuts, and a small amount of flour. As they bake, the batter melts into a thin lace-textured brittle cookie. Their one flaw is that they are sometimes so fragile they break easily. Adding some ground nuts and Lyle's Golden Syrup to the batter produces the ideal lace cookie that shatters when you eat it, but not before. The cookie's sophisticated appearance belies its simple preparation.

MAKES 32 COOKIES

4 tablespoons (^{1}/$_2$ stick) unsalted butter
^{1}/$_3$ cup sugar
2 tablespoons Lyle's Golden Syrup or light corn syrup
^{1}/$_3$ cup unbleached all-purpose flour
1 teaspoon vanilla extract
^{1}/$_2$ cup roasted cashew nuts, ground
^{3}/$_4$ cup roasted cashew nuts, coarsely chopped

1. Position 2 oven racks in the middle and upper third of the oven. Preheat the oven to 350°F. Line 2 baking sheets with nonstick liners or parchment paper.

2. Put the butter, sugar, and syrup in a medium saucepan and cook over low heat until the butter melts and the sugar dissolves, stirring often. Increase the heat to medium-high and bring to a boil, stirring constantly. The mixture will be smooth and syrupy. Remove from the heat and stir in the flour until it is incorporated. Stir in the vanilla, ground cashews, and chopped cashews. Drop teaspoons of batter 3 inches apart on the baking sheets.

3. Bake the cookies 8 to 9 minutes until the bottoms and edges are light brown and the centers are golden. Reverse the baking sheets after 4 minutes, front to back and top to bottom, to ensure that the cookies bake evenly. (One baking sheet of cookies may be done 1 minute sooner than the other.) Cool the cookies on the baking sheets for 5 minutes, then transfer them to wire racks to cool completely. They become crisp as they cool.

VARIATION   Substitute ground almonds and slivered almonds for the cashew nuts. To produce curved lace cookies, place warm cookies on a rolling pin or on small clean cans without paper labels, to cool.

To Freeze: Place the bottoms of 2 cookies together and wrap them in plastic wrap. Wrap curved cookies separately. Put the wrapped cookies in a metal or plastic freezer container and cover tightly. Label with the date and contents. Freeze up to 3 months. To Serve: Defrost the wrapped cookies at room temperature. Serve within 3 days, or within 1 day if the weather is humid.

Parisian Toffee Crisps

M ost people who dine at the Ambassade d'Auvergne in Paris try the *aligot*, an elastic purée of cheese, potatoes, and garlic, which the waiters lift several feet into the air as they serve it. But I go to this family restaurant so I can have these toffee crisps that are served with the house-made ice cream. They are dark cookies with the crunch of butter toffee candy and the intense taste of caramelized brown sugar and butter.

MAKES 26 COOKIES

> 1 cup plus 2 tablespoons unbleached all-purpose flour
> $^1/_4$ teaspoon salt
> 12 tablespoons ($1^1/_2$ sticks) soft unsalted butter
> $^2/_3$ cup packed dark brown sugar
> 2 teaspoons vanilla extract

1. Position 2 oven racks in the middle and upper third of the oven. Preheat the oven to 350°F. Line 2 baking sheets with nonstick liners or parchment paper.

2. Sift the flour and salt together and set aside.

3. Put the butter and dark brown sugar in the large bowl of an electric mixer and beat on low speed for about 1 minute, until the mixture is smooth and blended. Mix in the vanilla. Add the flour mixture, mixing just until it is incorporated and a smooth dough forms. Stop the mixer and scrape the sides of the bowl during this mixing. Form each cookie by rolling 1 tablespoon of dough between the palms of your hands into a 1-inch ball and flattening the ball into a $1^3/_4$-inch circle. Place the cookies 2 inches apart on the baking sheets.

4. Bake about 12 minutes, until the edges and bottoms darken slightly and the cookies flatten. Reverse the baking sheets after 7 minutes, front to back and top to bottom, to ensure that the cookies bake evenly. Cool them on the baking sheets for 5 minutes, then transfer them to wire racks to cool completely. The cookies become crisp as they cool.

VARIATION   Roll 1 tablespoon of the dough into a $1^1/_4$-inch ball. Place the balls 3 inches apart on the baking sheets and bake as directed above. These larger cookies will flatten toward the end of the baking time, but are somewhat thicker than the flattened balls and slightly soft in the center.

To Freeze: Place the bottoms of 2 cookies together and wrap them in plastic wrap. Put the wrapped cookies in a metal or plastic freezer container and cover tightly. Label with the date and contents. Freeze up to 3 months. To Serve: Defrost the wrapped cookies at room temperature. Serve within 4 days.

Butter Pecan Crisps

Sammye Williams and I became friends while participating in a Race for the Cure in Washington, D.C. When Sammye found out I was writing a cookie cookbook, she offered to share her recipe for what she described as "one of the best cookies in the world." By that afternoon, I had the recipe and knew she wasn't exaggerating. The ingredients are simple—butter, sugar, flour, egg, and pecans. It's the proportions that are unusual. The dough produces a crisp cookie because it has a large quantity of butter and sugar relative to the flour, and because it includes a large measure of pecans. The result is crisp, buttery cookie-coated pecans.

MAKES ABOUT 66 COOKIES

1/2 pound (2 sticks) soft unsalted butter
1 cup sugar
1 large egg
1 cup unbleached all-purpose flour
4 cups (1 pound) pecan halves

1. Position 2 racks in the lower middle and upper middle of the oven. Preheat the oven to 300°F. Line 4 baking sheets with nonstick liners or parchment paper. Or, bake 2 sheets, cool, and reuse them.

2. Put the butter and sugar in the large bowl of an electric mixer and beat on medium speed until lightened in color and thoroughly blended, about 1 minute. Mix in the egg until it is incorporated. Stop the mixer and scrape the sides of the bowl once during the mixing. Decrease the speed to low and add the flour, beating until it is incorporated and a smooth, sticky dough forms. Use a large spoon to stir in the pecans. Using a level tablespoon of batter for each cookie, place mounds of dough 2 inches apart on the prepared baking sheets. Each cookie has at least 4 or 5 pecan halves in it.

3. Bake just until the edges begin to change color, about 17 minutes. Reverse the baking sheets after 9 minutes, front to back and top to bottom, to ensure that the cookies bake evenly. Repeat with the remaining sheets of cookies. Cool on the baking sheets for 5 minutes. Carefully lift the baking liners from the sheets and put back down. Use a wide metal spatula to transfer the cookies to wire racks to cool completely. They become crisp as they cool.

Good Advice: Stir the pecans into the dough by hand; the electric mixer could break the nut halves. Sammye bakes the cookies just until the edges begin to change color. The tops are pale and become crisp when cool. If the color remains pale, the cookie will have a small chewy spot in the center. If they bake until the edges and bottoms are golden, about 3 additional minutes, they will be crisp all the way through. ✻ One batch of cookies requires 4 baking sheets, but you can bake 2 sheets, cool the pans, and reuse them. The remaining batter can sit at room temperature while the first batch bakes. **Doubling the Recipe:** Mix the dough in separate batches. **To Freeze:** Place the bottoms of 2 cookies together and wrap them in plastic wrap. Put the wrapped cookies in a metal or plastic freezer container and cover tightly. Label with the date and contents. Freeze up to 3 months. **To Serve:** Defrost the wrapped cookies at room temperature. Serve within 3 days.

Almond Tuiles

y friend Helen Hall is a master at making the most complicated recipe simple, even these fancy French cookies. I put off testing this recipe because I've had so many tuile flops, but I should have trusted Helen. Her recipe is foolproof. The batter is mixed quickly with a fork, and it keeps its shape during baking. ☀ Tuiles are curved cookies less than $^{1}/_{16}$ inch thick that imitate the shape of roof tiles. As soon as they come out of the oven, oval or round cookies are placed over a rolling pin or similar cylinder shape to curve them. The versatile batter can be spread into large rounds for molding into cups for ice cream or mousse, or long cookie strips that can be twisted into corkscrews for a fanciful garnish.

MAKES ABOUT FIFTEEN 4-INCH COOKIES

> 2 large egg whites
> $^{1}/_{2}$ cup sugar
> 6 tablespoons ($^{3}/_{4}$ stick) unsalted butter, melted and cooled
> $^{1}/_{2}$ cup cake flour
> 1 teaspoon vanilla extract
> $^{1}/_{2}$ teaspoon almond extract
> $^{2}/_{3}$ cup (about $1^{1}/_{2}$ ounces) sliced almonds (not toasted)

1. Position a rack in the middle of the oven. Preheat the oven to 350°F. Line 3 baking sheets with nonstick liners.

2. Put the egg whites and sugar in a medium bowl and beat with a fork until smooth and blended, about 20 seconds. Add the melted butter, cake flour, vanilla, and almond extract and mix until all of the flour is incorporated. The mixture will be smooth and shiny.

3. Using 1 tablespoon of batter for each cookie, spread five 4-inch circles on a prepared baking sheet. The batter looks translucent and in some spots you will see through to the baking sheet. Sprinkle about 2 teaspoons of sliced almonds over the top of each cookie. Prepare another sheet of cookies while the first sheet bakes.

4. Bake until a 1- to $1^{1}/_{2}$-inch border is evenly brown and the center is light golden, about 9 minutes. The almonds will be lightly toasted. Remove from the oven. Using a wide spatula, carefully lift a warm cookie and drape it over a rolling pin, clean bottle, or clean small can, with any labels removed. When it is firm and has cooled slightly, about 1 minute, move it to a wire rack to cool thoroughly. Be careful not to burn yourself.

5. Bake and shape the remaining cookies the same way, one baking sheet at a time.

VARIATIONS   Substitute $^{2}/_{3}$ cup sweetened coconut for the sliced almonds. The coconut toasts as the cookies bake.

To make corkscrews, use $^{1}/_{2}$ tablespoon of batter for each cookie and spread strips of batter about 1 × 7 inches, 1 inch apart. There will be about 30 strips. Sprinkle with the sliced almonds or coconut. Bake until evenly light brown, about 7 minutes. Quickly and carefully twist each cookie around the round handle of a wooden spoon. Cool until firm.

To make ruffled cups, use 2 tablespoons of batter for each cookie and spread the batter in 6- to 7-inch circles. Sprinkle with sliced almonds or coconut. Bake until a 2-inch border is evenly brown and the center is light golden, about 9 minutes. Lift the cookies carefully from the baking sheet and place each one in a small bowl with the almond side facing out. The cookie will form a ruffled cup. Cool until firm and move to a wire rack to cool thoroughly.

Good Advice: Although you can leave these cookies flat after they bake, it's fun to try the different shapes. As soon as they come out of the oven, form the soft cookies into the desired shape. They take only about 15 seconds to harden once they're removed from the baking sheet. If a cookie becomes too firm to bend, warm it in the oven just until it is pliable. ❦ Although you can only bake 1 sheet of 4 or 5 cookies at a time, they bake quickly. You can ready the next sheet of cookies while one is baking. ❦ I have tried baking these cookies on nonstick baking liners, parchment paper, and aluminum foil. The nonstick liner produces a superior, evenly golden brown cookie that the other baking liners do not. Cookies baked on the parchment and aluminum foil form spotty areas of light and brown, which is acceptable but not as appealing. **To Freeze:** Stack 3 curved cookies together and wrap in plastic wrap. Wrap each corkscrew or ruffled cup in plastic wrap. Carefully put the wrapped cookies in a single layer in a metal or plastic freezer container and cover tightly. Label with the date and contents. Freeze up to 1 month. **To Serve:** Defrost the wrapped cookies at room temperature. Store in a sealed container and serve within 2 days.

Sugar and Spice Cookies

ugar and spice and everything nice—that's what these cookies are made of. They're the kind of old-fashioned, dark brown spice- and sugar-coated cookies that build family baking traditions. Many of my relatives and friends have contributed their tried and true recipes that you'll find yourself baking repeatedly.

There are two types of possible coatings for sugar cookies. Rolling cookies in granulated sugar produces a crunchy coating, while rolling cookies in powdered sugar forms a decorative white coating. To balance the sweet coating, dough for powdered-sugar-covered cookies usually contains a small quantity of sugar. I coat cookies in powdered sugar before freezing them, so they're ready to serve when defrosted. On a humid day, or if the cookies have been roughed up in the freezer and need refreshing, it's easy give them a quick dusting just before serving.

Since spice cookies depend on spices rather than butter for their flavor, shortening's role is to create a particular texture. Vegetable shortening produces chewy interiors for Big Molasses Ginger Cookies, while oil gives the crisp snap to Gingersnaps.

The bottoms of dark spice cookies can quickly burn if not watched carefully, especially those with a sugar coating. This is the voice of many burnt cookie bottoms speaking. Checking them often toward the end of their baking time is the solution.

Old-Fashioned Sugar Cookies

or many years I searched for a certain kind of sugar cookie that I remembered from my southern childhood. They were thick three-inch cookies that were soft on the inside but had a crisp sugar-coated exterior. Then one afternoon, I was baking Big Molasses Ginger Cookies and realized that they had the exact texture that I sought. I used that recipe as a model to create just the cookie I wanted. It was right in my recipe box all along, but I hadn't realized it.

MAKES ABOUT TWENTY-TWO 3-INCH COOKIES

2 cups unbleached all-purpose flour
1 teaspoon baking soda
$^1/_2$ teaspoon salt
$^3/_4$ cup (12 tablespoons) cold vegetable shortening
$1^1/_4$ cups sugar
1 cold large egg
$^1/_4$ cup dark corn syrup
2 teaspoons vanilla extract
1 teaspoon almond extract

1. Position 2 oven racks in the lower middle and upper middle of the oven. Preheat the oven to 350°F. Line 2 baking sheets with parchment paper or heavy aluminum foil.

2. Sift the flour, baking soda, and salt together and set aside.

3. Put the vegetable shortening and 1 cup of the sugar in the large bowl of an electric mixer and beat on medium speed for about 1 minute, until smooth. Add the egg, corn syrup, and vanilla and almond extracts and blend on low speed for about 30 seconds. Stop the mixer and scrape the bowl during this mixing. On low speed add the flour mixture and mix until all of it is incorporated and the dough comes away from the sides of the bowl.

4. For each cookie, roll 2 level tablespoons of dough between the palms of your hands into a $1^1/_2$-inch ball. Roll each ball in the remaining $^1/_4$ cup of sugar to coat. Place the cookie balls about 2 inches apart on the prepared baking sheets. Bake about 11 minutes, reversing the baking sheets after 6 minutes, front to back and top to bottom, to ensure that the cookies bake evenly. The tops will be cracked and pale golden but the edges and bottoms will be light brown when they are done. Cool the cookies on the baking sheets for 5 minutes, then transfer them to wire racks to cool completely.

Good Advice: The centers of the tops of these cookies should remain light golden when baked; then the cookies will be soft rather than crisp in the middle. To Freeze: Place the bottoms of 2 cookies together and wrap them in plastic wrap. Put the wrapped cookies in a metal or plastic freezer container and cover tightly. Label with the date and contents. Freeze up to 3 months. To Serve: Defrost the wrapped cookies at room temperature. Store leftover cookies, wrapped in plastic wrap, up to 3 days at room temperature.

Cinnamon Sugar Mandel Bread

These cookies may have been responsible for my marriage. When I was in college my mother used to send me this mandel bread. After I began dating my future husband, Jeff, she put him on her mandel bread mailing list too. He knew if we stopped dating, the mandel bread would stop also—so who knows? 🏃 Mandel bread is not a bread but a twice-baked crisp cookie, sometimes referred to as Jewish biscotti. They're not very sweet and make a good choice for a snack or for dunking in tea.

MAKES 40 COOKIES

> 3 cups unbleached all-purpose flour
> 1¼ teaspoons baking powder
> ½ teaspoon salt
> 3 large eggs
> 1 cup sugar
> 1 cup canola oil or corn oil
> 2 tablespoons fresh lemon juice
> 1 teaspoon vanilla extract
> 1 teaspoon almond extract
> 1 cup coarsely chopped pecans, cold or frozen
> ¼ cup sugar mixed with 1½ teaspoons ground cinnamon

1. Position 2 oven racks in the middle and upper third of the oven. Preheat the oven to 325°F. Line 2 large baking sheets with parchment paper.

2. Sift the flour, baking powder, and salt together and set aside.

3. Put the eggs in the large bowl of an electric mixer and beat at medium speed for 10 seconds. Add the sugar and beat for 2 minutes, until the mixture thickens and lightens to a cream color. Mix in the oil, lemon juice, vanilla, and almond extract. Decrease the speed to low and mix in the flour mixture just until it is incorporated. Stir in the pecans. The batter will be soft and sticky.

4. Use a large spoon to form 2 strips of batter on each baking sheet, 3 inches apart. The strips will be about 11 inches long and will immediately spread to about 3½ inches wide. Bake about 35 minutes, reversing the baking sheets after 20 minutes, front to back and top to bottom, to ensure that the cookies bake evenly. The strips should be evenly golden but not crisp.

5. Reduce the oven temperature to 250°F.

6. Cool the strips 5 minutes on the baking sheets. Use a sharp knife to cut each strip at an angle into ten 1-inch-wide cookies. Spread the cinnamon sugar mixture on a plate and dip the cut sides of the cookies in the cinnamon sugar. Line the baking sheets with clean parchment paper. Place the cookies, with the flat (bottom) side down, $1/2$ inch apart on the baking sheets. Bake 30 minutes. Turn off the heat but leave the cookies in the oven for 1 hour. They become crisp as they cool. Put the cookies on wire racks to cool thoroughly.

Good Advice: Use cold or frozen pecans in the batter. Cold nuts thicken the batter and allow you to use less flour, which produces a lighter cookie. Since I store my nuts in the freezer, I don't defrost them before I use them in this recipe. **Doubling the Recipe:** Double the ingredients. Make 8 strips. **To Freeze:** Place 2 cookies side by side and wrap in plastic wrap. Put the wrapped cookies in a metal or plastic freezer container and cover tightly. Label with the date and contents. Freeze up to 2 months. **To Serve:** Defrost the wrapped cookies at room temperature. Serve within 4 days.

Pecan Crescents

ou may know these popular cookies as Russian tea cakes, Mexican wedding cookies, or powdered sugar cookies; but my mom's version is decidedly different. Hers uses a combination of butter and margarine to make them crisp, and chopped pecans rather than ground ones to emphasize the nuts. Even the dough, with its generous measure of vanilla and almond extracts, tastes good.

MAKES 48 COOKIES

2 cups unbleached all-purpose flour
1/2 teaspoon salt
8 tablespoons (1 stick) soft unsalted butter
8 tablespoons (1 stick) cold margarine
1/2 cup powdered sugar
1 teaspoon vanilla extract
1 teaspoon almond extract
1 cup pecans, coarsely chopped
1 cup powdered sugar, sifted, for coating cookies

1. Position an oven rack in the middle of the oven. Preheat the oven to 325°F. Line a baking sheet with parchment paper.

2. Sift the flour and salt together. Set aside.

3. Put the butter, margarine, and 1/2 cup powdered sugar in the large bowl of an electric mixer and beat on medium speed until smooth, 1 minute. Mix in the vanilla and almond extracts. On low speed add the flour mixture, blending just until it is incorporated and the dough looks smooth. Stir in the pecans.

4. For each cookie, roll a rounded teaspoon of dough between the palms of your hands into a cylinder with tapered ends. Place on the prepared sheet 3/4 inch apart, curving each cylinder into a crescent. The cookies do not spread a lot during baking.

5. Bake until the edges and pointed ends are light brown, about 25 minutes. Cool the cookies on the baking sheet for 5 minutes, then transfer them to a wire rack to cool completely. Put 1 cup of sifted powdered sugar in a shallow dish or pie tin and roll each cookie in it until evenly coated.

Good Advice: Even when cold, margarine combines easily with other ingredients, so I use a combination of cold margarine and soft butter to produce a dough that is firm enough to shape easily into crescents. 🏃 Chop the pecans with a knife rather than in a food processor so they remain in small pieces, not ground. *To Freeze:* Place the bottoms of 2 cookies together and wrap them in plastic wrap. Put the wrapped cookies in a metal or plastic freezer container and cover tightly. Label with the date and contents. Freeze up to 2 months. *To Serve:* Defrost the wrapped cookies at room temperature. Serve within 3 days.

Shortbread Rounds (PAGE 64)

 oasted Hazelnut Shortbread Hearts Dipped in Milk Chocolate (PAGE 66)

Cherry Orange Flaky Flats (PAGE 70)

ecan Crescents (PAGE 86)

Chocolate Chip Brownies (PAGE 100)

hocolate and Hazelnut Praline Cookie Tarts (PAGE 150)

orning Glory Tea Cakes (PAGE 186)

amden Cheese Ribbons (PAGE 214)

Gingersnaps

unt Alice Klivans is an expert baker who brings big tins of these gingersnaps whenever she comes to visit. Since these use oil for the shortening, the cookies are especially crisp, with just a bit of softness in the center. They form attractive deep cracks across the top during baking, and make a real snap if you break one in half. 🦎 Aunt Alice's recipe originated with Ellen Gingrich, whose Amish Raisin Cookies appear in this chapter.

MAKES 32 COOKIES

2 cups unbleached all-purpose flour
2 teaspoons baking soda
$1/4$ teaspoon salt
1 teaspoon ground cinnamon
$1/2$ teaspoon ground cloves
$1/2$ teaspoon ground ginger
$1/2$ teaspoon ground nutmeg
$3/4$ cup canola oil or corn oil
$1/2$ cup molasses
1 cup packed dark brown sugar
1 large egg
$1/3$ cup granulated sugar

1. Position 2 oven racks in the lower middle and upper middle of the oven. Preheat the oven to 375°F. Line 2 baking sheets with parchment paper.

2. Sift the flour, baking soda, salt, cinnamon, cloves, ginger, and nutmeg together and set aside.

3. Put the oil, molasses, brown sugar, and egg in the large bowl of an electric mixer and beat on medium speed until smoothly blended together, about 30 seconds. On low speed add the flour mixture and mix until incorporated. Put the granulated sugar in a small bowl. Roll the dough by level tablespoons between the palms of your hands into $1^{1}/4$-inch balls. Roll each ball in the sugar to coat. Place the cookie balls 2 inches apart on the prepared baking sheets. Bake the cookies for 8 minutes, reversing the baking sheets after 4 minutes, front to back and top to bottom, to ensure that they bake evenly. The cookies will be evenly brown and have large cracks across the top, and will flatten toward the end of their baking time. Cool them on the baking sheet for 2 minutes, then transfer them to wire racks to cool completely.

Good Advice: Measure the oil in a measuring cup, then use the same measuring cup to measure the molasses, and the molasses will not stick to the cup. **To Freeze:** Place the bottoms of 2 cookies together and wrap them in plastic wrap. Put the wrapped cookies in a metal or plastic freezer container and cover tightly. Label with the date and contents. Freeze up to 3 months. **To Serve:** Cover the cookies with plastic wrap and defrost at room temperature. Serve within 4 days.

Big Molasses Ginger Cookies

Heather Marston, who works with my husband, knows that I'm always eager to try a new cookie, so she sent me a ginger cookie recipe from her grandmother, Alice Black. When I read Heather's note on the recipe that the end result should be hard outside and chewy inside, I was pretty sure they would be just the type of big old-fashioned spice cookie that I wanted to know how to bake. And as soon as they cooled enough to take a bite, I knew I was right.

MAKES ABOUT EIGHTEEN 3- TO 3^1/$_2$-INCH COOKIES

2 cups unbleached all-purpose flour
1 teaspoon baking soda
^{1}/$_2$ teaspoon salt
^{1}/$_2$ teaspoon ground cloves
^{1}/$_2$ teaspoon ground cinnamon
^{3}/$_4$ teaspoon ground ginger
^{3}/$_4$ cup (12 tablespoons) cold vegetable shortening
1^1/$_4$ cups sugar
1 cold large egg
^{1}/$_4$ cup molasses

1. Position a rack in the middle of the oven. Preheat the oven to 325°F. Line 2 baking sheets with parchment paper or heavy aluminum foil.

2. Sift the flour, baking soda, salt, cloves, cinnamon, and ginger together and set aside.

3. Put the vegetable shortening and 1 cup of the sugar in the large bowl of an electric mixer and beat on medium speed for about 1 minute, until smooth. Add the egg and molasses and mix on low speed for about 30 seconds until blended thoroughly. Stop the mixer and scrape the bowl during this time. On low speed, add the flour mixture and beat until all the flour is incorporated and the dough comes away from the sides of the bowl. For each cookie, roll 2 tablespoons of dough between the palms of your hands into a 1^1/$_2$-inch ball; Heather says, "About the size of a Ping-Pong ball." Roll each ball in the remaining ^{1}/$_4$ cup of sugar to coat. Place the cookie balls about 2 inches apart on the prepared baking sheets.

4. Bake 1 baking sheet at a time about 17 minutes, reversing it after 8 minutes. The cookies will flatten toward the end of their baking time, and their tops will have cracks when they are done. Bake the second pan of cookies. Cool the cookies on the baking sheet for 5 minutes, then transfer them to wire racks to cool completely.

Good Advice: These cookies are rolled in sugar, which adds to the crisp outside but also makes the bottoms susceptible to burning. I bake 1 sheet at a time on the middle rack of the oven, and watch them carefully toward the end of the baking time. As soon as 1 baking sheet is filled with cookies, bake it while you form the cookies for the second pan. You will use only about 2 tablespoons of sugar to coat the cookies, but it is easier to use ^{1}/$_4$ cup of sugar and discard any that remains. 🏃 Vegetable shortening rather than butter gives these cookies their particular texture. Using cold shortening produces a slightly thicker cookie than room-temperature shortening does. ✻ These cookies are leavened with baking soda, which is activated by moisture. If the cookies sit a long time before they are baked, they will spread less than freshly prepared dough. I prefer to mix one batch at a time. ✻ The cookies begin to flatten after 10 minutes of baking. **Doubling the Recipe:** Double the ingredients. Use 4 baking pans and bake the cookies as quickly as possible. Use 2 ovens if possible. **To Freeze:** Place the bottoms of 2 cookies together and wrap them in plastic wrap. Put the wrapped cookies in a metal or plastic freezer container and cover tightly. Label with the date and contents. Freeze up to 3 months. **To Serve:** Defrost the wrapped cookies at room temperature. Store leftover cookies, wrapped in plastic wrap, up to 3 days at room temperature.

Spice Cookies

his recipe has traveled a long way to be included here. When Midwesterner Verda Bush's southern granddaughter Susan was married, Verda gave her a valuable present: a handwritten book of their family recipes. Susan shared the book with her Camden, Maine, cousin, Chris McLarty, who then shared this recipe with me. These are small crisp wafers with soft centers that will make you glad they made the journey.

MAKES ABOUT 138 COOKIES

> 2 cups unbleached all-purpose flour
> 1 teaspoon baking soda
> $^1/_2$ teaspoon salt
> 1 teaspoon ground cinnamon
> $^1/_2$ teaspoon ground cloves
> $^1/_2$ teaspoon ground ginger
> 12 tablespoons (1$^1/_2$ sticks) margarine, melted and cooled
> $^1/_4$ cup molasses
> 1$^1/_4$ cups sugar
> 1 large egg

1. Position 2 oven racks in the lower middle and upper middle of the oven. Preheat the oven to 325°F. Line 3 baking sheets with parchment paper.

2. Sift the flour, baking soda, salt, cinnamon, cloves, and ginger together and set aside.

3. Put the melted margarine, molasses, 1 cup of the sugar, and the egg in the large bowl of an electric mixer and beat on medium speed for about 1 minute, until smooth and light in color. On low speed add the flour mixture and mix until incorporated. The dough will be soft and sticky. Leave it in the bowl, cover, and refrigerate until firm, about 30 minutes.

4. Put the remaining $^1/_4$ cup of sugar in a small bowl. To form each cookie, roll 1 level teaspoon of dough between the palms of your hands into a $^3/_4$-inch ball. They will look like small olives. Roll each ball in the remaining sugar to coat. Place the cookie balls 1 inch apart on the prepared baking sheets. Set aside 1 sheet of cookies at room temperature.

5. Bake 2 sheets of cookies for 7 to 10 minutes, reversing the baking sheets after 4 minutes, front to back and top to bottom, to ensure that the cookies bake evenly. They will be evenly light brown and have small cracks on the tops. They will flatten toward the end of their baking time. Bake the remaining sheet of cookies on the middle rack of the oven, reversing the sheet after 5 minutes. Cool the cookies on the baking sheets for 1 minute, then transfer them to wire racks to cool completely. The tops will wrinkle slightly and the cookies flatten a bit more as they cool.

Good Advice: The dough should be rolled between your hands into ³/₄-inch balls. There's a tendency to make bigger balls as you go along, so I make a model ball and try to keep them all the same. ❧ These small cookies are affected by 1 or 2 minutes more or less of baking time, so watch them closely as they bake. After 4 minutes they look puffed, then they fall and flatten to make cookies about 1¹/₂ inches in diameter. Small cracks form on top and the cookies darken to an even light brown color. The bottoms shouldn't become any darker than the tops. Cookies that start baking on the lower rack may be done in as short a time as 7 minutes, while the final sheet of cookies that bakes by itself on the middle rack may take as long as 10 minutes. Perfectly baked cookies are crisp outside and soft only in the very center, with small cracks and wrinkles on the top. Underbaked cookies remain soft, overbaked ones are crisp all the way through, but all of them are still quite good. **To Freeze:** Line a 2-quart metal or plastic freezer container with plastic wrap. Fill the container with the cooled cookies, press plastic wrap onto them, and cover tightly. Label with the date and contents. Freeze up to 3 months. **To Serve:** Cover the cookies with plastic wrap and defrost at room temperature. Serve within 4 days.

Amish Raisin Cookies

n a recent visit to my Aunt Alice and Uncle Norman in Ohio, I met their Amish friend, Ellen Gingrich, who gave me this recipe for her grandmother's raisin cookies. Aunt Alice is a good cookie baker in her own right, but she gives Ellen credit for many of her recipes. 🏃 If you saw these cookies among others on a platter, you might pass them by; but that would be a big mistake. Like their Amish heritage, they look plain and simple on the outside, but they have a subtle spice flavor and an especially tender texture studded with soft raisins that makes them unique.

MAKES ABOUT 74 COOKIES

> 2 cups seedless raisins
> 4 cups unbleached all-purpose flour
> 1 teaspoon baking soda
> 1 teaspoon baking powder
> $^1/_2$ teaspoon ground cinnamon
> $^1/_2$ teaspoon ground nutmeg
> $^1/_4$ teaspoon ground allspice
> $^1/_2$ pound (2 sticks) softened margarine
> 2 cups sugar
> 3 large eggs
> 1 teaspoon vanilla extract
> 1 cup coarsely chopped pecans

1. Position 2 oven racks in the middle and upper third of the oven. Preheat the oven to 375°F. Line 2 baking sheets with parchment paper.

2. Put the raisins in a medium saucepan and add enough water to cover them (about 1$^1/_2$ cups). Bring the water to a gentle boil and boil for 5 minutes. Drain the raisins and set them aside to cool.

3. Stir the flour, baking soda, baking powder, cinnamon, nutmeg, and allspice together in a medium bowl.

4. Put the margarine, sugar, and eggs in the large bowl of an electric mixer and beat on medium speed until well blended and the pieces of margarine become small specks, about 1 minute. Mix in the vanilla. Decrease the speed to low and mix in the cooled raisins. Add the flour mixture, blending just until the flour is incorporated. Stir in the pecans.

5. Pinch off pieces of dough 1 tablespoon at a time and place 1 inch apart on the prepared baking sheets. They look like rough mounds. Put the remaining dough in the refrigerator.

6. Bake the cookies 9 to 10 minutes, or until the bottoms and several spots on the top are light brown. Reverse the baking sheets after 5 minutes, front to back and top to bottom, to ensure that the cookies bake evenly. Cool the cookies on the baking sheets for 5 minutes,

then transfer them to wire racks to cool completely. Cool the 2 baking sheets and line them with clean parchment paper. Form the remaining dough into cookies and bake and cool as directed above.

Good Advice: The unbaked cookies should have a rough rather than smooth texture so they form bumpy mounds. ❀ This amount of cookie dough requires 4 baking sheets, so I bake 2 sheets at a time and refrigerate the remaining dough while the first batch bakes. Cool the baking sheets before using them again to bake more cookies. **Doubling the Recipe:** Mix the cookies in 2 batches. **To Freeze:** Place the bottoms of 2 cookies together and wrap them in plastic wrap. Put the wrapped cookies in a metal or plastic freezer container and cover tightly. I use two 2-quart containers for this large number of cookies. Label with the date and contents. Freeze up to 3 months. **To Serve:** Defrost the wrapped cookies at room temperature. Serve within 3 days.

Chocolate Chip Cookies and Bars

When some people can't sleep, they count sheep; I spend the time concocting chocolate chip cookie recipes. It doesn't put me to sleep, but it's a great way to spend a sleepless night.

My night thoughts produced this assortment of chocolate chip cookies. Chocolate Chip Galettes bake in ramekins that mold them into perfectly rounded cookies. These galettes are thicker and moister than a cookie baked free-form on a baking sheet could ever be. I finally figured out how to reproduce the crisp-all-the-way-through chocolate chip mounds that Jeff's Grandmother Tillie used to bake. And one of my midnight fantasies produced the "best of everything" combination. It's a chocolate chip cookie that's half all-chocolate chip dough and half brown sugar chocolate chip dough. Finally, birthdays are for indulging in favorite desserts, and for that I've dreamed up a giant decorated cookie for all of us chocolate chip cookie lovers.

Chocolate Chip Bars

hese are like eating a triple-thick chocolate chip cookie, and I'll bet you can't eat just one! I can't.

MAKES 12 TO 16 BARS

    1 cup unbleached all-purpose flour
    $1/2$ teaspoon baking soda
    $1/4$ teaspoon salt
    8 tablespoons (1 stick) soft unsalted butter
    $1/2$ cup packed light brown sugar
    $1/2$ cup granulated sugar
    1 large egg
    2 teaspoons vanilla extract
    1 cup (6 ounces) semisweet chocolate chips

1. Position a rack in the middle of the oven. Preheat the oven to 350°F. Butter an $8 \times 8 \times 2$-inch pan.

2. Stir the flour, baking soda, and salt together in a small bowl. Set aside.

3. Put the butter, brown sugar, and granulated sugar in the large bowl of an electric mixer and beat on low speed for about 30 seconds until smooth. Stir in the egg and vanilla and mix until blended thoroughly. Add the flour mixture, beating just until it is incorporated. Mix in the chocolate chips. Spread the batter evenly in the prepared pan.

4. Bake for 30 to 35 minutes, or until a toothpick inserted in the center comes out with a few crumbs clinging to it. Cool thoroughly in the baking pan on a wire rack. Use a sharp knife to cut the bars into 2 or 3 large pieces or 16 individual pieces.

VARIATION   Stir $1/2$ cup chopped pecans into the batter along with the chocolate chips.

To Freeze: Wrap large pieces in plastic wrap, then heavy aluminum foil, or individual bars in plastic wrap. Place in a metal or plastic freezer container and cover tightly. Label with the date and contents. Freeze up to 1 month. **To Serve:** Defrost the wrapped bars at room temperature. If you have frozen large pieces, cut them into smaller bars. Serve within 3 days.

A Big Chocolate Chip Birthday Cookie

ookies can even become birthday "cakes." Recently, I baked a batch of chocolate chip cookie dough in a round pan, wrote "Happy Birthday" on the top of the giant cookie, and sent it to my daughter, Laura, for her birthday. It was birthday cake and present all in one chocolate chip package.

MAKES ONE 13-INCH COOKIE IN A PIZZA PAN OR
ONE 10-INCH COOKIE IN A SPRINGFORM PAN

1 cup plus 2 tablespoons unbleached all-purpose flour
1 teaspoon baking soda
$^1/_2$ teaspoon salt
6 tablespoons ($^3/_4$ stick) unsalted butter, softened slightly for about 30 minutes
2 tablespoons vegetable shortening
$^1/_2$ cup packed light brown sugar
6 tablespoons granulated sugar
1 large egg
1 teaspoon vanilla extract
$1^1/_2$ cups (9 ounces) semisweet chocolate chips
2 ounces semisweet chocolate, chopped (optional)

MAKE THE COOKIE

1. Position an oven rack in the middle of the oven. Preheat the oven to 350°F. Butter a 15-inch flat pizza pan or a 10-inch springform pan.

2. Sift the flour, baking soda, and salt together and set aside.

3. Put the butter and shortening in the large bowl of an electric mixer and beat on medium speed just to combine. Add the brown sugar and granulated sugar and mix for about 1 minute, until smooth. Add the egg and vanilla and mix on low speed for about 15 seconds, until they are blended thoroughly. Stop the mixer and scrape the bowl during this mixing. Add the flour mixture, mixing just until it is incorporated. Stir in the $1^1/_2$ cups chocolate chips. Use your fingers to spread the dough in a 10-inch circle on the pizza pan and smooth the edges. Or, spread the dough evenly in the springform pan.

4. If using the pizza pan, bake for about 14 minutes, or until the edges are light brown and the center is golden. Cool the cookie thoroughly on the pan. If using the springform pan, bake for about 18 minutes, or until it is evenly light brown. The cookie sinks slightly in the center as it cools. Loosen the edges from the springform pan as soon as you remove it from the oven, then cool it thoroughly in the pan. Remove the sides of the springform pan before adding any chocolate decoration.

1. Preheat the oven to 175°F. Place the chocolate in a small ovenproof container and melt it in the oven for about 8 minutes. Remove the chocolate from the oven as soon as it is melted and stir it smooth.

2. Put the melted chocolate in a small self-sealing freezer bag, press out the air, and seal the bag. Cut a small hole (about $1/16$ inch) in one corner of the bag. Hold the bag at a slight angle about 1 inch above the cookie. Write your message by twisting the bag and gently squeezing to release a thin stream of chocolate. Move the bag slowly and guide it to form thin chocolate letters or designs.

Good Advice: I bake this cookie two ways—on a pizza pan or in a springform pan. The cookie baked on the pizza pan spreads as it bakes, so it is crisp on the outside and soft on the inside, while the cookie baked in the springform pan comes out chewy, more like a bar. ✻ If you plan to mail the cookie, bake it in the springform pan, which produces a sturdy cookie in a manageable size that arrives safely. When the chocolate decoration on top is cool and firm, wrap the cookie tightly in plastic wrap. Place cardboard on top of and under the cookie and tape the cardboard pieces together to secure them. Cardboard cake circles work well. Pack the cookie package in a box as directed on pages 17–18 of Freezing and Shipping cookies. Try to avoid shipping this cookie during hot weather, since the chocolate decoration might melt. ✻ Two ounces of melted chocolate will be plenty for writing on the cookie and drawing some decorations, but for just a few words, one ounce of melted chocolate is sufficient. *Doubling the Recipe:* Use $1^{1}/_{2}$ teaspoons baking soda and $3/_{4}$ teaspoon salt and double the remaining ingredients. Bake the cookies in 2 pans. *To Freeze:* Chill the cookie, uncovered but still on the pizza pan or the base of the springform, in the freezer for about 1 hour, until the chocolate is firm. Loosen the cookie from the bottom of the pizza pan or springform pan. Slide the removable bottom of a tart pan under the cookie to move it to a serving plate or cardboard cake circle. Wrap tightly in plastic wrap, then heavy aluminum foil. Label with the date and contents. Freeze up to 2 months. *To Serve:* Defrost the wrapped cookie at room temperature for about 3 hours. Store any leftover cookie, wrapped tightly in plastic wrap, up to 3 days at room temperature.

The Best of Everything Chocolate Chip Cookies

ere's one brilliant cookie idea, if I do say so myself. One side of the cookie is a brown sugar chocolate chip cookie and one side is a chocolate chocolate chip cookie. It's all made from one dough so it's simple to mix.

MAKES ABOUT 34 COOKIES

1 ounce semisweet chocolate, chopped
1¼ cups all-purpose flour
1 teaspoon baking soda
½ teaspoon salt
8 tablespoons (1 stick) soft unsalted butter
½ cup firmly packed light brown sugar
6 tablespoons granulated sugar
1 large cold egg
1 teaspoon vanilla extract
1 tablespoon unsweetened Dutch process cocoa powder, such as Droste or
    Hershey's European
2 cups (12 ounces) semisweet chocolate chips

1. Position 2 oven racks in the lower middle and upper middle of the oven. Preheat the oven to 175°F. Line 2 baking sheets with parchment paper.

2. Place the ounce of semisweet chocolate in a small ovenproof container and melt it in the oven for about 5 minutes. Remove it as soon as it is melted and stir it smooth. Set aside. Increase the oven temperature to 350°F.

3. Sift the flour, baking soda, and salt together and set aside.

4. Put the butter, brown sugar, and granulated sugar in the large bowl of an electric mixer and beat on medium speed for about 1 minute until smooth. Add the egg and vanilla and mix on low speed for about 15 seconds until blended thoroughly. Stop the mixer and scrape the bowl during this mixing. Decrease the speed to low and add the flour mixture, mixing just until it is incorporated.

5. Transfer half the dough to a medium bowl. With the mixer running on low speed, stir in the melted chocolate and cocoa powder until combined. Stir 1 cup of chocolate chips into each bowl of dough. Using a small spoon, scoop a rounded teaspoon of chocolate dough onto the spoon, then dip the spoon into the plain dough and scoop a rounded teaspoon of that dough beside the chocolate dough. Place paired dark and light dough mounds on the baking sheets, spacing them 2 inches apart. The cookies will spread as they bake.

6. Bake the cookies for about 11 minutes, or until the edges are dark golden, reversing the baking sheets after 6 minutes, front to back and top to bottom, to ensure even browning. Watch carefully as the cookies near the end of their baking time. Cool them on the baking sheet for 5 minutes, then transfer them to wire racks to cool completely.

To Freeze: Place the bottoms of 2 cookies together and wrap them in plastic wrap. Put the wrapped cookies in a metal or plastic freezer container and cover tightly. Label with the date and contents. Freeze up to 3 months. **To Serve:** Defrost the wrapped cookies at room temperature. Serve within 3 days. If you prefer cookies with warm, soft chocolate chips, spread the defrosted cookies in a single layer on a baking sheet and warm them in a preheated 200°F oven for 5 minutes before serving.

Chocolate Chip Brownies

ometimes a person has to be flexible. Although I normally think that brownies should be as fudgy as possible, with this brownie too much of a fudgy texture would obscure the chocolate chips. I made these just cakelike enough for the chocolate chips throughout to stand up and be noticed.

MAKES 12 TO 16 BROWNIES

6 tablespoons (³/4 stick) unsalted butter, cut into 3 pieces
3 ounces unsweetened chocolate, chopped
³/4 cup plus 2 tablespoons unbleached all-purpose flour
¹/2 teaspoon baking powder
¹/2 teaspoon salt
2 large eggs
1 cup plus 2 tablespoons sugar
1 teaspoon vanilla extract
1 cup (6 ounces) semisweet chocolate chips

1. Position a rack in the middle of the oven. Preheat the oven to 325°F. Butter an 8 × 8 × 2-inch pan.

2. Put the butter, unsweetened chocolate, and 2 tablespoons water in a large heatproof container set over, but not touching, a saucepan of barely simmering water. Stir the mixture over the hot water until the butter and chocolate are melted and smooth. Set aside to cool slightly.

3. Stir the flour, baking powder, and salt together and set aside.

4. Put the eggs and sugar in the large bowl of an electric mixer and beat on medium speed until fluffy and lightened in color, about 1 minute. Add the vanilla. On low speed add the chocolate mixture, blending until it is incorporated. Add the flour and mix just until incorporated and the dough is smooth. Stir in the chocolate chips. Spread the batter evenly in the prepared pan.

5. Bake for about 35 minutes, or until a toothpick inserted in the center comes out with moist crumbs clinging to it. Cool the brownies in the pan on a wire rack about 1¹/2 hours. Cut into 12 to 16 pieces.

Good Advice: When these brownies are done, they will be firm around the edges but soft in the center. The center becomes firm as it cools. If the toothpick tester penetrates a chocolate chip, test another spot. **To Freeze:** Wrap each brownie tightly in plastic wrap. Place in a metal or plastic freezer container and cover tightly. Or, put the wrapped brownies in a plastic freezer bag and seal. Label with the date and contents. Freeze up to 3 months. **To Serve:** Defrost the wrapped brownies at room temperature for about 3 hours. Leftover brownies can be covered with plastic wrap and stored at room temperature up to 3 days.

Breakaway Chocolate Chip Cookie Crunch

These cookies reminded me of how one slight change in a recipe can make a big difference in the result. I was trying to make a pan of brittle, candylike chocolate chip bars that I could break into crisp random-shaped cookies, but I kept producing ones with soft centers. Then I remembered that when I had substituted melted butter for solid butter in crumb toppings, the crumbs became crisp. So I tried melting the butter before adding it to these cookies, and it worked. The dough baked into this crunchy cookie confection that breaks easily into appealing irregular pieces.

MAKES ABOUT TWENTY 2- TO 4-INCH IRREGULAR-SHAPED COOKIES

2 cups unbleached all-purpose flour
$^3/_4$ teaspoon baking soda
$^3/_4$ teaspoon salt
$^1/_2$ pound (2 sticks) unsalted butter, melted and cooled slightly
$^1/_2$ cup packed light brown sugar
$^3/_4$ cup granulated sugar
2 teaspoons vanilla extract
$1^1/_2$ cups (9 ounces) semisweet chocolate chips

1. Position a rack in the middle of the oven. Preheat the oven to 350°F. Have ready a $17 \times 11^3/_4 \times 1$-inch baking sheet.

2. Stir the flour, baking soda, and salt together in a small bowl. Set aside.

3. Put the melted butter, brown sugar, granulated sugar, 2 tablespoons water, and the vanilla in the large bowl of an electric mixer and beat on low speed for about 30 seconds until smooth. Add the flour mixture, blending just until it is incorporated. Mix in the chocolate chips. Use a thin metal spatula to spread the dough evenly over the baking sheet. If it doesn't quite reach the edges, the dough will spread to the edges during baking.

4. Bake for about 15 minutes, or until the top is an even light brown and feels evenly firm on top. Cool thoroughly on the baking sheet. The cookie will crisp as it cools. The baked cookie is $^3/_8$ to $^1/_2$ inch thick. Break the large cookie into about twenty 2- to 4-inch irregular pieces.

Good Advice: The baking sheet for these cookies has inside measurements of $17 \times 11^3/_4 \times 1$ inches and is often called a baker's half sheet. It's not necessary to line it with paper. The cookie lifts easily from the baking sheet, and butter from the dough would seep through parchment paper. **To Freeze:** Put the bottoms of 2 cookies together and wrap in plastic wrap. Place in a metal or plastic freezer container and cover tightly. Or, put the wrapped cookies in a plastic freezer bag and seal. Label with the date and contents. Freeze up to 3 months. **To Serve:** Defrost the wrapped cookies at room temperature for about 3 hours. Leftover cookies can be covered with plastic wrap and stored at room temperature up to 4 days.

Chocolate Chip Raisin Cookies

eff's Grandma Tillie used to make chocolate chip cookies that were like no others. The cookies were exceptionally crisp, had a rough-topped mound shape, a distinct taste of brown sugar, and a subtle taste of coffee. She mixed raisins and chocolate chips into the cookies, but not so many that they would overpower the cookie taste. I often asked Grandma Tillie for the recipe and she always said they were from the recipe on the chocolate chip bag. She must have had some unusual sort of bag because my cookies never tasted like hers. Over the years I gave up trying to reproduce her cookies and thought we would never taste them again. When I was testing the Breakaway Chocolate Chip Cookie Crunch, Jeff tasted it and said the flavor reminded him of his grandmother's cookies. I was off and running into the kitchen, and baked several hundred cookies until I finally received the "Jeff seal of approval" for these.

MAKES ABOUT 42 COOKIES

> 2 cups unbleached all-purpose flour
> 1 teaspoon baking soda
> $^3/_4$ teaspoon salt
> 12 tablespoons ($1^1/_2$ sticks) unsalted butter, melted and cooled
> $^1/_2$ cup packed light brown sugar
> $^3/_4$ cup granulated sugar
> 1 tablespoon instant decaffeinated coffee granules dissolved in 2 tablespoons warm
>   water
> 2 teaspoons vanilla extract
> $^2/_3$ cup (4 ounces) semisweet chocolate chips
> $^2/_3$ cup seedless raisins

1. Position 2 oven racks in the lower middle and upper middle of the oven. Preheat the oven to 350°F. Line 2 baking sheets with parchment paper.

2. Sift the flour, baking soda, and salt together and set aside.

3. Put the melted butter, brown sugar, granulated sugar, dissolved coffee, and vanilla in the large bowl of an electric mixer and beat on low speed for about 30 seconds until smooth. Add the flour mixture, mixing just until it is incorporated and the dough forms large crumbs. Mix in the chocolate chips and raisins. Pinch off clumps of dough that are 1 tablespoon in size and squeeze gently to form 1-inch mounds. Leave the mounds rough-textured rather than smooth. Place the cookies $1^1/_2$ inches apart on the baking sheets.

4. Bake for about 12 minutes, or until the bottoms of the cookies are light brown. The tops will darken slightly. Reverse the baking sheets after 7 minutes, front to back and top to bottom, to ensure even browning. Watch the cookies carefully as they near the end of their baking time. Cool them on the baking sheets for 5 minutes, then transfer them to wire racks to cool completely. The cookies become crisp as they cool.

Good Advice: When it is mixed, the dough forms large crumbs rather than a smooth mixture. Press clumps of dough together to form the cookies. 🏃 I bake these cookies no longer than 12 minutes. The top of the hot cookie feels soft, but the cookies crisp as they cool. If these cookies bake too long, they become quite hard when cooled. **To Freeze:** Place the bottoms of 2 cookies together and wrap them in plastic wrap. Put the wrapped cookies in a metal or plastic freezer container and cover tightly. Label with the date and contents. Freeze up to 3 months. **To Serve:** Defrost the wrapped cookies at room temperature. Serve within 3 days.

Cherry Chocolate Chip Oatmeal Cookies

hese are not your mother's oatmeal cookies. Like a good oatmeal cookie, they're chewy on the inside and crisp on the outside, but you'll find them loaded with dried cherries, toasted almonds, and chocolate chips.

MAKES 36 COOKIES

1 cup unbleached all-purpose flour
$^1/_2$ teaspoon baking soda
$^1/_4$ teaspoon salt
10 tablespoons (1$^1/_4$ sticks) unsalted butter, at room temperature
$^1/_2$ cup packed dark brown sugar
$^1/_2$ cup granulated sugar
1 large egg
1 teaspoon vanilla extract
$^1/_2$ teaspoon almond extract
1 cup oatmeal (not quick-cooking)
1 cup dried pitted cherries
$^1/_2$ cup slivered almonds, toasted
1$^1/_2$ cups (9 ounces) semisweet chocolate chips

1. Position 2 oven racks in middle and upper third of oven. Preheat the oven to 350°F. Line 2 baking sheets with parchment paper.

2. Sift the flour, baking soda, and salt together and set aside.

3. Put the butter, brown sugar, and granulated sugar in the large bowl of an electric mixer and beat on medium speed for about 1 minute until smooth. Add the egg, vanilla, and almond extract and mix on low speed for about 15 seconds until thoroughly blended. Stop the mixer and scrape the bowl during this mixing. Decrease the speed to low and add the flour mixture and oatmeal. Mix in the dried cherries, almonds, and chocolate chips. Drop rounded tablespoons of the dough 2 inches apart on the prepared baking sheets.

4. Bake until the edges are light brown, about 13 minutes. Reverse the baking sheets after 7 minutes, front to back and top to bottom, to ensure even browning. Watch the cookies carefully as they near the end of their baking time. Cool them on the baking sheets for 5 minutes, then transfer them to wire racks to cool completely.

To Freeze: Place the bottoms of 2 cookies together and wrap them in plastic wrap. Put the wrapped cookies in a metal or plastic freezer container and cover tightly. Label with the date and contents. Freeze up to 3 months. To Serve: Defrost the wrapped cookies at room temperature. Store leftover cookies, wrapped in plastic wrap, up to 3 days at room temperature.

Chocolate Chubbies

've had versions of this half-brownie, half-cookie at bakeries around the country. It's crisp on the outside, fudgy on the inside, and loaded with chocolate chips and pecans. It's my choice for finest chubby.

MAKES 24 COOKIES

6 tablespoons (³/₄ stick) unsalted butter, cut into 3 pieces
3 ounces unsweetened chocolate, chopped
1 cup unbleached all-purpose flour
¹/₂ teaspoon baking powder
¹/₂ teaspoon salt
2 large eggs
1¹/₄ cups sugar
1 teaspoon vanilla extract
1¹/₂ cups (9 ounces) semisweet chocolate chips
³/₄ cup coarsely chopped pecans

1. Position a rack in the middle of the oven. Preheat the oven to 350°F. Line 2 baking sheets with parchment paper.

2. Put the butter and unsweetened chocolate in a large heatproof container set over, but not touching, a saucepan of barely simmering water. Stir the mixture over the hot water until the butter and chocolate are melted and smooth. Remove from over the hot water and set aside to cool and thicken slightly, about 15 minutes.

3. Stir the flour, baking powder, and salt together and set aside.

4. Put the eggs, sugar, and vanilla in the large bowl of an electric mixer and mix on medium speed until fluffy and lightened in color, about 1 minute. On low speed add the chocolate mixture, beating until it is incorporated. Add the flour mixture and mix just until it is incorporated and the dough is smooth. Stir in the chocolate chips and pecans. The batter will be thick and hold its shape when dropped onto the cookie sheet. Place rounded tablespoons of dough 2 inches apart on the prepared baking sheets (you will have 2-inch mounds). Bake 1 sheet of cookies at a time until the tops feel crusty when touched gently, about 10 minutes. Reverse the baking sheet after 5 minutes to ensure that the cookies bake evenly. Watch them carefully at the end of the baking time. Bake the second sheet of cookies. Cool the cookies on the baking sheet for 5 minutes, then transfer them to a wire rack to cool completely.

Good Advice: Cool the melted chocolate and butter mixture until it thickens slightly. This produces a thick batter that holds its shape and makes a plump cookie, a generous ¹/₂ inch thick when baked. **To Freeze:** Place the bottoms of 2 cookies together and wrap them in plastic wrap. Put the wrapped cookies in a metal or plastic freezer container and cover tightly. Label with the date and contents. Freeze up to 3 months. **To Serve:** Defrost the wrapped cookies at room temperature. Serve within 3 days.

Chocolate Chip Galettes

I spotted this French version of a chocolate chip cookie in a Parisian bakery. It was nice to see the French imitating an American dessert and certainly worth bringing the idea back across the ocean. These galettes bake in ramekins, so you get perfectly rounded moist, thick, chocolate chip cookies that are actually half-bar and half-cookie. Their slightly sunken centers are just right for holding a scoop of ice cream topped with warm Chocolate Truffle Sauce.

MAKES NINE 3-INCH COOKIES

1 cup unbleached all-purpose flour
1/2 teaspoon baking soda
1/2 teaspoon salt
8 tablespoons (1 stick) unsalted butter, melted and cooled slightly
1/2 cup packed light brown sugar
6 tablespoons granulated sugar
1 large egg
2 teaspoons vanilla extract
2/3 cup (4 ounces) miniature semisweet chocolate chips

1. Position an oven rack in the middle of the oven. Preheat the oven to 350°F. Cut parchment or wax paper to fit the bottom of nine 3-inch-wide ramekins (small soufflé cups) with a 5- or 6-ounce capacity and line the bottom of each ramekin with the paper. Put the ramekins on a baking sheet.

2. Sift the flour, baking soda, and salt together. Set aside.

3. Put the melted butter, brown sugar, and granulated sugar in the large bowl of an electric mixer and beat on low speed for about 30 seconds, until the mixture is smooth and the butter is incorporated. Mix in the egg and vanilla. Add the flour mixture, blending just until it is incorporated. Stir in the chocolate chips. Spoon 3 level tablespoons of batter into each of the prepared ramekins. The batter will be 1/2 inch thick in each ramekin. The bumpy tops become smooth during baking.

4. Bake the galettes just until the tops are light brown and a toothpick inserted in the center comes out clean, about 21 minutes. Cool the galettes 5 minutes in the ramekins. Use a small, sharp knife to loosen them and turn them out of the ramekins onto a wire rack to cool. (Be careful lifting the hot ramekins; they are slippery.) Remove the wax paper and turn the galettes right side up. Cool thoroughly. The galettes sink slightly in the center as they cool.

Good Advice: Ramekins are small porcelain soufflé cups with straight sides. Muffin tins can be substituted. My ramekins measure 3 inches, but my muffin tins measure 2 1/2 inches across the top so they produce eleven rather than nine galettes with slightly slanted sides. To Freeze: Wrap each galette in plastic wrap, put them in a metal or plastic freezer container, and cover tightly. Label with the date and contents. Freeze up to 3 months. To Serve: Defrost the wrapped galettes at room temperature. If desired, serve each galette topped with a scoop of ice cream and several tablespoons of warm Chocolate Truffle Sauce (page 20). Wrap leftover galettes in plastic wrap and store up to 3 days at room temperature. Defrosted galettes can be warmed in a preheated 250°F oven for about 8 minutes to make them taste as if they were just baked.

Brownies

rownie baking is one time when you're after a dense, almost fallen cake texture rather than a light and fluffy one. Several factors produce the qualities you're looking for in a brownie. By comparing brownie ingredients to cake ingredients, you'll notice that the brownies have a large proportion of sugar and butter to flour. Melted chocolate, nut butters, or brown sugar are the most common ingredients added to encourage a fudgelike texture.

Brownie batters are not fussy about their mixing and seldom benefit from long beating. It's more important to combine ingredients smoothly. You can use an electric mixer to blend them, but a whisk works just as well in most recipes. Flour is seldom sifted, but I often stir it with the salt and the leavening (if it is used) to break up lumps. I once mistakenly sifted the flour when I was making A Really Good Brownie recipe and was amazed at the difference. As they baked, the brownies formed a sugary crust over the top that crumbled and fell off when the brownies were cut. They were not really good brownies.

Most brownies become thick enough to require baking in a two-inch-high pan, but the recipes tell you when some thinner brownies, such as Cappuccino Brownies, can bake in a 1-inch-high pan. Remember to grease the sides of the pan so the batter rises evenly. Most brownies have no leavening and need all the help they can get to expand as they bake. To ensure moist brownies, bake them only to the point that a toothpick inserted in the center has moist crumbs clinging to it.

For freezing, I usually cut brownies into serving-size pieces or into several large sections. A thin, flexible metal spatula is a useful tool for removing brownies from the pan. When I include brownies as a part of a cookie platter assortment, I cut them into bite-size pieces. An eight-or nine-inch square pan produces about forty-eight dainty bite-size brownies. Brownies don't break easily if moved around in the freezer, so they can be packed in plastic containers or plastic freezer bags.

I can't think of any occasion that wouldn't suit a brownie sundae, and all of these brownies can become one. Just match them with a complementary ice cream and sauce.

A Really Good Brownie

his brownie has been our family fudge brownie since Doris Kovner shared her recipe with me over twenty years ago. That's a pretty long track record for a family of brownie lovers. The secret of its success is twofold. Unsweetened chocolate gives the brownies an almost black color and a rich chocolate taste that isn't too sweet, and a combination of butter and vegetable shortening creates an especially dense fudge texture.

MAKES 12 TO 16 BROWNIES

8 tablespoons (1 stick) unsalted butter, cut into 4 pieces
$^1/_2$ cup (8 tablespoons) vegetable shortening, cut into 4 pieces
5 ounces unsweetened chocolate, chopped
4 large eggs
$^1/_4$ teaspoon salt
2 cups sugar
2 teaspoons vanilla extract
1 cup unbleached all-purpose flour

1. Position a rack in the middle of the oven. Preheat the oven to 325°F. Lightly grease the bottom and sides of a $9 \times 9 \times 2$-inch pan with vegetable shortening.

2. Put the butter, vegetable shortening, and chocolate in a heatproof container and place it over, but not touching, a saucepan of barely simmering water. Stir the mixture over the hot water until it is melted and smooth. Remove the container from over the water and cool 5 minutes.

3. Put the eggs and salt in the large bowl of an electric mixer and mix at medium speed for about 30 seconds until the eggs just begin to look fluffy. Add the sugar and beat for 1 minute until the mixture thickens and the color lightens. Decrease the speed to low and mix in the melted chocolate mixture and vanilla until thoroughly combined. Add the flour, mixing just until it is incorporated. Spread the batter evenly in the prepared pan.

4. Bake for about 50 minutes, until a toothpick inserted in the center comes out with moist crumbs clinging to it. Cool the brownies in the pan on a wire rack about $1^1/_2$ hours. Cut into 12 to 16 pieces.

VARIATION   Stir 1 cup coarsely chopped walnuts or pecans into the batter. Bake as directed.

Good Advice: Using some vegetable shortening in these brownies gives them their particular texture. Read the label carefully and buy shortening that is not butter-flavored. To Freeze: Wrap individual brownies tightly in plastic wrap. Place in a metal or plastic freezer container and cover tightly. Or, put the wrapped brownies in a plastic freezer bag and seal. Label with the date and contents. Freeze up to 3 months. To Serve: Defrost the wrapped brownies at room temperature for about 3 hours. Leftover brownies can be covered with plastic wrap and stored at room temperature up to 3 days.

Peppermint Patty Brownies

ince candy makes a good addition to many brownies, I've strewn dark chocolate-covered peppermint patties throughout these. As the brownies bake, chocolate from the candy melts into the batter and adds to the fudgy texture, while the peppermint candy centers hold their shape and dot the brownies with bursts of cool mint.

MAKES 12 TO 16 BROWNIES

8 tablespoons (1 stick) unsalted butter, cut into 4 pieces
4 ounces unsweetened chocolate, chopped
2 large eggs
1¼ cups sugar
¼ teaspoon salt
1 teaspoon vanilla extract
¾ cup unbleached all-purpose flour
1 cup small peppermint patties cut in quarters (about twelve ½-ounce patties)

1. Position an oven rack in the middle of the oven and preheat to 325°F. Butter the bottom and sides of an 8 × 8 × 2-inch square baking pan.

2. Put the butter and unsweetened chocolate in a large heatproof container set over, but not touching, a saucepan of barely simmering water. Stir the mixture over the hot water until the butter and chocolate are melted and smooth.

3. Put the eggs, sugar, and salt in a large bowl and whisk them together to blend them thoroughly. Whisk in the warm chocolate mixture and vanilla. Add the flour and whisk just to incorporate the flour. Use a large spoon to stir in the peppermint candy pieces. Spread the batter in the prepared pan.

4. Bake for about 30 minutes, or until a toothpick inserted in the center comes out with a few moist crumbs clinging to it. If the toothpick penetrates a piece of candy, test another spot. Cool the brownies in the pan on a wire rack about 1 hour. Cut them into 12 to 16 pieces.

To Freeze: Wrap individual brownies tightly in plastic wrap. Put the wrapped brownies in a metal or plastic freezer container and cover tightly. Or, put the wrapped brownies in a plastic freezer bag and seal. Label with the date and contents. Freeze up to 3 months. **To Serve:** Defrost the wrapped brownies at room temperature for about 3 hours. Leftover brownies can be covered with plastic wrap and stored at room temperature up to 3 days.

Pecan Praline Brownies

 These blond brownies have the remarkable flavor of the brown sugar pecan pralines that are a specialty of New Orleans. Crushed pecan praline provides a crunchy topping.

MAKES 16 TO 20 BROWNIES

1¹/₂ cups unbleached all-purpose flour
1 teaspoon baking powder
³/₄ teaspoon salt
12 tablespoons (1¹/₂ sticks) soft unsalted butter
1¹/₂ cups packed light brown sugar
2 large eggs
2 teaspoons instant decaffeinated coffee granules dissolved in 1 tablespoon water
2 teaspoons vanilla extract
1¹/₂ cups Nut Pralines made with pecans, crushed in ¹/₄- to ³/₈-inch pieces (page 26)

1. Preheat the oven to 325°F. Position a rack in the middle of the oven. Butter the bottom and sides of a 13 × 9 × 2-inch baking pan.

2. Stir the flour, baking powder, and salt together in a small bowl and set aside.

3. Put the butter in the large bowl of an electric mixer and beat on medium speed for 15 seconds. Add the brown sugar and cream thoroughly with the butter, about 1 minute. Decrease the speed to low and add the eggs, dissolved coffee, and vanilla, mixing just until the eggs are incorporated. The batter will look curdled. Stop the mixer and scrape the sides of the bowl once during this mixing. Slowly add the flour mixture and blend just until it is incorporated and the mixture is smooth. Stir in 1 cup of the crushed pecan praline. Spread the batter evenly in the prepared pan.

4. Bake for 15 minutes. Sprinkle the remaining ¹/₂ cup of pecan praline evenly over the top and return the pan to the oven. Bake for about 10 minutes more, just until a toothpick inserted in the center no longer has liquid clinging to it. Cool the brownies in the pan on a wire rack about 2 hours, then cut them into 16 to 20 pieces.

Good Advice: Crush the praline carefully into small pieces, ¹/₄ to ³/₈ inches, before adding it to the brownie batter. Large pieces of praline could settle to the bottom of the pan and stick, which doesn't ruin the brownies but could make them difficult to remove from the pan. **To Freeze:** Wrap each brownie tightly in plastic wrap. Place in a metal or plastic freezer container and cover tightly. Or, put the wrapped brownies in a plastic freezer bag and seal. Label with the date and contents. Freeze up to 3 months. **To Serve:** Defrost the wrapped brownies at room temperature for about 3 hours. Leftover brownies can be covered with plastic wrap and stored at room temperature up to 3 days.

Cappuccino Brownies

s coffee houses sprang up on every street corner, it seemed to me that a foamy cup of cappuccino dusted with cinnamon should inspire a new brownie. Although these contain white chocolate to give them a dense, moist brownie texture, it's the coffee and cinnamon that deliver the cappuccino jolt.

MAKES 12 TO 16 BROWNIES

6 ounces white chocolate, chopped (preferably Callebaut, Lindt, or Baker's Premium)
$1/2$ cup unbleached all-purpose flour
$1/4$ teaspoon salt
2 teaspoons ground cinnamon
4 tablespoons ($1/2$ stick) soft unsalted butter
$1/2$ cup sugar
2 large eggs
1 tablespoon instant decaffeinated coffee dissolved in 1 tablespoon hot water
1 teaspoon vanilla extract

1. Position a rack in the middle of the oven. Preheat the oven to 175°F. Butter the bottom and sides of an 8 × 8-inch pan with 1- to 2-inch sides.

2. Put the white chocolate in a small nonreactive heatproof container and melt it in the oven about 10 to 12 minutes. Remove it as soon as it is melted and stir until smooth. Set aside to cool slightly. Increase the oven to 325°F.

3. Stir the flour, salt, and cinnamon together in a small bowl and set aside.

4. Put the butter and sugar in the large bowl of an electric mixer and beat on medium speed until smooth, or about 1 minute. Decrease the speed to low and add the eggs, dissolved coffee, and vanilla, blending until the eggs are incorporated. You will see pieces of butter. Stop the mixer and scrape the sides of the bowl once during this mixing. Mix in the melted chocolate. Mix in the flour mixture just until it is incorporated and the batter is smooth. Spread it evenly in the prepared pan.

5. Bake for about 25 minutes, just until a toothpick inserted in the center comes out clean. The brownies will feel soft. Cool them thoroughly in the pan on a wire rack about 1 hour. Cut into 12 to 16 pieces.

Good Advice: Watch these brownies carefully during baking. They are thin and the edges can quickly become too crisp. **To Freeze:** Wrap each brownie tightly in plastic wrap. Place in a metal or plastic freezer container and cover tightly. Or, put the wrapped brownies in a plastic freezer bag and seal. Label with the date and contents. Freeze up to 3 months. **To Serve:** Defrost the wrapped brownies at room temperature for about 3 hours. Leftover brownies can be covered with plastic wrap and stored at room temperature up to 3 days.

Roasted Almond Butter Brownies

eanut butter is a familiar brownie ingredient, but I bake brownies with a variety of nut butters. Since nut butters are rich in natural oils, they add the desired moist, dense texture to a brownie, plus the unique taste of each nut used. Roasted almond butter is easy to find in most natural food stores.

MAKES 12 TO 16 BROWNIES

$^1\!/_2$ cup unbleached all-purpose flour
$^1\!/_2$ teaspoon salt
4 tablespoons ($^1\!/_2$ stick) soft unsalted butter
$^3\!/_4$ cup (7 ounces) roasted almond butter, at room temperature
1 cup packed light brown sugar
2 large eggs
1 teaspoon vanilla extract
$^3\!/_4$ teaspoon almond extract
2 teaspoons fresh lemon juice

1. Position a rack in the middle of the oven. Preheat the oven to 325°F. Butter the bottom and sides of an 8 × 8-inch pan with 1- to 2-inch sides.

2. Stir the flour and salt together in a small bowl and set aside.

3. Put the butter and almond butter in the large bowl of an electric mixer and beat on low speed until blended together, 30 seconds. Add the brown sugar and beat until the mixture is creamed thoroughly, about 30 seconds. Add the eggs, vanilla and almond extracts, and lemon juice, blending until smooth. Stop the mixer and scrape the sides of the bowl once during this mixing. Add the flour mixture, mixing just until it is incorporated. Spread the batter evenly in the prepared pan.

4. Bake for about 35 minutes, or until a toothpick inserted in the center comes out with a few crumbs clinging to it. Cool the brownies in the pan on a wire rack about 1 hour, then cut them into 12 to 16 pieces.

Good Advice: Check to see that any nut butter used is made from roasted nuts. Unroasted nuts have a mild flavor that doesn't assert itself in brownies. I use smoothly ground nut butters, but crunchy ones work fine if you want to add some crunch. 🐜 Bring nut butters to room temperature before using them so they combine smoothly with the other ingredients. Pour off any oil that has accumulated at the top. To Freeze: Wrap each brownie tightly in plastic wrap. Place in a metal or plastic freezer container and cover tightly. Or, put the wrapped brownies in a plastic freezer bag and seal. Label with the date and contents. Freeze up to 3 months. To Serve: Defrost the wrapped brownies at room temperature for about 3 hours. Leftover brownies can be covered with plastic wrap and stored at room temperature up to 3 days.

Peanut Butter Chocolate Chunk Brownies

lthough my son, Peter, eats them for breakfast, these brownies are just right for packing in lunch boxes or taking along on picnics. They are thick, with a smooth peanut butter texture and an abundance of milk chocolate pieces scattered throughout.

MAKES 12 TO 16 BROWNIES

1 cup unbleached all-purpose flour
$^3/_4$ teaspoon baking powder
$^1/_2$ teaspoon salt
6 tablespoons ($^3/_4$ stick) soft unsalted butter
$^3/_4$ cup smooth peanut butter (low sodium preferred), at room temperature
$^3/_4$ cup packed light brown sugar
$^1/_2$ cup granulated sugar
2 large eggs
1 teaspoon vanilla extract
6 ounces milk chocolate, cut into about $^1/_2$-inch pieces

1. Position a rack in the middle of the oven. Preheat the oven to 325°F. Butter the bottom and sides of an $8 \times 8 \times 2$-inch pan.

2. Sift the flour, baking powder, and salt together and set aside.

3. Put the butter and peanut butter in the large bowl of an electric mixer and blend on low speed until smooth, 1 minute. Beat in the brown sugar and granulated sugar until the mixture is creamed thoroughly, about 30 seconds. Add the eggs and vanilla, mixing until smooth. Stop the mixer and scrape the sides of the bowl once during this time. Add the flour mixture, mixing just until it is incorporated. Stir in the chopped chocolate. Spread the batter evenly in the prepared pan.

4. Bake for about 30 minutes, or until a toothpick inserted in the center comes out with moist crumbs clinging to it. Cool the brownies in the pan on a wire rack about 1 hour, then cut them into 12 to 16 pieces.

Good Advice: You can substitute milk chocolate chips for the chopped milk chocolate. If the peanut butter has been refrigerated, soften it to room temperature so that it combines smoothly with the butter. Peanut butter can create a heavy texture in brownies, but sifting the flour lightens these. I use low-sodium but not low-fat peanut butter. **To Freeze:** Wrap each brownie tightly in plastic wrap. Place in a metal or plastic freezer container and cover tightly. Or, put the wrapped brownies in a plastic freezer bag and seal. Label with the date and contents. Freeze up to 3 months. **To Serve:** Defrost the wrapped brownies at room temperature for about 3 hours. Leftover brownies can be covered with plastic wrap and stored at room temperature up to 3 days.

White Chocolate and
Raspberry Ripple Brownies

hite chocolate and raspberries turn any dessert into something elegant, even a familiar brownie. The white chocolate batter is rippled with sweetened raspberry purée that turns rosy pink inside the brownies and forms a lovely pattern of red swirls over the top.

MAKES 12 TO 16 BROWNIES

1 cup sweetened frozen raspberries, defrosted and drained, or fresh raspberries mixed
    with 2 teaspoons sugar
9 ounces white chocolate, chopped (preferably Callebaut, Lindt, or Baker's Premium)
$^3/_4$ cup unbleached all-purpose flour
$^1/_2$ teaspoon salt
6 tablespoons ($^3/_4$ stick) soft unsalted butter
$^3/_4$ cup sugar
3 large eggs
1 teaspoon vanilla extract
$^1/_2$ teaspoon almond extract
Powdered sugar for dusting

1. Position a rack in the middle of the oven and preheat to 175°F. Butter the bottom and sides of an 8 × 8 × 2-inch pan.

2. Use the back of a spoon to press the sweetened raspberries through a strainer to remove the seeds. Measure $^1/_4$ cup strained purée into a small bowl. Set the purée aside and save any additional for another use.

3. Place the white chocolate in a nonreactive ovenproof container and melt it in the oven about 12 minutes. As soon as it is melted, remove it from the oven and stir it smooth. Set aside to cool. Increase the oven to 325°F.

4. Stir the flour and salt together in a small bowl and set aside.

5. Put the butter and sugar in the large bowl of an electric mixer and beat on medium speed until smooth, about 1 minute. Decrease the speed to low and add the eggs, vanilla, and almond extract, blending until the eggs are incorporated. You will see pieces of butter. Stop the mixer and scrape the sides of the bowl once during this time. Beat in the melted white chocolate. Mix in the flour mixture just until it is incorporated and the batter is smooth.

6. Spread the batter evenly in the prepared pan. Drizzle the $^1/_4$ cup raspberry purée over the top. Draw a thin metal spatula gently through the purée to swirl it with the white chocolate batter until the top is marbleized.

7. Bake for about 30 minutes, or until a toothpick inserted in the center comes out with a few moist crumbs clinging to it. Cool the brownies in the pan on a wire rack about 1 hour. Dust with powdered sugar and cut into 12 to 16 pieces.

Good Advice: Lightly sweetened raspberry purée adds more flavor to the brownies than unsweetened raspberry purée. Use sweetened frozen raspberries or add sugar to a purée made with fresh raspberries. Defrost frozen raspberries before puréeing them. *To Freeze:* Wrap each brownie tightly in plastic wrap. Place in a metal or plastic freezer container and cover tightly. Or, put the wrapped brownies in a plastic freezer bag and seal. Label with the date and contents. Freeze up to 3 months. *To Serve:* Defrost the wrapped brownies at room temperature for about 3 hours. Refresh them with a light dusting of powdered sugar if necessary. Leftover brownies can be covered with plastic wrap and stored at room temperature up to 3 days. The brownies can be served with raspberry ice cream or sorbet and garnished with fresh raspberries.

Banana Caramel Brownies

 hese comforting brownies belong with a cup of tea on a cold winter day. They are made from a caramel and banana batter, streaked with pure caramel, and topped with pecans that become glazed with caramel during baking.

MAKES 12 TO 16 BROWNIES

1¹/₃ cups unbleached all-purpose flour
1 teaspoon baking powder
¹/₄ teaspoon salt
8 tablespoons (1 stick) soft unsalted butter
1¹/₃ cups packed light brown sugar
1 teaspoon vanilla extract
1¹/₂ cups sliced and mashed bananas (about 3)
2 large eggs
³/₄ cup Caramel Filling (page 25), cooled or defrosted to room temperature
1 cup coarsely chopped pecans

1. Position a rack in the middle of the oven. Preheat the oven to 325°F. Butter the bottom and sides of a 9 × 9 × 2-inch pan.

2. Sift the flour, baking powder, and salt together and set aside.

3. Put the butter in the large bowl of an electric mixer and beat on low speed for 15 seconds. Add the brown sugar and vanilla and beat until the mixture is creamed thoroughly, about 1 minute. Mix in the mashed bananas. Small pieces of banana will remain visible. Add the eggs, blending until they are incorporated. The mixture will look curdled. Stop the mixer and scrape the sides of the bowl once during this time. Slowly add the flour mixture and mix just until it is incorporated and the batter is smooth. Stir in ¹/₄ cup of the caramel filling until it is blended with the batter.

4. Spread the batter evenly in the prepared pan. Drizzle the remaining ¹/₂ cup of caramel filling over the top. Draw a thin metal spatula gently through the batter to swirl in the caramel, leaving swirls of caramel on the top. Sprinkle on the pecans evenly, trying to drop them wherever caramel is showing through.

5. Bake for about 50 minutes, or just until a toothpick inserted in the center comes out clean. Cool the brownies in the pan on a wire rack about 1 hour. Cut into 12 to 16 pieces.

Good Advice: The caramel filling should be soft, pourable, and at room temperature. Cold caramel is too thick to swirl in the thin streaks desired, and warm caramel might cause changes in the unbaked batter. *To Freeze:* Wrap each brownie tightly in plastic wrap. Place in a metal or plastic freezer container and cover tightly. Or, put the wrapped brownies in a plastic freezer bag and seal. Label with the date and contents. Freeze up to 3 months. *To Serve:* Defrost the wrapped brownies at room temperature for about 3 hours. Leftover brownies can be covered with plastic wrap and stored at room temperature up to 3 days.

Bars with Chocolate or Nuts

aramel and cashews, fudge soufflé, coffee toffee, and cinnamon crisps—you get the idea. They're the bars filled with chocolate, nuts, coconut, or toffee that disappear instantly from cookie platters.

When I want a cookie that mixes together quickly and produces a large quantity, I turn to my recipes for bar cookies. Forming them is as simple as spreading them in a pan, recipes double easily, and they only need to be cut for serving. They can become a cookie for any occasion. Small pieces look dainty on a cookie plate, while large pieces fit nicely into lunch boxes, travel safely in their baking pan to picnics, or sit on the counter ready for snacking. Many of these bars expand into stand-alone desserts with the addition of ice cream or sundae sauces.

Cooled bars lift easily from baking pans, so take the time to cool them thoroughly before removing them. I cut bars into individual pieces or 2 or 3 large sections when freezing them. When I know what size I'm going to want, I cut individual pieces before freezing. Large pieces are ready for multiple uses. Wide offset metal spatulas that look like pancake turners with long blades are handy for lifting large sections of bars from pans. The larger pieces stack efficiently in the freezer and save space.

Caramel Cashew Triangles

F or a cookie that requires almost no baking, these are pretty fancy-looking bars. The crisp crust is filled with roasted cashew nuts and caramel, and the cookies are cut into triangles and half spread with white chocolate. The crust bakes in a springform pan so it unmolds easily into a perfect circle, and if you use Caramel Filling from the freezer, the bars assemble quickly.

MAKES 12 TRIANGLES

Crust

    1 cup unbleached all-purpose flour
    $1/2$ cup packed light brown sugar
    4 tablespoons ($1/2$ stick) cold unsalted butter, cut into pieces

Caramel Layer

    1 cup Caramel Filling (page 25), cooled or defrosted and warmed to pouring
        consistency
    $1^1/2$ cups coarsely chopped roasted, unsalted cashews nuts
    6 ounces white chocolate, chopped (preferably Callebaut, Lindt, or
        Baker's Premium)
    1 tablespoon vegetable shortening, such as Crisco

PREPARE THE CRUST

1. Position a rack in the center of the oven. Preheat the oven to 350°F. Butter a 9-inch springform pan.

2. Put the flour, brown sugar, and butter in the large bowl of an electric mixer. Beat on low speed until pea-size crumbs form. Press the crust firmly into the bottom and $1/2$ inch up the sides of the prepared pan.

3. Bake about 25 minutes until the crust is golden. Cool in the pan on a rack.

PREPARE THE FILLING

1. Put $3/4$ cup of the Caramel Filling in a medium bowl and stir in the cashew nuts until they are evenly coated. Spread the nut mixture evenly over the prepared crust. Spoon the remaining $1/4$ cup caramel filling on top, covering any bare spaces. Refrigerate until the caramel is firm, at least 1 hour.

2. Put the white chocolate and vegetable shortening in a heatproof container and place it over, but not touching, a saucepan of barely simmering water. Stir over the hot water until the chocolate melts and the mixture is smooth. Pour the coating into a small bowl and let sit 5 minutes to cool and thicken slightly.

3. Remove the springform pan from the refrigerator. Use a small, sharp knife to loosen the crust all around, then remove the sides of the springform pan. Use a large, sharp knife to cut 12 equal wedges and transfer the wedges to a wire rack.

4. Put wax paper under the rack to catch and recycle white chocolate drips. Beginning at the pointed end of each triangle, spoon melted white chocolate over the top and sides of half of each. (The tips look as if they had been dipped in white chocolate.) Leave them on the rack and return them to the refrigerator until the white chocolate is firm.

Good Advice: The crust is not as rich as my usual Press-in Butter Crust for Bars (page 21). It makes a good contrast to the rich filling, and a firm base for the bars. ❄ Chill the finished bars until the filling is firm before cutting them so they cut into neat slices. Spread the white chocolate over the bars rather than dipping them in it. If dipped in the warm white chocolate, the caramel can soften and drip off. I know; it happened to me. *To Freeze:* Wrap individual wedges in plastic wrap, place in a metal or plastic freezer container, and cover tightly. Label with the date and contents. Freeze up to 2 months. *To Serve:* Defrost the wrapped triangles in the refrigerator, about 3 hours. Serve cold. Store in the refrigerator up to 3 days.

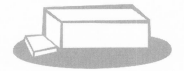

D.C. Oatmeal Toffee Bars

 ver on the lookout for a new cookie, I found these bars at a coffee shop while visiting our children in Washington, D.C. I wrote down on a piece of paper "D.C. toffee bars," that's all. When I returned home, I remembered the bar but not the details, so I asked my son, Peter, to mail some to me. He went to the shop every day for two weeks on his way to school and on his way home. The toffee bars never appeared again, and the people in the shop didn't remember them. I was on my own. 🏃 I remembered that they were moist bars but also had a crisp, crumbly texture. They were full of chocolate-covered toffee candy; some of the toffee melted into the bars and added a hint of caramel but some remained solid and crunchy. The top was appealingly bumpy. As soon as I reproduced these bars, I recognized the taste. I won't forget them again.

MAKES 16 TO 20 BARS

1 cup unbleached all-purpose flour
$1/2$ teaspoon baking soda
$1/4$ teaspoon salt
12 tablespoons ($1^1/2$ sticks) soft unsalted butter
$1/2$ cup granulated sugar
$3/4$ cup packed light brown sugar
1 large egg
2 teaspoons vanilla extract
$1^1/2$ cups oatmeal (not quick-cooking)
1 cup coarsely chopped pecans
2 cups (about 10 ounces) coarsely crushed toffee candy, such as Heath Bars or Skor

1. Position a rack in the middle of the oven. Preheat the oven to 350°F. Butter a $13 \times 9 \times 2$-inch pan.

2. Stir the flour, baking soda, and salt together in a small bowl. Set aside.

3. Put the butter, sugar, and brown sugar in the large bowl of an electric mixer and beat on low speed for about 30 seconds until smooth. Stir in the egg and vanilla and mix until thoroughly blended. Stir in the oatmeal. Mix in the flour mixture just until it is incorporated. Stir in the pecans and crushed toffee. Spread the batter evenly in the prepared pan.

4. Bake until a toothpick inserted in the center comes out sticky but not dripping with batter and the edges are light brown, about 25 minutes. Cool thoroughly in the baking pan on a wire rack. Use a sharp knife to cut into 2 or 3 large pieces or 16 to 20 individual bars.

Good Advice: Break the toffee into random pieces. Most pieces will be about $1/2$ inch, but an assortment with smaller and larger pieces works best. I leave the candy in its wrapper and crush it with the flat side of a meat pounder. **To Freeze:** Wrap large pieces in plastic wrap, then in heavy aluminum foil. Wrap individual bars in plastic wrap, place in a metal or plastic freezer container, and cover tightly. Label with the date and contents. Freeze up to 1 month. **To Serve:** Defrost the wrapped bars at room temperature. Serve within 3 days.

Double Deckers

y Aunt Mutzi, who moved to California over forty years ago, is considered the pioneer in our family. When we spent some time in California, she always had these two-layered bars on hand. They have a soft base and a crisp brown sugar–pecan meringue topping. The almond flavor is actually in the meringue, but it mysteriously seems to come from the base.

MAKES 35 BARS

3 cups unbleached all-purpose flour
1 teaspoon salt
1 teaspoon baking powder
$^{1}/_{2}$ pound (2 sticks) soft unsalted butter
2 cups granulated sugar
4 large eggs, separated
2 teaspoons vanilla extract
$^{1}/_{4}$ teaspoon cream of tartar
1 cup packed light brown sugar
1 teaspoon almond extract
1 cup coarsely chopped pecans
Powdered sugar

1. Position a rack in the middle of the oven. Preheat the oven to 325°F. Butter a $10^{1}/_{2} \times 15^{1}/_{2} \times 1$-inch baking sheet.

2. Sift the flour, salt, and baking powder together and set aside.

3. Put the butter and granulated sugar in the large bowl of an electric mixer and beat on medium speed until blended and lightened in color, 1 minute. Decrease the speed to low and add the egg yolks and vanilla, mixing until the batter is smooth. Add the flour mixture and mix just until it is incorporated and a soft dough forms. Use a thin metal spatula to spread the dough evenly in the prepared baking sheet.

4. Put the egg whites and cream of tartar in the clean large bowl of an electric mixer and beat with clean beaters on low speed until foamy. Increase the speed to medium-high and beat until soft peaks form. Reduce the speed to low and slowly beat in the brown sugar, 2 tablespoons at a time. Mix in the almond extract. Spread the meringue evenly over the prepared dough to the edges of the baking pan. Sprinkle the pecans evenly over the meringue.

5. Bake until a toothpick inserted in the center comes out clean or with a few crumbs clinging to it and the meringue is evenly light brown, about 40 minutes. Cool thoroughly in the baking pan on a wire rack. Sift powdered sugar over the top. Use a sharp knife to cut into 2 or 3 large pieces or 35 individual bars.

To Freeze: Wrap large pieces in plastic wrap, then in heavy aluminum foil. Wrap individual bars in plastic wrap, place in a metal or plastic freezer container, and cover tightly. Label with the date and contents. Freeze up to 1 month. **To Serve:** Defrost the wrapped bars at room temperature. Refresh with an additional dusting of powdered sugar if necessary. Serve within 3 days.

Chocolate Fudge Soufflé Bars

hese bars have a chocolate fudge filling sandwiched between a crunchy brown sugar crust and a thin, crisp chocolate top. Beaten egg whites lighten the filling, creating the soufflélike texture, but a generous quantity of chocolate adds a dark fudge quality.

MAKES 12 TO 16 BARS

> 1 Press-in Butter Crust for Bars (page 21), prepared with light brown sugar and
>   unbaked in a 9 × 9 × 2-inch pan, not defrosted if frozen
> 3 tablespoons unsalted butter, cut in pieces
> 5 ounces semisweet chocolate, chopped
> 2 large eggs, separated
> 1/8 teaspoon cream of tartar
> 3 tablespoons sugar
> 1 teaspoon instant decaffeinated coffee dissolved in 1 teaspoon hot water
> 1 tablespoon unbleached all-purpose flour

1. Position a rack in the middle of the oven. Preheat the oven to 350°F. Bake the prepared crust until the top is golden, 20 to 25 minutes if fresh, 25 to 30 minutes if frozen.

2. Put the butter and chocolate in a heatproof container and place it over, but not touching, a saucepan of barely simmering water. Stir over the hot water until melted and smooth. Pour the chocolate mixture into a medium bowl and set aside.

3. Put the egg whites and cream of tartar in the large bowl of an electric mixer and beat on low speed until foamy. Increase the speed to medium-high and beat until soft peaks form. Reduce the speed to medium and slowly beat in the sugar, 1 tablespoon every 30 seconds.

4. Whisk the egg yolks, dissolved coffee, and flour into the chocolate mixture until blended thoroughly. Fold in half of the beaten egg whites, then fold in the remaining egg whites. Spread the filling evenly over the baked crust.

5. Bake just until a toothpick inserted in the center comes out with a few crumbs clinging to it, and the top looks firm, about 15 minutes. Cool thoroughly in the pan on a wire rack. Use a sharp knife to cut into 2 or 3 large pieces or 12 to 16 individual bars.

VARIATION   Spread 1 cup (6 ounces) semisweet chocolate chips evenly over the baked crust. Spread the chocolate batter over the chocolate chips and bake and cool as directed above.

Good Advice: The filling doesn't bake long enough for the crust to cook, so you bake the crust without the filling until it is golden. This adds a browned butter and toasted brown sugar taste to the crust. 🏃 As the chocolate filling bakes, it separates into a soft middle layer and a crisp top layer. To Freeze: Wrap large pieces in plastic wrap, then in heavy aluminum foil. Wrap individual bars in plastic wrap, place in a metal or plastic freezer container, and cover tightly. Label with the date and contents. Freeze up to 1 month. To Serve: Defrost the wrapped bars at room temperature. Serve within 3 days.

Coffee Toffee Bars

ertain combinations, such as coffee and toffee, bring out the best in each other. Coffee cuts the sweetness of toffee, while toffee mellows any sharpness that coffee could add. These cake-type bars have a rich coffee color and a crunchy toffee and crumb topping. Some of the bar mixture is reserved and used without liquid to make the crumb topping.

MAKES 12 TO 16 BARS

2 cups unbleached all-purpose flour
$^1/_2$ teaspoon salt
1 cup granulated sugar
1 cup packed light brown sugar
8 tablespoons (1 stick) soft unsalted butter, cut into 8 pieces
1 cup (about 5 ounces) coarsely crushed toffee candy, such as Heath Bars or Skor
1 teaspoon baking soda
1 cup buttermilk
1 large egg
1 tablespoons plus 2 teaspoons instant decaffeinated coffee dissolved in 1 tablespoon plus 1 teaspoon hot water
1 teaspoon vanilla extract

1. Position a rack in the middle of the oven. Preheat the oven to 350°F. Butter a $9 \times 9 \times 2$-inch pan.

2. Sift the flour and salt into the large bowl of an electric mixer. Add the granulated sugar, brown sugar, and butter and mix on low speed until fine crumbs form. Put $^3/_4$ cup of the mixture in a small bowl and stir in the toffee. Set aside to use for the crumb topping. Stir the baking soda into the remaining flour mixture. Add the buttermilk, egg, dissolved coffee, and vanilla, beating until completely blended. Spread the batter evenly in the prepared pan. Sprinkle the reserved crumb toffee mixture evenly over the batter.

3. Bake until the edges are light brown and a toothpick inserted in the center comes out with moist crumbs clinging to it, about 40 minutes. Use a large, sharp knife to cut into 2 or 3 large pieces or 12 to 16 individual bars while the toffee is warm. Cool the bars thoroughly in the baking pan on a wire rack.

Good Advice: Nonfat buttermilk works fine for these bars. To Freeze: Wrap large pieces in plastic wrap, then in heavy aluminum foil. Wrap individual bars in plastic wrap, place in a metal or plastic freezer container, and cover tightly. Label with the date and contents. Freeze up to 1 month. To Serve: Defrost the wrapped bars at room temperature. Serve within 3 days.

Pure Pine Nut Toffee Bars

ince pine nuts are grown in New Mexico, they're as common there as pecans are in Georgia. On my first visit to Santa Fe, I realized that New Mexican cooks serve them during any course of a meal, but there was one dish that stood out from all the others. It was a pine nut tart with a filling of almost solid pine nuts enrobed in a soft, buttery toffee glaze. When I came home, I began efforts to duplicate it and finally turned the filling into this bar. While I was testing, it became apparent that any crust I tried overpowered the filling, so I simplified matters by baking the filling by itself. As it bakes, it forms a firm bottom. Now you can concentrate on pure pine nuts and toffee.

MAKES 12 TO 16 BARS

1 cup whipping cream
¾ cup sugar
2 tablespoons (¼ stick) unsalted butter
1 teaspoon vanilla extract
1½ cups pine nuts, toasted (page 3)

1. Position a rack in the middle of the oven. Preheat the oven to 325°F. Line an 8 × 8 × 2-inch pan with heavy aluminum foil, letting the foil extend over the ends of the pan. Butter the bottom and sides of the aluminum foil generously.

2. Put the cream, sugar, and butter in a 2-quart saucepan and cook over low heat until the butter melts and the sugar dissolves, stirring often. Increase the heat to medium-high and bring to a boil. Boil for 7 minutes, stirring occasionally. The mixture will be smooth and syrupy. Remove from the heat and stir in the vanilla and pine nuts. Pour into the prepared pan.

3. Bake until the edges are brown and the center is golden, about 30 minutes. (The mixture bubbles during baking.) The square is soft when it comes out of the oven, but will firm as it cools. Cool at room temperature until firm, about 1 hour. Use the overhanging ends of foil to lift the square out of the pan, then peel the foil from the bottom. Use a large, sharp knife to cut into 2 or 3 large pieces or 12 to 16 individual bars. Cool thoroughly on a wire rack.

VARIATIONS   Substitute 1½ cups sliced, toasted almonds for the pine nuts.

Or, stir ½ cup raisins into the pine nut mixture. Bars baked with raisins are softer than those baked only with nuts, so remove the aluminum foil slowly and carefully. It can stick.

Good Advice: Peel the aluminum foil from the bars and cut them as soon as they are firm enough to hold their shape. They will be cool enough to handle. Cold bars are so hard that they are difficult to cut. To Freeze: Wrap large pieces in plastic wrap, then in heavy aluminum foil. Wrap individual bars in plastic wrap, place in a metal or plastic freezer container, and cover tightly. Label with the date and contents. Freeze up to 1 month. To Serve: Defrost the wrapped bars at room temperature. Serve within 3 days.

Coconut Pecan Southland Bars

ne of my earliest cookie memories is of coming home from school to a house filled with the aroma of butter and brown sugar from these bars baking. I was a lucky kid! ✦ The bars have a distinctive not-too-sweet filling that is soft from the brown sugar batter, crunchy from the pecans, chewy from the coconut flakes, and held together by a soft butter crust. During baking, the top becomes crisp and the brown sugar in the center becomes slightly caramelized.

MAKES 12 TO 16 BARS

1 Press-in-Butter Crust for Bars (page 21), prepared with powdered sugar and unbaked in a 9 × 9 × 2-inch pan, not defrosted if frozen
1 cup packed dark brown sugar
2 large eggs
1 teaspoon vanilla extract
2 tablespoons unbleached all-purpose flour
$1/2$ teaspoon baking powder
$1/4$ teaspoon salt
$1/4$ teaspoon ground cinnamon
1 cup chopped pecans
$1^{1}/4$ cups shredded sweetened coconut

1. Position a rack in the middle of the oven. Preheat the oven to 350°F. Bake the prepared crust 15 minutes if fresh, 20 minutes if frozen.

2. Beat the brown sugar, eggs, and vanilla in the large bowl of an electric mixer on medium speed until smooth and lightened in color, 1 minute. Decrease the speed to low and mix in the flour, baking powder, salt, and cinnamon until incorporated and no white flecks of flour remain. Stir in the pecans and coconut. Pour the batter over the partially baked crust.

3. Bake until a toothpick inserted in the center comes out sticky and the center remains set if you give the pan a gentle shake, about 25 minutes. Cool thoroughly in the baking pan on a wire rack. Use a sharp knife to cut into 2 or 3 large pieces or 12 to 16 individual bars.

To Freeze: Wrap large pieces in plastic wrap, then in heavy aluminum foil. Wrap individual bars in plastic wrap, place in a metal or plastic freezer container, and cover tightly. Label with the date and contents. Freeze up to 1 month. **To Serve:** Defrost the wrapped bars at room temperature. Serve within 3 days.

Pecan Cinnamon Crisps

hese thin, crisp bars are just right with a cup of tea, go well with any flavor of ice cream, ship easily, and store well. They'll even fit into your time schedule, since you can make a lot in a short time. Long slow baking and a combination of butter and margarine produce a bar that is crisp throughout. The kitchen fills with the fragrance of roasting pecans as the bars bake and the nut topping toasts.

MAKES 35 BARS ABOUT 3 × 1¼ INCHES

2 cups unbleached all-purpose flour
1½ teaspoons ground cinnamon
8 tablespoons (1 stick) soft unsalted butter
8 tablespoons (1 stick) soft margarine
1 cup sugar
1 large egg, separated
1 cup coarsely chopped pecans

1. Position a rack in the middle of the oven. Preheat the oven to 300°F. Butter a 15½ × 10½ × 1-inch baking pan.

2. Sift the flour and cinnamon together and set aside.

3. Put the butter, margarine, and sugar in the large bowl of an electric mixer and beat on medium speed for about 1 minute, until the mixture is smooth and creamy. Blend in the egg yolk. Stop the mixer and scrape the bowl during this mixing. Decrease the speed to low and add the flour mixture, mixing just until it is incorporated and a dough forms that holds together. Press the dough evenly into the prepared pan. Smooth the top by putting a piece of wax paper over the dough and drawing the edge of a ruler over the paper. Discard the wax paper. Use a fork to beat the egg white until foamy, about 30 seconds. Brush the egg white evenly over the dough. You will have about 1 tablespoon of egg white left; discard it. Sprinkle the pecans evenly over the egg white and press them gently into the dough.

4. Bake until the top is golden, about 50 minutes. Immediately cut into rectangles. To cut 35 bars, cut 7 rows lengthwise and 5 rows across. Or, cut into diamond shapes by cutting strips at an angle rather than straight across. Cool 10 minutes in the pan. Transfer the bars to a wire rack to cool completely.

To Freeze: Put the bottoms of 2 cookies together and wrap them in plastic wrap. Put the wrapped cookies in a metal or plastic freezer container and cover tightly. Label with the date and contents. Freeze up to 3 months. **To Serve:** Defrost the wrapped bars at room temperature. Serve within 5 days.

White Chocolate and Toasted Almond Bars

 here is no skimping on the white chocolate in these bars. The butter-crust base holds a moist white chocolate filling studded with pieces of white chocolate, and the crisp topping is a combination of almonds and white chocolate.

MAKES 16 BARS

1 Press-in Butter Crust for Bars (page 21), prepared with light brown sugar and
    unbaked in a $9 \times 9 \times 2$-inch pan, not defrosted if frozen
10 ounces white chocolate, chopped in $^1/_2$-inch pieces
4 tablespoons ($^1/_2$ stick) unsalted butter
$^3/_4$ cup unbleached all-purpose flour
$^1/_2$ teaspoon baking powder
$^1/_4$ teaspoon salt
$^1/_2$ cup packed light brown sugar
2 large eggs
1 teaspoon vanilla extract
$^1/_2$ teaspoon almond extract
$^1/_2$ cup sliced almonds

1. Position a rack in the middle of the oven. Preheat the oven to 325°F. Bake the prepared crust 15 minutes, or 20 minutes if the crust is frozen.

2. Melt 2 ounces of the white chocolate with the butter in a large heatproof container set over, but not touching, a saucepan of barely simmering water, stirring until the chocolate and butter melt and the mixture is smooth. Remove from over the water and set aside.

3. Sift the flour, baking powder, and salt together and set aside.

4. Beat the brown sugar and eggs in the large bowl of an electric mixer on medium speed until smooth and slightly thickened, 2 minutes. Decrease the speed to low and blend in the melted white chocolate mixture, vanilla, and almond extract. Mix in the flour just until it is incorporated. Stir in 6 ounces of chopped white chocolate. Pour the batter over the crust and spread evenly. Mix the remaining 2 ounces of chopped white chocolate with the almonds and sprinkle evenly over the batter.

5. Bake for about 35 minutes, or until a toothpick inserted in the center comes out clean or with a few crumbs clinging to it. Cool thoroughly in the baking pan on a wire rack. Use a sharp knife to cut into 2 or 3 large pieces or 16 individual bars.

Good Advice: Use sliced almonds, either blanched or unblanched, which make a thin, crisp topping that is easy to cut. 🏃 Check to see that any white chocolate you choose contains cocoa butter. The 10 ounces of chopped white chocolate is used as 2 ounces for melting, 6 ounces for the filling, and 2 ounces for the topping. Two ounces of chopped white chocolate measures a heaping $^1/_3$ cup and 6 ounces of chopped white chocolate measures 1 heaping cup. *To Freeze:* Wrap large pieces in plastic wrap, then in heavy aluminum foil. Wrap individual bars in plastic wrap, place in a metal or plastic freezer container, and cover tightly. Label with the date and contents. Freeze up to 1 month. *To Serve:* Defrost the wrapped bars at room temperature. Serve within 3 days.

New York Bakery
Almond Raspberry Tall Bars

arolyn Marsh, the editor of our local paper, is a former New Yorker who used to carry these bars back to Camden after she visited Manhattan. Three years ago Carolyn gave me a small piece so I could duplicate them. I recognized them at once from the Brooklyn bakeries of my childhood. They have two layers of thin, moist almond cake spread with raspberry jam that is topped with chopped almonds and powdered sugar. 🦎 Since I had only seen this cake in bakeries, I looked in William Sultan's professional baking book, *Practical Baking*, for inspiration. It gave me a start, as well as the idea for the thrifty bakery technique of adding leftover cake crumbs to the batter.

MAKES 20 BARS ABOUT 2 × 1¹/₂ INCHES

1 cup cake flour
1 teaspoon ground cinnamon
1 teaspoon baking powder
1 cup plus 3 tablespoons sugar
¹/₂ teaspoon salt
¹/₃ cup packed almond paste (about 3 ounces)
2 large whole eggs plus 3 large eggs, separated
¹/₂ pound (2 sticks) cold or slightly softened margarine, cut in pieces
2 tablespoons corn syrup
¹/₄ cup milk
1¹/₂ teaspoons almond extract
1³/₄ cups finely chopped unblanched almonds
1 cup yellow cake crumbs
¹/₂ cup seedless raspberry jam
Powdered sugar

1. Position a rack in the middle of the oven. Preheat the oven to 350°F. Line a 10¹/₂ × 15¹/₂ × 1-inch baking pan with heavy aluminum foil, letting the foil extend over the edges of the pan. Butter the foil.

2. Sift the flour, cinnamon, and baking powder together and set aside.

3. Put 1 cup of the sugar, the salt, almond paste, and 1 egg in the large bowl of an electric mixer and beat on medium speed until the almond paste is blended smoothly, about 1 minute. Add the margarine and corn syrup and mix until blended, 1 minute. Add the remaining egg and the 3 yolks 1 at a time, beating for 1 minute. Stop the mixer and scrape the bowl during this process. Decrease the speed to low and add the milk and almond extract. The mixture may look curdled. Add 1¹/₄ cups of the chopped almonds, the cake crumbs, and the flour mixture, mixing just until the flour and cake crumbs are incorporated and the batter looks smooth. Set aside while beating the egg whites.

4. Put the egg whites in the clean large bowl of an electric mixer and beat with clean beaters on medium-high speed until soft peaks form. Reduce the speed to medium and slowly beat in the remaining 3 tablespoons of sugar. Use a large rubber spatula to fold the egg whites into the almond batter, folding just until no white streaks remain. Spread the batter evenly in the prepared pan.

5. Bake until the top is golden brown and a toothpick inserted in the center comes out clean, about 22 minutes. Cool thoroughly in the pan. Use the overhanging edges of aluminum foil to lift the bars out of the pan, then peel the foil away from the sides. Invert the bars onto the back of the baking pan and remove the foil carefully. With the bottom side up and the long side facing you, cut the bars in half. You will have two pieces measuring about 10 × 7½ inches each. Spread one piece with ¼ cup raspberry jam. Use the removable bottom of a tart pan to invert the remaining piece and slide it, top side up, on top of the jam-covered layer. Spread the remaining ¼ cup jam over the top. Sprinkle the remaining ½ cup ground almonds evenly over the top and dust the top with powdered sugar. You will have one double-layered piece measuring about 10 × 7½ inches. To cut 20 rectangles, cut 4 rows the long way and 5 rows across.

VARIATION   These can be prepared as single-layered rather than double-layered bars. Spread all the raspberry jam over the cooled bars in the pan. Sprinkle the ½ cup almonds thinly over the top, dust with powdered sugar, and cut into 40 bars.

Good Advice: Use almonds with skins. They add a more intense almond flavor to the bars. Process the almonds in a food processor just until some are ground but larger pieces up to ¼ inch in size remain. A combination of ground and finely chopped almonds gives the best result. ❧ A food processor works well for grinding the cake into crumbs. If I don't have a yellow cake layer in my freezer, I buy a good-quality pound cake. One Sara Lee pound cake is enough for 3 batches of these bars. *To Freeze:* Leave each row of 5 pieces touching each other and wrap each 5-piece row in plastic wrap. Place in a single layer in a metal or plastic freezer container and cover tightly. Label with the date and contents. Freeze up to 1 month. *To Serve:* Defrost the wrapped bars at room temperature. (If the day or your kitchen is hot and humid, defrost them in the refrigerator to reduce sweating on the wrapper.) Serve at room temperature within 3 days.

Bars with Fruit

More than any other category, these bars lend themselves to being served as complete desserts. Although you can add a dollop of whipped cream, they really don't need any embellishment. There are thin cheesecakes in the form of fruit and cream cheese bars, individual key lime pies as Key Lime Bars, fruit crumbles as Blueberry Crisp Squares, and snacking cakes as New England Raisin Spice Bars with Simple Caramel Glaze.

The fruit in these bars can be dried, fresh, freshly squeezed juice, or even fruit jam. Similar fruits can substitute for each other. Summer Berry Picnic Bars change as each summer berry reaches its peak, and Apricot Bars can be prepared with peach jam rather than apricot. You can swap dates and raisins for each other in the Banana Date Bars with Cinnamon Cream Cheese Frosting or New England Raisin Spice Bars with Simple Caramel Glaze.

Several of the bars have a graham cracker crust. I line the pans for them with heavy aluminum foil and let the ends of the foil overlap the pan rims. After the bars cool, the foil ends act as handles to lift them out of the pan. The crust won't crumble, the bars slice easily, and the pieces slide right off the foil. Use heavy aluminum foil, since the regular weight can tear. I generally cut cheesecake bars into large dessert-size pieces. If they bake in a 13 × 9-inch pan, I cut twelve or sixteen pieces rather than the sixteen to twenty I would normally cut for other bars.

I seldom reverse the pans for bars in the oven during baking. About two-thirds of the way into the baking time, I check that they are baking evenly, and reverse the pan only if one end seems to be darkening more than the other.

Since the Blueberry Crisp Squares have a fresh fruit filling, they are frozen unbaked so that no juice releases until the crisp is baked. That's the secret to keeping the crust and topping crisp.

Marvelous Mango Macadamia Bars

I'm an armchair dessert traveler. As soon as the cold winter winds begin to howl and mangoes begin arriving from tropical islands, I take my annual vicarious trip to the warm places where they grow. I put on some macarena music, bake these bright golden mango and cream cheese bars, and pretend I'm on a tropical vacation.

MAKES 12 TO 16 BARS

3 cups peeled, pitted, sliced ripe mango (about 3 mangoes)
1 pound cream cheese, softened 3 to 4 hours at room temperature
3 tablespoons unbleached all-purpose flour
One 14-ounce can sweetened condensed milk
2 tablespoons fresh lemon juice
2 teaspoons vanilla extract
1/4 teaspoon coconut extract
2 large eggs, at room temperature
1 Graham Cracker Crust (page 22) cooled or frozen, baked in a 13 × 9 × 2-inch pan lined with heavy aluminum foil that extends over the ends of the pan
1 cup crushed Nut Pralines made with macadamia nuts (page 26)

1. Position a rack in the middle of the oven. Preheat the oven to 325°F.

2. Put the mango slices in the work bowl of a food processor fitted with the steel blade. Process to a purée, about 30 seconds, then pour the purée into a bowl. You will have about 2³/4 cups. Put the cream cheese, flour, condensed milk, lemon juice, vanilla, and coconut extract in the food processor. (It is not necessary to clean the bowl after puréeing the mango.) Start with a few short bursts to break up the cream cheese, then process until the mixture is smooth, about 30 seconds. Add the eggs and process to incorporate them, about 10 seconds. Add the mango purée and process until the mixture is smooth, about 10 seconds. Pour the filling into the prepared crumb crust.

3. Bake for about 35 minutes, until the bars look set when you give the pan a gentle shake. Cool in the pan for 1 hour at room temperature, then refrigerate, uncovered, for 1 hour. Cover with plastic wrap and chill thoroughly in the refrigerator, at least 6 hours or overnight. Use the overhanging ends of aluminum foil to lift the cold bars out of the pan. Cut it into 12 to 16 pieces. Use a wide spatula to slide each bar off the aluminum foil.

Good Advice: Use ripe mangoes; they will have smooth skins that yield to gentle pressure, a mild, sweet scent, and a fragrant mango odor when peeled. Unripe mangoes will add color but little flavor. To keep the praline topping crisp, sprinkle it over the bars when you're ready to serve them. **Doubling the Recipe:** Use 2 pans and 2 crumb crusts. Mix the filling in 2 batches. Double the macadamia praline. **To Freeze:** Wrap individual bars in plastic wrap. Place in a metal or plastic freezer container and cover tightly. Label with the date and contents. Freeze up to 1 month. **To Serve:** Defrost the wrapped bars in the refrigerator for 5 hours or overnight. Unwrap the bars and sprinkle the macadamia praline over the top. Serve cold. Leftover bars can be covered with plastic wrap and stored in the refrigerator up to 5 days, but the praline softens after 1 day.

Apricot Bars

W hen our family has a wedding, graduation, or celebration of any kind, we can count on my Aunt Elaine to supply the cookies. She bakes for months in advance, freezes everything, and then sends big cartons of cookies via overnight delivery so they arrive at the event before she does. The center of attention is always these apricot bars that have a lemon crust spread with apricot jam and topped with a walnut meringue. Dusted with powdered sugar, they're pretty enough for a wedding table, yet easy enough to make and serve any day.

MAKES 12 TO 16 BARS

> 1 cup unbleached all-purpose flour
> 1/4 teaspoon baking soda
> 1/2 teaspoon salt
> 8 tablespoons (1 stick) soft unsalted butter
> 3/4 cup sugar
> 1 teaspoon grated lemon zest
> 2 large eggs, separated
> 1 cup apricot jam
> 1/8 teaspoon cream of tartar
> 1/2 cup finely chopped walnuts
> Powdered sugar

1. Position a rack in the middle of the oven. Preheat the oven to 325°F. Butter a 9 × 9 × 2-inch pan.

2. Sift the flour, baking soda, and salt together. Set aside.

3. Put the butter, 1/2 cup of the sugar, and the lemon zest in the large bowl of an electric mixer and beat on medium speed for about 1 minute, until the mixture is fluffy and lightened in color. Blend in the egg yolks 1 at a time, beating after each addition until the yolk is incorporated. Decrease the speed to low and mix in the flour mixture just until it is incorporated. Spread the batter evenly in the prepared pan. Spread the apricot jam evenly over the batter.

4. Put the egg whites and cream of tartar in the clean large bowl of an electric mixer and beat with clean beaters on low speed until frothy. Increase the speed to medium-high and beat until soft peaks form. Reduce the speed to low and slowly beat in the remaining 1/4 cup sugar about 2 tablespoons at a time. Use a rubber spatula to fold the walnuts gently into the meringue. Use a thin metal spatula to spread the meringue evenly over the jam to the edges of the pan.

5. Bake until a toothpick inserted in the center comes out clean, about 35 minutes. Remove from the oven and use a small, sharp knife to loosen the meringue from the edges of the pan. Cool in the pan. Dust the top with powdered sugar. Use a sharp knife to cut into 2 or 3 large pieces or 12 to 16 individual bars.

Good Advice: Apricot fruit spread that is sweetened with fruit juice can be substituted for the jam. ✿ Humidity softens the meringue topping. If the weather is humid or rainy, keep the cookies frozen until the day you want to serve them. **To Freeze:** Wrap large pieces in plastic wrap, then in heavy aluminum foil. Wrap individual bars in plastic wrap, place in a metal or plastic freezer container, and cover tightly. Label with the date and contents. Freeze up to 1 month. **To Serve:** Defrost the wrapped bars at room temperature. Serve within 3 days.

Key Lime Bars

W hen my friend Carole Emanuel saw these bars, she exclaimed, "What a good idea! Now I can have Key lime pie in my freezer all the time, but I don't have to make a whole pie." I realized how right she was after stocking my freezer with a dozen of these sweet and tart lime bars. They never freeze hard so they can be served straight from the freezer— at the drop of a Key lime craving.

MAKES 12 TO 16 BARS

Key Lime Filling
> 1 large egg
> 3 large egg yolks
> Two 14-ounce cans sweetened condensed milk
> 1 teaspoon grated fresh lime zest
> $3/4$ cup plus 2 tablespoons Key lime juice or fresh Persian lime juice

> 1 Graham Cracker Crust (page 22), cooled or frozen, baked in a $13 \times 9 \times 2$-inch pan
>> lined with heavy aluminum foil that extends over the ends of the pan

Sour Cream Topping
> $1^1/_2$ cups sour cream
> 2 tablespoons sugar
> 1 teaspoon vanilla extract

1. Position a rack in the middle of the oven. Preheat the oven to 300°F.

2. Put the egg and egg yolks in a large bowl and mix with a whisk just to break up. Whisk in the condensed milk until incorporated. Add the lime zest and lime juice and whisk until the mixture is smooth. Pour the filling into the baked crust.

3. Bake for 25 minutes until firm. Meanwhile, put the sour cream, sugar, and vanilla in a small bowl and stir them smooth. Remove the pan from the oven and carefully spread the sour cream mixture evenly over the filling. Bake for 10 minutes more.

4. Cool in the pan for 30 minutes. Put the uncovered pan in the freezer and freeze until firm, about 5 hours or overnight. Remove from the freezer and use the overhanging ends of aluminum foil to lift the cold bars out of the pan. Loosen the aluminum foil from the sides and cut into 12 to 16 bars. Use a wide spatula to slide the bars off the aluminum foil.

VARIATION Omit the sour cream topping and bake 35 minutes. Serve the frozen bars with whipped cream flavored with 1 teaspoon vanilla extract and 1 tablespoon powdered sugar for each cup of whipping cream used.

Good Advice: Good quality Key lime juice is now available in bottles at a reasonable price. I buy it at our local co-op market, but Simpson and Vail, listed in the mail order sources, ships the juice. When using bottled Key lime juice, I grate the peel from a Persian lime for the fresh zest. Fresh Persian limes can be substituted for the Key limes or Key lime juice. Wash the limes, grate the zest, then squeeze the juice. **Doubling the Recipe:** Use 2 pans and 2 crumb crusts. Double the remaining ingredients. **To Freeze:** Wrap individual bars in plastic wrap. Place in a metal or plastic freezer container and cover tightly. Label with the date and contents. Freeze up to 1 month. **To Serve:** Remove only as many bars as you need from the freezer, unwrap, and serve. The bars do not freeze hard and do not need to be defrosted.

Banana Date Bars with Cinnamon Cream Cheese Frosting

ananas are so dependable. Even in the depths of winter, when desperate for good fruit, we can count on finding trusty bananas to give an ultrasmooth texture to these bars. Soft, chewy dates contribute to their remarkable moistness, while cinnamon added to a cream cheese frosting produces its appealing creamy tan color.

MAKES 16 TO 20 BARS

Banana Date Bars

> 1 cup ¹/₂-inch pieces dates (about 6 ounces) or seedless raisins
> 1¹/₄ cups unbleached all-purpose flour
> ³/₄ teaspoon baking powder
> ¹/₂ teaspoon baking soda
> ¹/₄ teaspoon salt
> ¹/₂ teaspoon ground cinnamon
> ¹/₂ teaspoon allspice
> 8 tablespoons (1 stick) soft unsalted butter
> ³/₄ cup sugar
> 2 large eggs
> 1³/₄ cups mashed bananas (about 3 large)
> ¹/₂ cup sour cream
> 2 teaspoons vanilla extract

Cinnamon Cream Cheese Frosting

> 4 tablespoons (¹/₂ stick) soft unsalted butter
> 3 ounces cream cheese, full fat or reduced fat, softened about 2 hours at room
>   temperature
> 1 teaspoon vanilla extract
> 1 teaspoon ground cinnamon
> 1¹/₂ cups powdered sugar

PREPARE THE BARS

1. Position a rack in the middle of the oven. Preheat the oven to 325°F. Butter a 13 × 9 × 2-inch pan.

2. Put the dates in a medium bowl and pour on enough boiling water to cover them, about 1 cup. Let sit for 15 minutes. Drain off the water and set the dates aside.

3. Sift the flour, baking powder, baking soda, salt, cinnamon, and allspice together. Set aside.

4. Put the butter in the large bowl of an electric mixer and beat on medium speed for 15 seconds. Add the sugar and beat until smooth and creamy, 1 minute. Add the eggs and beat for 1 minute. Stop the mixer and scrape the bowl once during this beating. Blend in the mashed bananas, sour cream, and vanilla. Add the flour mixture, mixing just until it is incorporated. Stir in the dates. The batter will have small lumps. Spread it evenly in the prepared pan.

5. Bake until a toothpick inserted in the center comes out feeling sticky, about 30 minutes. Cool thoroughly in the baking pan on a wire rack.

PREPARE THE CINNAMON CREAM CHEESE FROSTING

1. Put the butter, cream cheese, vanilla, and cinnamon in the large bowl of an electric mixer and beat on medium-low speed for about 1 minute, until the mixture is smooth and the butter and cream cheese are thoroughly combined. Decrease the speed to low, add the powdered sugar, and beat until it is incorporated and the frosting is smooth, about 1 minute. Use a thin metal spatula to spread the frosting evenly over the top of the cooled cake.

2. Put the pan in the freezer and freeze until the frosting is firm, about 1 hour. Use a sharp knife to cut into 2 or 3 large pieces or 16 to 20 individual bars.

To Freeze: Wrap large pieces in plastic wrap, then in heavy aluminum foil. Wrap individual bars in plastic wrap, place in a metal or plastic freezer container, and cover tightly. Label with the date and contents. Freeze up to 1 month. **To Serve:** Defrost the wrapped bars in the refrigerator for 3 hours or overnight. Serve cold; will keep for 5 days.

New England Raisin Spice Bars with Simple Caramel Glaze

arly New England sailing vessels took lumber and forest products around the world and returned loaded with molasses, rum, and sugar from the West Indies and spices from Asia. The adventurous sailors supplied Colonial cooks with a surprising variety of imported ingredients from which they created the traditional spice cakes and cookies that we associate with New England desserts. These golden bars, with their blend of molasses, raisins, and spices and a brown sugar caramel glaze topping, carry on that proud tradition.

MAKES 16 TO 20 BARS

Raisin Bars

1 1/2 cups seedless raisins
1 3/4 cups unbleached all-purpose flour
1 teaspoon baking powder
1/2 teaspoon baking soda
1/4 teaspoon salt
1 teaspoon ground cinnamon
1/2 teaspoon ground ginger
1/2 teaspoon ground mace
1/4 teaspoon ground cloves
8 tablespoons (1 stick) soft unsalted butter
1 1/4 cups packed light brown sugar
2 large eggs
1/4 cup molasses

Simple Caramel Glaze

1/4 cup whipping cream
6 tablespoons packed light brown sugar
1 tablespoon light corn syrup

PREPARE THE BARS

1. Position a rack in the middle of the oven. Preheat the oven to 325°F. Butter a 13 × 9 × 2-inch pan.

2. Put the raisins in a medium bowl and pour on enough boiling water to cover them, about 1 cup. Let sit for 15 minutes. Drain off the water and set aside.

3. Sift the flour, baking powder, baking soda, salt, cinnamon, ginger, mace, and cloves together. Set aside.

4. Put the butter and brown sugar in the large bowl of an electric mixer and beat on medium speed for about 1 minute until smooth. Stir in the eggs, mixing until smooth.

Stir in the molasses and blend smooth. On low speed add the flour mixture, mixing just until it is incorporated. Stir in the raisins. Spread the batter evenly in the prepared pan.

5. Bake until a toothpick inserted in the center comes out feeling sticky, about 23 minutes. Cool 5 minutes, then pour the warm caramel glaze over the top.

PREPARE THE GLAZE

1. While the bars bake, prepare the glaze. Put the cream, brown sugar, and corn syrup in a small saucepan and cook over medium heat, stirring occasionally, until the mixture is blended together and the brown sugar dissolves in the cream. Increase the heat to medium-high and bring to a boil. Boil the mixture for 2 minutes, stirring constantly. Pour the glaze evenly over the warm cake. It thickens as it cools. If the prepared glaze becomes too thick to pour while the cake bakes, rewarm it over low heat. Cool thoroughly in the baking pan on a wire rack.

2. Freeze until the glaze is firm, about 30 minutes. Use a sharp knife to cut into 2 or 3 large pieces or 16 to 20 individual bars.

To Freeze: Wrap large pieces in plastic wrap, then in heavy aluminum foil. Wrap individual bars in plastic wrap, place in a metal or plastic freezer container, and cover tightly. Label with the date and contents. Freeze up to 1 month. **To Serve:** Defrost the wrapped bars in the refrigerator for 5 hours or overnight. Serve cold; will keep for 5 days.

Spice Leather

any years ago I received a squashed box in the mail from my friend Mary Pennell. The box contained these thin spicy bars with a moist and chewy yet firm, leathery consistency. Even the bashing in the mail couldn't hurt these bars, and Jeff and I loved them from the very first bite, not that we stopped after one bite. It took many tries to get these cookies right, but here they are.

MAKES 96 BARS

2¹/₄ cups seedless raisins
1¹/₄ cups unbleached all-purpose flour
1 cup cake flour
1 teaspoon baking soda
¹/₂ teaspoon salt
2 teaspoons ground cinnamon
1 teaspoon ground cloves
8 tablespoons (1 stick) softened margarine
1¹/₂ cups packed dark brown sugar
1 large egg
1 cup dark corn syrup
2 cups yellow cake crumbs

1. Put the raisins in a medium bowl and pour 2 cups boiling water over them. Let sit for 1 to 2 hours. Put the raisins in a strainer and drain them over a bowl. Measure the liquid in the bowl and press on the raisins until you have 1 cup plus 2 tablespoons liquid. Discard the liquid. That will ensure the raisins have the proper amount of moisture remaining in them. Put the raisins in a food processor fitted with a metal blade and process for about 30 seconds, until a thick purée forms. Set aside.

2. Position 2 racks in the lower middle and upper middle of the oven. Preheat the oven to 350°F. Line three 17 × 12 × 1-inch baking sheets with parchment paper, letting the paper come up the side at one end of the pan so you can lift out the baked bars. Spray the paper with vegetable oil spray.

3. Stir the flours, baking soda, salt, cinnamon, and cloves together in a small bowl.

4. Put the margarine and brown sugar in the large bowl of an electric mixer and beat on medium speed until smooth, about 45 seconds. Mix in the egg, corn syrup, and raisin purée until blended into the creamed mixture. Stop the mixer and scrape the bowl. Add the cake crumbs and mix until they dissolve, about 30 seconds. Decrease the speed to low and add the flour mixture, mixing just until it is incorporated. The batter will be soft and sticky.

5. Use a thin metal spatula to spread about 2 cups of batter evenly over a prepared baking sheet all the way to the edges. Repeat with a second baking sheet.

6. Bake for about 12 minutes, until you can press your fingers gently on top of the bars and they feel as firm in the center as at the edges. Remove from the oven and let sit for 5 minutes. Use a small, sharp knife to loosen the bars from the edges of the pan. Using the parchment liner that is exposed at one end, slide the liner and bars onto the counter to cool thoroughly. Repeat spreading and baking the third sheet.

7. Use clean kitchen scissors to trim the crisp edges from the bars, about $1/2$ inch on all sides. Use the scissors to cut each rectangle into 8 strips lengthwise, cutting through the bars and paper. Cut each strip into 4 pieces. Each bar will measure about $3^3/4 \times 1^3/8$ inches. Remove the paper from the bottoms of the bars.

Good Advice: To prevent the bars from sticking to the pans, line the baking sheets with parchment paper and spray the paper with a vegetable oil spray. ❧ A food processor works well for grinding cake into crumbs. If I don't have a cake layer in my freezer, I buy a good quality pound cake. One Sara Lee pound cake is enough for two batches of spice leather with a few slices left over. ❧ If you don't have three 17×12-inch baking sheets, reuse and reline a cooled baking sheet after you remove a batch of bars from it. ❧ These are thin bars that require careful timing as they bake. If underbaked, they will be sticky and soft and will not have the desired firm leather quality. If overbaked, they will be hard and dry. The top of the bars should feel firm at both the center and the edges when they are properly baked. **Doubling the Recipe:** Mix and bake the batter in separate batches so it won't have to wait too long until it bakes. **To Freeze:** Stack 5 bars together and wrap in plastic wrap. Put them in a metal or plastic freezer container and cover tightly. Label with the date and contents. Freeze up to 3 months. **To Serve:** Defrost the wrapped bars in the refrigerator. Separate defrosted bars into a single layer and cover with plastic wrap. Serve at room temperature within 3 days.

Fruit Jelly Squares

 few years ago I developed some recipes for the Chocolate Manufacturers and Confectionery Association. Every recipe contained some sort of candy, and all types of candy companies needed to be represented, even those that produced candy without chocolate. I went down to our neighborhood drugstore's candy counter for inspiration and spotted large fruit-flavored, sugar-coated jellies that were similar to giant gumdrops. I added them along with dates, walnuts, and raisins to a spice bar batter and came up with these colorful bars.

MAKES 25 SQUARES

1½ cups unbleached all-purpose flour
1½ teaspoons baking powder
¼ teaspoon salt
1 teaspoon ground cinnamon
½ teaspoon ground ginger
1 cup ½-inch pieces soft sugar-coated fruit jellies (about 8 ounces)
½ cup ½-inch pieces pitted dates
1 cup coarsely chopped walnuts
½ cup golden raisins
8 tablespoons (1 stick) soft unsalted butter
1½ cups packed light brown sugar
2 large eggs
2 teaspoons vanilla extract
Powdered sugar, optional

1. Position a rack in the middle of the oven. Preheat the oven to 300°F. Butter the bottom and sides of a 9 × 9 × 2-inch pan.

2. Sift the flour, baking powder, salt, cinnamon, and ginger into a large bowl. Add the fruit jellies, dates, walnuts, and golden raisins to the flour mixture, stirring just to combine the fruit and nuts with the dry ingredients.

3. Put the butter and brown sugar in the large bowl of an electric mixer. Beat on low speed until the mixture is smooth. Blend in the eggs and vanilla until incorporated, about 1 minute. Stop the mixer and scrape the bowl once. Add the flour mixture and mix just until it is incorporated. The batter will be thick. Spread the batter evenly in the prepared pan.

4. Bake until a toothpick inserted in the center comes out clean or with just a few crumbs clinging to it, about 1 hour. Cool thoroughly in the baking pan on a wire rack. Dust with powdered sugar, if desired. Use a large, sharp knife to cut into 2 or 3 large pieces or 25 individual bars, cutting 5 rows in each direction.

Good Advice: Check to see that the jellies are fruit-flavored rather than spice-flavored. To Freeze: Wrap large pieces in plastic wrap, then in heavy aluminum foil. Wrap individual bars in plastic wrap, place in a metal or plastic freezer container, and cover tightly. Label with the date and contents. Freeze up to 3 months. To Serve: Defrost the wrapped bars at room temperature. Serve within 5 days.

Summer Berry Picnic Bars

he harvest may come late in Maine, but July brings a two-month parade of all the juicy raspberries, blueberries, and blackberries that we can gather. That's when we take advantage of the precious few warm summer days to celebrate with a picnic, and these bars filled with whatever berry is in season. They have a crisp crumb topping, a light cake and berry filling, and a butter crust that makes them especially picnic-portable.

MAKES 16 TO 20 BARS

1 Press-in Butter Crust for Bars (page 21), prepared with light brown sugar and
    unbaked in a 13 × 9 × 2-inch pan, not defrosted if frozen
1³/₄ cups unbleached all-purpose flour
1³/₄ cups packed light brown sugar
1¹/₂ teaspoons ground cinnamon
8 tablespoons (1 stick) slightly softened unsalted butter, cut into 8 pieces
3 tablespoons unsalted butter, melted
1 teaspoon baking soda
¹/₂ teaspoon salt
1 cup sour cream
1 large egg
1 teaspoon vanilla extract
¹/₂ teaspoon almond extract
2 cups raspberries, blueberries, blackberries, or a combination of berries

1. Position a rack in the middle of the oven. Preheat the oven to 350°F. Bake the prepared crust 15 minutes, or 20 minutes if frozen.

2. Put the flour, brown sugar, and cinnamon in the large bowl of an electric mixer and mix on low speed just to blend the ingredients. Add the softened butter and mix until fine crumbs form (the largest pieces will be about ¹/₄ inch). Put 2 cups of the flour mixture in a small bowl and stir in the melted butter. Larger moist crumbs will form. Set aside for the crumb topping.

3. Stir the baking soda and salt into the remaining flour mixture. Add the sour cream, egg, vanilla, and almond extract, beating just until they are blended completely. Gently stir in the berries. Spread the batter evenly over the baked crust. Sprinkle the reserved crumb mixture evenly over the batter.

4. Bake until the edges are light brown and a toothpick inserted in the center comes out with moist crumbs clinging to it, about 35 minutes. Cool thoroughly in the baking pan on a wire rack. Use a large, sharp knife to cut into 2 or 3 large pieces or 16 to 20 individual bars.

To Freeze: Wrap large pieces in plastic wrap, then in heavy aluminum foil. Wrap individual bars in plastic wrap, place in a metal or plastic freezer container, and cover tightly. Label with the date and contents. Freeze up to 1 month. **To Serve:** Defrost the wrapped bars at room temperature. Serve within 3 days.

Blueberry Crisp Squares

orking in a restaurant had certain perks. There were always desserts-in-progress on the counter to inspire new combinations. One day I mixed fresh blueberries with some graham cracker crumb crust mixture for a snack. It became one of my favorite combinations and led to these bars, which have a thick graham cracker crumb crust topped with blueberries and crisp crumbs.

MAKES 9 BARS

Blueberry Filling

2¹/₂ cups blueberries, fresh or frozen unsweetened, not defrosted
2 tablespoons packed light brown sugar
1 tablespoon unbleached all-purpose flour
¹/₂ teaspoon ground cinnamon

1 Thick Graham Cracker Crust (page 22), cooled or frozen, baked in a 9-inch square
    pan lined with heavy aluminum foil that extends over the ends of the pan

Crumb Topping

²/₃ cup unbleached all-purpose flour
¹/₃ cup packed light brown sugar
3 tablespoons granulated sugar
Pinch salt
6 tablespoons (³/₄ stick) cold unsalted butter, cut into 6 pieces

MIX THE FILLING

Put the blueberries, brown sugar, flour, and cinnamon in a large bowl and stir together. Spread the blueberry mixture over the prepared crust.

MIX THE CRUMB TOPPING

Put the flour, brown sugar, granulated sugar, and salt in a large bowl and stir them together. Add the butter, and use your fingertips, a pastry blender, or an electric mixer on low speed to combine until you get crumbs about ¹/₂ inch in size. Sprinkle the crumbs evenly over the blueberry filling.

Good Advice: If using frozen blueberries, do not defrost them before preparing the squares. Assemble the bars and store them unbaked in the freezer until you want to serve them. ✸ Cool the baked bars thoroughly before cutting them so that they cut into neat pieces and hold their shape. ✸ If the bars are not frozen when they are baked, shorten the baking time by about 10 minutes. **Doubling the Recipe:** Use 2 graham cracker crumb crusts baked in 2 pans and double the remaining ingredients. **To Freeze:** Cover the unbaked bars tightly with plastic wrap, then heavy aluminum foil, gently pressing the foil against the crumbs. Seal the wrapping tightly. Label with the date and contents. Freeze in the pan up to 1 month. After it is frozen, you can lift the frozen bars and their wrapping from the pan. When you are ready to bake, carefully return the frozen bars with their foil liner to the original baking pan. **To Bake and Serve:** Position a rack in the middle of the oven. Preheat the oven to 350°F. Unwrap the frozen bars. Bake about 55 minutes, until the crumb topping is golden brown and the blueberry filling is just beginning to bubble in one or two places. Cool thoroughly. Carefully lift the aluminum foil and bars from the baking pan and loosen the foil from the sides. Cut into 9 bars. Use a wide spatula to slide the bars off the foil. These bars are good served warm with vanilla ice cream. Warm them in a 250°F oven for 10 to 12 minutes. They are best served within 2 days.

Cookie Sandwiches and Filled Cookies

ookie sandwiches are so extravagant. Each one has two cookies, a filling, and some even have a topping. They look as if you've put a lot of work into them, but it's just a matter of gluing two cookies together with some Chocolate Truffle Sauce, melted chocolate, or jam. The cookies should be thin and soft enough to break easily when you take a bite so that the filling stays put rather than squishing out.

Cookie sandwiches that have a rolled dough are usually made from rounds, but you can also cut out hearts, trees, ovals, or even letters that spell out a name. The shapes are limited only by your selection of cookie cutters. The size of the cookie sets its style and influences when it's served. Large cookie sandwiches make knife and fork cookie tart desserts, medium ones are convenient for picnics and lunch boxes, and small ones fit into more refined tea party occasions.

Filled cookies have fruit and nut combinations rolled inside a cold dough. When properly chilled, the dough is easy to handle. It rolls out smoothly, won't stick to the rolling surface, and won't tear when rolled around the filling. Breaks in the dough allow the filling to leak out, so if you find a tear, patch it carefully with dough scraps.

Chocolate-Filled Almond Lace Cookies

y childhood summers spent in Brooklyn actually lasted well into September. I remember the abrupt change as soon as Labor Day arrived. Summer was officially over and the weather became cooler. The neighborhood bakeries began baking their cool weather specialties that would have melted in the heat or become soft from summer humidity. I knew it was time to begin my daily bakery checks for these crisp lace-textured cookies that were flavored with ground almonds and held together by a creamy chocolate filling. There were only a few weeks to enjoy them before we returned to Florida, so I could never get my fill. Now I can store these cookies in my freezer and enjoy them in any season.

MAKES 15 COOKIE SANDWICHES

6 tablespoons (³/₄ stick) unsalted butter
¹/₃ cup sugar
2 tablespoons Lyle's Golden Syrup
¹/₃ cup all-purpose flour
1 cup plus 2 tablespoons ground blanched almonds
1 teaspoon vanilla extract
³/₄ teaspoon almond extract

1 cup Chocolate Truffle Sauce (page 20), warmed just until spreadable

1. Position 2 racks in the middle and upper third of the oven. Preheat the oven to 350°F. Line 2 baking sheets with a nonstick liner or parchment paper.

2. Put the butter, sugar, and syrup in a medium saucepan and cook over low heat until the butter melts and the sugar dissolves, stirring often. Increase the heat to medium-high and bring to a boil, stirring constantly. The mixture will be smooth and syrupy. Remove from the heat and stir in the flour until it is incorporated. Stir in the ground almonds, vanilla, and almond extract. Drop teaspoons of batter 3 inches apart on the baking sheets.

3. Bake the cookies 8 to 9 minutes, until the bottoms and edges are light brown and the centers are golden. Reverse the baking sheets after 4 minutes front to back and top to bottom to ensure that the cookies bake evenly. The cookies begin to spread during the final 2 to 3 minutes of baking. One baking sheet of cookies may be done 1 minute sooner than the other. Cool the cookies on the baking sheets for 5 minutes until firm, then transfer them to wire racks to cool completely. The cookies become crisp as they cool.

4. Arrange the cookies in pairs of similar size. Turn half of the cookies bottom side up. Leaving a ³/₈-inch plain edge, carefully spread about 1 tablespoon of Chocolate Truffle Sauce over the bottoms of half the cookies. Gently place the remaining cookies bottom side down on the truffle sauce. Let the cookies sit until the filling is firm, about 30 minutes.

To Freeze: Wrap each cookie sandwich in plastic wrap. Put the wrapped cookies in a metal or plastic freezer container and cover tightly. Label with the date and contents. Freeze up to 1 month. **To Serve:** Defrost the wrapped cookies in the refrigerator. I prefer these cookies at room temperature. Leftover cookies can be wrapped and stored in the refrigerator up to 3 days.

Crumb-Topped
Lemon Cream Sandwiches

I'd probably put crumbs on shoe leather if I thought it would taste good, but they really belong on these cookies. These crumbs bake on top of delicate multilayered cookies that are filled with lemon cream frosting. The sandwiches go from crunchy to flaky to creamy in one bite. Although I usually cut round cookies, the dough holds its shape well during baking and can be cut into hearts, squares, triangles, or ovals.

MAKES 20 COOKIE SANDWICHES

Crisp Crumb Topping
6 tablespoons unbleached all-purpose flour
6 tablespoons sugar
2 tablespoons unsalted butter, melted

Flaky Cookies
1 1/2 cups unbleached all-purpose flour
12 tablespoons (1 1/2 sticks) cold unsalted butter, cut into 12 pieces
1 tablespoon cold fresh lemon juice
1 large egg white, lightly beaten

Lemon Cream Filling
4 tablespoons (1/2 stick) soft unsalted butter
3/4 cup powdered sugar, sifted
1/4 teaspoon vanilla extract
1 teaspoon fresh lemon juice
3/4 teaspoon grated lemon zest

PREPARE THE CRUMB TOPPING

Put the flour and sugar in a small bowl. Use a mixing spoon to stir them together. Pour on the melted butter and stir the mixture until it is evenly moistened and fine crumbs form. Set aside.

PREPARE THE COOKIES

1. Preheat the oven to 375°F. Position 2 oven racks in the upper middle and lower middle of the oven. Line 2 baking sheets with parchment paper.

2. Put the flour in the large bowl of an electric mixer. Add the butter pieces and mix on low speed just until they are the size of small lima beans, about 45 seconds. They will not all be the same size, and you will still see loose flour. Add the lemon juice, then slowly add 3 to 4 tablespoons ice water, a tablespoon at a time. Stop beating as soon as the mixture

begins to hold together, about 30 seconds. Turn the dough out onto a lightly floured rolling surface and divide it in half. Form each piece of dough into a 4-inch square disk and refrigerate for about 20 minutes, until the dough is cold and firm.

3. Remove one piece of dough from the refrigerator. Lightly flour the rolling surface and rolling pin and roll the dough into a circle about 10 inches in diameter and $\frac{1}{8}$ inch thick. Using a $2\frac{1}{4}$-inch-diameter pastry cutter, cut out circles and place them on the baking sheets $\frac{3}{4}$ inch apart. The cookies do not spread when they bake. Repeat with the second piece of dough. Press the dough scraps together, roll, and cut in circles. You will have 40 cookies. Use a pastry brush to brush each cookie lightly with egg white. Leaving a $\frac{1}{4}$-inch plain edge, sprinkle each cookie with about 1 teaspoon of the crumb topping. (A few crumbs will fall off the cookies.) Gently press the crumbs onto the cookies.

4. Bake until the bottoms are golden, about 11 minutes, reversing the baking sheets from top to bottom and back to front after 6 minutes. Cool the cookies on the baking sheet for 5 minutes, then transfer them to wire racks to cool completely.

PREPARE THE FILLING

Put the butter, powdered sugar, vanilla, lemon juice, and lemon zest in a small bowl and beat with an electric mixer on low speed or with a large spoon until smooth. Spread a thin layer of frosting on the bottoms of half of the cookies. Press another cookie, bottom side down, onto each frosted cookie.

VARIATIONS   Serve the cookies as single cookies without filling.

Lemon Curd (page 24) can be substituted for the lemon frosting. Use about $\frac{2}{3}$ cup of Lemon Curd and spread a thin layer over the bottom of half of the cookies. Press the remaining cookies, bottom sides down, onto each curd-topped cookie.

Good Advice: When you add the crumbs to the cookies, a few will fall off. You can leave them on the baking sheet and discard them after the cookies bake. ✯ Try other shapes and different sizes. Pointed shapes such as stars and trees are difficult to fill smoothly with frosting, but they'll work fine if the cookies are not filled. *To Freeze:* Wrap each cookie sandwich in plastic wrap. Put the wrapped cookies in a metal or plastic freezer container and cover tightly. Label with the date and contents. Freeze up to 1 month. Cookies without filling can be wrapped in pairs and frozen up to 3 months. *To Serve:* Defrost the wrapped cookies in the refrigerator. I prefer these cookies at room temperature so I let the wrapped cookies sit at room temperature about 1 hour before serving them. Leftover cookies can be stored in the refrigerator up to 3 days.

Chocolate and Hazelnut Praline Cookie Tarts

his recipe reminds me of one of those old Cecil B. DeMille movie advertisements—it's been five years in the making. Years ago when I was testing the Raspberry Sandwich Cookies for my first book, *Bake and Freeze Desserts*, I decided a chocolate and hazelnut version would be good, so this was one of the first cookies I tried out for this book. I started with a basic butter shortbread dough, added hazelnut praline to it, and sandwiched the baked cookies together with chocolate. I couldn't decide whether I preferred a dark or white chocolate filling, so I've included both versions.

MAKES TWELVE 2-INCH COOKIE SANDWICHES

1 cup unbleached all-purpose flour
1/4 teaspoon salt
8 tablespoons (1 stick) soft unsalted butter
6 tablespoons powdered sugar
1/2 teaspoon vanilla extract
1/4 teaspoon ground cinnamon
1/2 cup hazelnut Nut Pralines powder (page 26)

1/2 cup Chocolate Truffle Sauce (page 20) warmed just until spreadable
1 1/2 ounces semisweet chocolate, chopped

1. Position 2 racks in the middle and upper third of the oven. Preheat the oven to 325°F. Line 2 large baking sheets with parchment paper.

2. Sift the flour and salt together and set aside.

3. Put the butter and powdered sugar in a large bowl. Beat with an electric mixer on medium speed for 30 seconds until smooth. Decrease the speed to low and beat in the vanilla and cinnamon, then the hazelnut praline powder. Add the flour mixture and blend just until it is completely incorporated and the dough holds together. Stop the mixer and scrape down the sides of the bowl once during the mixing. Form the dough into a 6-inch disk and wrap in plastic wrap. Refrigerate until the dough is cold and just firm enough to roll, about 40 minutes.

4. Remove the dough from the refrigerator, put it between 2 pieces of wax paper, and roll it 1/4 inch thick. Remove the top piece of wax paper. Use a metal cutter to cut out 2-inch circles from the dough. Turn the bottom piece of wax paper over and release the circles. Place them 1 inch apart on the prepared baking sheets, using a wide spatula to move the cookies. Gather together the dough scraps into a disk and put them between 2 clean pieces of wax paper. Repeat the rolling and cutting process to form circles from the remainder of the dough. You should have 24 cookies. Cut a 1-inch circle from the centers of half of the cookies and remove the circles. (The wide, round end of a pastry tube works well for cutting the circles.) The dough holes can be baked with the cookies for snacks.

5. Bake the cookies for 23 to 26 minutes, or until the bottoms are light brown and the tops evenly golden, reversing the baking sheets after 10 minutes, front to back and top to bottom, to ensure that the cookies bake evenly. The cookies may be finished at different times.

6. Cool the cookies in the pans for 5 minutes. Use a wide metal spatula to transfer the cookies to a wire rack to cool completely. Leaving a ¼-inch plain edge, spread about 2 teaspoons of the truffle sauce evenly over the cookies without the holes.

7. Preheat the oven to 175°F. Place the semisweet chocolate in a small ovenproof container and melt it in the oven for about 5 minutes. Remove the chocolate from the oven as soon as it is melted and stir it smooth. Dip a fork in the melted chocolate and sprinkle thin lines of chocolate over the tops of cookies with the holes, moving the fork quickly to create a random pattern. Place the decorated tops on the sauce-covered cookies.

VARIATION   Chop 5 ounces of white chocolate. Preheat the oven to 175°F. Place the white chocolate in a small ovenproof container and melt it in the oven for about 9 minutes. Remove it from the oven as soon as it is melted and stir it smooth. Let the white chocolate thicken slightly at room temperature, about 10 minutes. Leaving a ¼-inch plain edge, spread 1 teaspoon of white chocolate over the cookies without the holes. Dip a fork in the remaining white chocolate and sprinkle thin lines over the cookies with the holes, then fit them on top of the white-chocolate-covered cookies.

Good Advice: Even when cold, this soft dough usually sticks to the rolling surface, but rolling the dough between 2 sheets of wax paper solves the problem. ❧ These cookies hold their shape when baked and can be cut into heart, star, or other decorative shapes. To Freeze: Chill the cookies, un-covered, until the chocolate is firm. Wrap each cookie sandwich in plastic wrap. Put the wrapped cookies in a metal or plastic freezer container and cover tightly. Label with the date and contents. Freeze up to 3 months. To Serve: Defrost the wrapped cookies at room temperature. Leftover cookies can be covered with plastic wrap and stored at room temperature up to 3 days.

Black and White Hazelnut Cookie Tarts

T he more I bake the more ideas I get. Testing the Chocolate and Hazelnut Praline Cookie Tarts led me to this dark chocolate and hazelnut cookie filled with white chocolate. The top cookie has a hole cut out of the center to let the white chocolate show through, and it is decorated with thin lines of white chocolate. The total effect makes a stunning black and white finish.

MAKES TWELVE 2-INCH COOKIE SANDWICHES

³/₄ cup unbleached all-purpose flour
¹/₄ cup unsweetened Dutch process cocoa powder, such as Droste or Hershey's European
¹/₄ teaspoon salt
8 tablespoons (1 stick) soft unsalted butter
¹/₂ cup plus 1 tablespoon powdered sugar
1 teaspoon vanilla extract
¹/₂ cup hazelnut Nut Pralines powder (page 26)
6 ounces chopped white chocolate (preferably Callebaut, Lindt, or Baker's Premium)

1. Position a rack in the middle of the oven. Preheat the oven to 325°F. Line 2 large baking sheets with parchment paper.

2. Sift the flour, cocoa powder, and salt together and set aside.

3. Put the butter and powdered sugar in a large bowl. Beat with an electric mixer on medium speed for 30 seconds until smooth. Decrease the speed to low and beat in the vanilla, then the hazelnut praline powder. Add the flour mixture and blend just until it is completely incorporated and a smooth dough forms. Stop the mixer and scrape down the sides of the bowl once during the mixing. Form the dough into a 6-inch disk and wrap in plastic wrap. Refrigerate until the dough is cold and just firm enough to roll, about 40 minutes.

4. Remove the dough from the refrigerator. Lightly flour the rolling surface and rolling pin and roll the dough ¹/₄ inch thick. Use a metal cutter to cut out 2-inch circles. Using a metal spatula, loosen the circles of dough and place them 1 inch apart on the prepared baking sheets. Gather together the dough scraps and repeat the rolling and cutting process to form circles from the remainder of the dough. You should have 24 cookies. Cut a 1-inch circle from the centers of half the cookies and remove the circles. (The wide, round end of a pastry tube works well for cutting out the circles.) The dough holes can be baked with the cookies for snacks.

5. Bake 1 sheet of cookies at a time until the tops feel firm, about 13 minutes, reversing the baking sheet after 7 minutes to ensure that the cookies bake evenly. Bake the second

pan of cookies. Cool the cookies on the baking sheets for 5 minutes, then transfer them to wire racks to cool completely.

6. Decrease the oven to 175°F. Place the white chocolate in a small ovenproof container and melt it in the oven for about 10 minutes. Remove the white chocolate from the oven as soon as it is melted and stir it smooth. Let it thicken slightly at room temperature, about 10 minutes. Leaving a $1/4$-inch plain edge, spread 1 teaspoon of white chocolate over the cookies without the holes. Dip a fork in the remaining white chocolate, sprinkle thin lines of white chocolate over the cookies with the holes, and place them gently on top of the white-chocolate-covered cookies.

Good Advice: Chocolate cookies can burn easily, so I bake one sheet of these cookies at a time on the middle rack. *To Freeze:* Chill the cookies, uncovered, until the white chocolate is firm. Wrap each cookie sandwich in plastic wrap. Put the wrapped cookies in a metal or plastic freezer container and cover tightly. Label with the date and contents. Freeze up to 3 months. *To Serve:* Defrost the wrapped cookies at room temperature. Leftover cookies can be covered with plastic wrap and stored at room temperature up to 3 days.

Oatmeal Date Cookie Sandwiches

ates and cream cheese may be a classic combination, but these cookies pair them in an original way. Crisp oatmeal cookies are studded with dates, then sandwiched together with cream cheese frosting. Try them as a sweet sandwich surprise for your next picnic, being sure to take along several for each person.

MAKES 12 COOKIE SANDWICHES

Oatmeal Date Cookies

1 cup unbleached all-purpose flour
$^1/_2$ teaspoon baking soda
$^1/_4$ teaspoon salt
$^1/_2$ teaspoon ground cinnamon
8 tablespoons (1 stick) soft unsalted butter
$^1/_2$ cup granulated sugar
$^1/_2$ cup packed light brown sugar
1 large egg
1 teaspoon vanilla extract
1 cup oatmeal (not quick-cooking)
$^1/_2$ cup $^1/_2$-inch pieces pitted dates

Cream Cheese Frosting

2 tablespoons ($^1/_4$ stick) soft unsalted butter
2 ounces cream cheese, full fat or reduced fat, softened about 2 hours at room
   temperature
1 teaspoon vanilla extract
1 cup powdered sugar

MAKE THE COOKIES

1. Position 2 oven racks in the lower middle and upper middle of the oven. Preheat the oven to 350°F. Line 2 baking sheets with parchment paper.

2. Sift the flour, baking soda, salt, and cinnamon together and set aside.

3. Put the butter, granulated sugar, and brown sugar in the large bowl of an electric mixer and beat on medium speed for about 1 minute until smooth. Add the egg and vanilla and mix on low speed for about 15 seconds until thoroughly blended. Stop the mixer and scrape the bowl during this time. Add and mix in the flour mixture and oatmeal. Stir in the date pieces. Using 1 tablespoon of dough for each cookie, roll the dough between the palms of your hands to form 1-inch balls. Place them about 2 inches apart on the prepared baking sheets.

4. Bake the cookies about 13 minutes, or until they are golden. Reverse the baking sheets after 7 minutes, front to back and top to bottom, to ensure even browning, watching them carefully as they near the end of their baking time. Cool the cookies on the baking sheets for 5 minutes, then transfer them to wire racks to cool completely.

FILL THE COOKIES

Put the butter, cream cheese, and vanilla in the large bowl of an electric mixer and beat on medium-low speed for about 1 minute until the mixture is smooth and thoroughly combined. Decrease the speed to low and add the powdered sugar. Beat until it is incorporated and the frosting is smooth, about 1 minute. Use a thin metal spatula to spread a slightly rounded tablespoon of cream cheese filling over the flat bottoms of half the cooled cookies. Press the flat bottoms of the remaining cookies on the cream cheese frosting. Refrigerate until the frosting is firm, about 30 minutes.

Good Advice: Before filling the cookies, arrange them in pairs of equal size. ✻ Use whole pitted dates, not date pieces that may have been rolled in sugar. *To Freeze:* Wrap each cookie sandwich in plastic wrap. Place the cookies in a metal or plastic freezer container and cover tightly, packing them in loosely so they do not break. Label with the date and contents. Freeze up to 1 month. *To Serve:* Remove the cookie sandwiches you need from the freezer. Defrost the wrapped cookies for 3 hours or overnight in the refrigerator. Serve cold or at room temperature. Cover leftover cookie sandwiches with plastic wrap and store up to 3 days in the refrigerator.

Pumpkin Whoopie Pies

lthough the A-1 Diner in Gardiner, Maine, is thirty-five miles from Camden, we create excuses to eat there often. It's a restaurant with two delicious personalities. The printed menu features the typical diner fare of sandwiches, chili, or meat loaf with mashed potatoes and gravy—very good gravy. Then, posted on the daily specials board, is a list of a dozen global choices that could include pad thai, vegetable samosas, leek and onion cobbler, Bombay chicken pie, pesto lasagne, fried smelts, and Santa Fe pork stew. Although I seldom have room for dessert, I always check the offerings as soon as I walk in the door. Recently, I spotted what looked like two thick golden cookies sandwiched together with a white filling. The waitress told me they were pumpkin whoopie pies and added "The locals love them." You can bet we saved room for dessert that day.

MAKES FOURTEEN 3-INCH FILLED COOKIES

Pumpkin Cookies
2$^1/_4$ cups unbleached all-purpose flour
1 teaspoon baking powder
$^1/_2$ teaspoon baking soda
$^1/_4$ teaspoon salt
$^1/_2$ teaspoon ground cinnamon
8 tablespoons (1 stick) soft unsalted butter
1$^1/_4$ cups sugar
2 large eggs
1 teaspoon vanilla extract
$^1/_2$ cup sour cream
$^3/_4$ cup canned pumpkin
$^3/_4$ cup coarsely chopped walnuts

Cream Cheese Filling
6 tablespoons ($^3/_4$ stick) soft unsalted butter
4 ounces cream cheese, full fat or reduced fat, softened about 2 hours at room
        temperature
1 teaspoon vanilla extract
2 cups powdered sugar

PREPARE THE COOKIES

1. Position 2 racks in the middle and upper third of the oven. Preheat the oven to 350°F. Line the bottoms of 3 baking sheets with parchment paper and butter the paper.

2. Sift the flour, baking powder, baking soda, salt, and cinnamon together and set aside.

3. Put the butter and sugar in the large bowl of an electric mixer and beat on medium speed for 1 minute until smooth. Add the eggs and vanilla and beat for 30 seconds. Decrease the speed to low and mix in the sour cream and pumpkin just until incorporated. Add the flour mixture and blend just until it is incorporated. Stir in the walnuts. Drop 28 rounded tablespoons of batter 3 inches apart on the prepared baking sheets. The batter is thick enough to hold its mound shape on the sheets.

4. Bake 2 sheets of cookies for about 12 minutes, or until the tops are firm to the touch and a toothpick inserted in the center of the cookies comes out clean. Reverse the baking sheets after 7 minutes, front to back and top to bottom, to ensure that the cookies bake evenly. Immediately bake the third sheet of cookies. Cool the cookies for 5 minutes on the baking sheets. Use a wide metal spatula to loosen them from the paper, then cool them thoroughly on the sheets.

FILL THE COOKIES

Put the butter, cream cheese, and vanilla in the large bowl of an electric mixer and beat on medium-low speed for about 1 minute, until the mixture is smooth and thoroughly combined. Decrease the speed to low and add the powdered sugar in 2 additions. Beat until it is incorporated and the frosting is smooth, about 1 minute. Use a thin metal spatula to spread a slightly rounded tablespoon of cream cheese filling over the flat bottoms of half the cooled cookies. Press the flat bottoms of the remaining cookies on the cream cheese frosting. Refrigerate until the frosting is firm, about 30 minutes.

Good Advice: Be sure you buy a can of plain pumpkin, not pumpkin pie filling. 🍂 I often use reduced-fat cream cheese for the frosting and find the results to be the same as for the full-fat version. Reduced-fat cream cheese is softer and requires less softening time, only about 30 minutes. **Doubling the Recipe:** Mix and bake the batter in separate batches so it doesn't have to sit for a long time before it bakes. A double recipe of cookie batter would require 6 baking sheets and 2 ovens, which few of us have. Double the ingredients for the filling. **To Freeze:** Wrap each whoopie pie in plastic wrap. Loosely pack them in a metal or plastic freezer container and cover tightly. Label with the date and contents. Freeze up to 1 month. **To Serve:** Defrost the wrapped whoopie pies for 5 hours or overnight in the refrigerator. Serve cold or at room temperature. Cover leftovers with plastic wrap and store up to 3 days in the refrigerator.

Apple Raisin Rugelach

raditional rugelach have a cream cheese pastry filled with fruit and nuts and are formed into a crescent shape. I stuff these rugelach with an especially moist all-fruit filling of apples and raisins that breaks slightly with tradition but complements the crisp cream cheese pastry.

MAKES 48 RUGELACH

Cream Cheese Dough

2 cups unbleached all-purpose flour
3 tablespoons sugar
$^1/_4$ teaspoon salt
12 ounces soft cream cheese, cut into pieces
12 tablespoons ($1^1/_2$ sticks) cold unsalted butter, cut into 12 pieces
3 tablespoons sour cream
2 teaspoons vanilla extract

Apple Raisin Filling

$^1/_2$ cup sugar
2 teaspoons ground cinnamon
$^1/_2$ cup chopped dried apples ($^1/_2$-inch pieces)
$^1/_2$ cup raisins

$^1/_4$ cup apricot preserves

PREPARE THE CREAM CHEESE DOUGH

Put the flour, sugar, and salt in the large bowl of an electric mixer and mix on low speed just to blend. Add the cream cheese and butter and mix until all of the flour is incorporated, about 45 seconds. Stir the sour cream and vanilla together. With the mixer running, add the sour cream mixture and mix until all of it is incorporated, about 15 seconds. The dough will be soft and sticky. Divide it into 4 equal pieces, form each piece into a ball, then flatten to a 4-inch disk. Wrap each disk in plastic wrap and refrigerate until firm, at least 2 hours or overnight.

PREPARE THE APPLE AND RAISIN FILLING

Put the sugar and cinnamon in a small bowl and stir together. Stir in the apples and raisins.

ASSEMBLE AND BAKE THE RUGELACH

1. Position 2 oven racks in the middle and upper third of the oven. Preheat the oven to 375°F. Line 2 baking sheets with parchment paper.

2. Remove the disks from the refrigerator and unwrap them. If the dough has become cold and hard, let it sit at room temperature for about 10 minutes or until it is easy to roll. Lightly flour the rolling surface and rolling pin. Roll 1 disk into a $10^1/2$-inch-diameter circle and trim the edges even. The trimmed circle will be $9^1/2$ to 10 inches in diameter. Leaving a $^3/4$-inch plain border, use a thin spatula to spread 1 tablespoon of apricot preserves evenly over the dough, removing any large pieces of apricot. Leaving a $^3/4$-inch plain border and a $1^1/2$-inch-diameter plain circle in the center, sprinkle a fourth of the filling (a scant $^1/3$ cup) evenly over the preserves. Press the filling into the dough. Use a large knife to cut the dough into 12 wedges. Roll each wedge up tightly from the wide edge to the point. Place, point side down, 1 inch apart on the prepared baking sheets. Bend the ends slightly to curve each rugelach into a crescent. Repeat with the remaining dough to form 48 small rugelach.

3. Bake for 20 to 23 minutes, or until the pastry is golden brown. Reverse the baking sheets after 10 minutes, front to back and top to bottom, to ensure even browning. Transfer the rugelach immediately to a wire rack to cool thoroughly.

Good Advice: When preparing the dough, use soft cream cheese so that it blends into the other in- gredients, but use cold butter to form the little butter pockets that make the pastry flaky. This rich dough is sticky when it is mixed, but it firms during chilling and rolls out easily. ❧ The dried apples can be chopped in a food processor. Apricot fruit spread sweetened with fruit juice can be substituted for the apricot preserves. *Doubling the Recipe:* Double the ingredients. Roll the dough into 8 circles. *To Freeze:* Place the bottoms of 2 rugelach together and wrap them in plastic wrap. Place in a metal or plastic freezer container and cover tightly. Label with the date and contents. Freeze up to 3 months. *To Serve:* Defrost the wrapped pastries at room temperature, about 3 hours. To restore the just-baked taste, preheat the oven to 225°F. Unwrap the rugelach and bake just until warm, about 10 minutes. Leftover rugelach may be covered with plastic wrap and stored at room temperature up to 3 days.

Carrot Strudel

hen Louise Shames sent me this recipe for her family's carrot strudel, she also included several dozen pieces of strudel. As soon as I tasted it, I knew what made it unique. The thin dough remains soft after baking and there is a generous proportion of fruit filling to crust. The shredded carrot in the dough gives the crust a beautiful golden color, but you would never know it was there. The lightly sweetened filling reminded several friends who tasted it of homemade mincemeat.

MAKES ABOUT 60 PIECES

Carrot Strudel Dough

2 cups unbleached all-purpose flour
1 1/2 teaspoons baking powder
1/2 cup (8 tablespoons) soft vegetable shortening
1/2 cup sugar
2 large eggs
1/2 teaspoon vanilla extract
1/2 cup finely grated carrot (1 large carrot)

Filling

1/2 lemon, washed, seeded, and cut in 3 pieces
1 orange, washed, seeded, and cut in 8 pieces
3 cups (15 ounces) seedless raisins
3 tablespoons granulated sugar

Powdered sugar

PREPARE THE STRUDEL DOUGH

1. Sift together the flour and baking powder. Set aside.

2. Put the vegetable shortening and sugar in the large bowl of an electric mixer and beat on medium speed for about 1 minute, until smooth. Decrease the speed to low and add the eggs and vanilla, beating for about 30 seconds until they are blended thoroughly. Stop the mixer and scrape the bowl during this time. On low speed add the flour mixture and carrots alternately, beginning and ending with the flour mixture (3 flour, 2 carrot), and blend until all the flour is incorporated. The dough will be soft.

3. Divide the dough into 4 pieces and pat each piece into a small, round disk. Wrap each disk in plastic wrap and refrigerate overnight.

Put the lemon, orange, raisins, and granulated sugar in the work bowl of a food processor fitted with the steel blade. Start with a few short bursts to break up the fruit, then process until the fruit is finely chopped, about 30 seconds. Put the fruit mixture in a medium saucepan and cook uncovered over low heat, stirring often, for about 20 minutes until it is thick and has the moist consistency of jam. When it is stirred, the mixture should come away easily from the pan. If it begins to stick to the bottom of the pan, don't cook it any longer. Cool thoroughly. The filling firms as it cools.

FILL AND BAKE THE STRUDEL

1. Position a rack in the middle of the oven. Preheat the oven to 350°F. Grease a baking sheet that has open ends lightly with vegetable shortening.

2. Remove one piece of dough from the refrigerator and unwrap it. Flour the rolling surface and rolling pin generously. Roll the dough into a 12- to 13-inch circle. Slide a thin metal spatula under the dough about halfway through the rolling and sprinkle flour under the dough to keep it from sticking. Flour the rolling pin again if it begins to stick. Leaving a $\frac{1}{2}$-inch plain border, use a thin spatula to spread a fourth of the filling (about $\frac{2}{3}$ cup) evenly over the dough. Using the metal spatula to loosen the dough from the rolling surface as you roll it, roll up the strudel tightly. Press the edges and seam together to seal. Trim the plain dough from the end of the roll and use it to patch any holes. The roll will be 12 to 13 inches long. Slide it onto the prepared baking sheet. Repeat with the remaining 3 pieces of dough and place the strudel rolls 1 inch apart on the baking sheet.

3. Bake 20 minutes. The pastry will not change color. Cool completely on the baking sheet. Use a serrated knife and a slight sawing motion to trim off and discard the crisp ends. Then cut each strip into $\frac{3}{4}$-inch pieces. Dust the tops lightly with powdered sugar.

Good Advice: Shred the carrot fine so it blends into the dough and adds the desired color. I grate the carrot on the small teardrop holes of a box grater. ✻ The dough is soft even when cold, but is rolled to a scant $\frac{1}{8}$ inch thick. You will need to flour the rolling surface and rolling pin often and generously. ✻ Don't worry if there is a small crack in the dough; the filling is so thick that it won't leak out during baking. ✻ Bake on a cookie sheet with open sides. Then it will be easy to cut the warm strudel on the sheet. Raised sides on a baking sheet can burn you as you cut. *Doubling the Recipe:* Double the ingredients and make 8 rolls. *To Freeze:* Place 6 pieces of strudel side by side and wrap them in plastic wrap. Place in a metal or plastic freezer container and cover tightly. Label with the date and contents. Freeze up to 3 months. *To Serve:* Remove as much strudel as you need from the freezer, cover it with plastic wrap, and defrost at room temperature. Serve within 4 days.

Sicilian Fig Cookies

ince my friend, the cookbook author Melanie Barnard, has a passion for figs, I knew just whom to ask when I was looking for a fig cookie recipe. She promptly offered this cookie from her Sicilian grandmother; the recipe has been in her family for three generations. The cookies are formed by cutting slices from unbaked logs of fig-filled pastry. It's the generous proportion of soft filling to crisp crust and the particular combination of figs and almonds spiced with cinnamon, lemon, and orange that makes these cookies exceptional. From the first time I made this recipe, it hasn't needed the slightest adjustment. Three generations have honed it to perfection.

MAKES ABOUT 48 COOKIES

Dough
> 2 large eggs
> $1/4$ cup milk
> $2^1/2$ cups unbleached all-purpose flour
> $1/3$ cup sugar
> $3/4$ teaspoon baking powder
> $1/2$ teaspoon salt
> $1/2$ cup (8 tablespoons) cold vegetable shortening, cut in 8 pieces

Fig Filling
> 2 cups (about 12 ounces) calimyrna figs cut in half, stems removed
> $1/2$ cup raisins
> $1/3$ cup slivered blanched almonds
> $1/4$ cup sugar
> $1/4$ teaspoon ground cinnamon
> 1 teaspoon grated lemon zest
> Pinch freshly ground black pepper
> $1/4$ cup fresh orange juice

Icing
> $1^1/2$ cups powdered sugar
> 2 to 3 tablespoons milk
> $1/4$ teaspoon vanilla extract
> Colored sprinkles, optional

MAKE THE DOUGH

1. Mix the eggs and milk in a small bowl until blended. Set aside.

2. Put the flour, sugar, baking powder, and salt in the large bowl of an electric mixer and mix on low speed just to blend, about 10 seconds. Add the shortening and beat until most of the pieces are the size of split peas, about 1 minute. The dough looks crumbly, and the

crumbs vary in size. With the mixer running, add the egg mixture and blend until a soft dough forms that pulls away from the sides of the bowl, about 30 seconds. Divide it in 4 parts and wrap each piece in plastic wrap. Refrigerate at least 30 minutes or up to 2 days.

PREPARE THE FILLING

Put the figs, raisins, almonds, sugar, cinnamon, lemon zest, and black pepper in the work bowl of a food processor fitted with the steel blade. Start with a few short bursts to break up the fruit, then process until the fruit and nuts are finely chopped, about 1 minute. With the motor running, add the orange juice through the feed tube and process just until it is blended in, about 15 seconds. The filling will be sticky and firm.

FILL THE COOKIES

Remove 1 piece of dough from the refrigerator and unwrap it. If the dough has become cold and hard, let it sit at room temperature for about 10 minutes until it is easy to roll. Lightly flour the rolling surface and rolling pin. Roll the dough into a 14 by 4-inch rectangle. The edges will not be even. Using your hands, put a fourth of the filling in a 1-inch strip down the center of the dough. Slide a thin metal spatula under the dough to loosen it from the rolling surface, then use the spatula to help roll the long sides of the dough over the filling to enclose it. Pinch the edges of the seam together to seal tightly. Repeat with the remaining dough and filling to form 4 rolls.

BAKE AND FROST THE COOKIES

1. Position a rack in the middle of the oven. Preheat the oven to 350°F. Line 2 baking sheets with parchment paper. Refrigerate as many filled rolls as you want to bake for about 2 hours or overnight, until soft enough to cut easily. Unwrap the rolls and use a sharp knife and a slight sawing motion to cut each filled roll into diagonal slices about 1 inch wide. Put the slices, seam side down, 1 inch apart on the baking sheets.

2. Bake for about 16 minutes, until the bottoms are pale golden and the tops just lightly colored. Cool the cookies for 5 minutes on the baking sheets, then use a wide metal spatula to transfer them to a wire rack to cool completely. Place the cookies so they are touching each other and it will be easier to frost them.

3. Whisk the powdered sugar, 2 tablespoons of the milk, and vanilla together. Add more milk by $1/2$ teaspoonfuls until the icing has a thick drizzling consistency. Use a small spoon to drizzle icing over the tops of the cookies. Immediately sprinkle the cookies with colored sprinkles, if desired. If using the colored sprinkles, place the cookies close together before adding them.

Good Advice: The filling can be made up to 2 days ahead and stored in the refrigerator. The flavor develops overnight, so if the filling is freshly made, these cookies taste better the day after they are baked.  Unbaked strips can be frozen and baked as needed. **Doubling the Recipe:** Mix the dough and filling in 2 batches and double the icing ingredients. **To Freeze Unbaked Rolls:** Wrap each unbaked roll in plastic wrap, then in heavy aluminum foil. Label with the date and contents. Freeze up to 1 month. **To Freeze:** Let the cookies sit at room temperature until the icing is firm. Put the bottoms of 2 cookies together and wrap them in plastic wrap. Put them in a metal or plastic freezer container and cover tightly. Label with the date and contents. Freeze up to 1 month. **To Serve:** Defrost the wrapped cookies at room temperature. Leftover cookies can be covered with plastic wrap and stored at room temperature up to 3 days.

Meringues, Macaroons, and Parisian Macaroon Sandwiches

everal years ago on a visit to Paris, I was doing my usual bakery window-shopping and became intrigued by the colorful macaroon sandwiches displayed in almost every pâtisserie window. The neat rows of pink raspberry, pale yellow lemon, soft brown coffee, and dark chocolate rounds lured me inside more than one pastry shop. All the cookies had a moist nut center, a crisp outside that was a cross between a macaroon and meringue, and they were filled with either jam, chocolate, fruit curds, or a simple frosting. That day of French macaroon shopping and tasting was the inspiration for the eight macaroon sandwiches that follow.

Both macaroons and meringues form crisp shells if baked on a dry day. On a humid summer day, it's difficult to keep the moisture in the air from softening them. The Almond Macaroon Horns are soft and moist throughout, so you can bake them in any weather.

Meringues are the lightest of cookies. Egg whites beaten with sugar are their main ingredients, so it's a challenge to keep the sugar from overshadowing other flavors. Inside the crisp shell of these meringue cookies, there is a soft nutty or chocolate center, and it's the walnuts, almonds, or melted chocolate that you notice.

Almond Macaroon Horns

hildhood summers spent in Brooklyn were like living in "bakery paradise." Our two-block shopping street held one bakery that specialized in cakes and pies, another in butter cookies and fancy French pastries, and a third in breads, coffee cakes, rugelach, and almond horns. The almond horns had a soft smooth interior and a shiny crisp coating that glistened in the glass cases. Where I live in Camden, Maine, there are no bakeries that make almond horns. You can imagine my pleasure when I decided to bake them myself and discovered how simple they were. Store-bought almond paste is the main ingredient, and it is responsible for the intense almond flavor, moist texture, and simple preparation.

MAKES TEN 3-INCH-LONG COOKIES

Almond Macaroon Horns
- $1/3$ cup sliced almonds
- 8 ounces almond paste (about 1 cup packed), at room temperature
- 2 tablespoons soft unsalted butter
- $1/3$ cup superfine sugar
- 1 large egg white
- 2 teaspoons fresh lemon juice
- $1/2$ teaspoon vanilla extract
- 1 large egg white, lightly beaten with a fork

Sugar Syrup for Glazing
- 2 tablespoons water
- 2 tablespoons plus 1 teaspoon sugar
- 1 teaspoon light corn syrup

MAKE THE COOKIES

1. Position a rack in the middle of the oven. Preheat the oven to 325°F. Line a baking sheet with parchment paper.

2. Spread the sliced almonds on a piece of wax paper and set aside.

3. Put the almond paste and butter in the large bowl of an electric mixer and beat on low speed until blended. Add the sugar, the egg white, the lemon juice, and the vanilla and mix until smooth. Roll 2 tablespoons of the mixture between your hands into a sausage shape, about 3 inches long and 1 inch thick. Pinch the ends to taper them. Wet your fingers if the mixture sticks to them. Brush the tops and sides with the lightly beaten egg white. Dip the egg white–coated dough in the sliced almonds, pressing gently so the almonds stick to the dough. Place the cookies 2 inches apart, plain side down, on the baking sheet, curving the ends to form a crescent shape.

4. Bake about 20 minutes, until the tops are light golden and the bottoms are light brown, reversing the baking sheet after 10 minutes. (The almonds will be lightly toasted.) Transfer the cookies to a wire rack. Carefully brush the warm sugar syrup over the almond coating while warm, being careful not to disturb the nuts. Cool completely.

PREPARE THE SUGAR SYRUP

While the cookies bake, prepare the syrup. Put the water, sugar, and corn syrup in a small saucepan. Cook the syrup over low heat until all the sugar is dissolved, stirring occasionally. Increase the heat to medium-high and boil the syrup without stirring for 2 minutes, until it is thick and sticky. The syrup can be prepared up to a week ahead, stored covered in the refrigerator, and warmed before it is brushed on the cookies.

Good Advice: Almond paste is a finely ground mixture of almonds and sugar. When fresh, it is soft, malleable, and easy to mix. Make sure that you buy almond paste rather than marzipan, which contains more sugar than almond paste does. Almond paste in cans or sealed tubes of plastic is available in the baking section of most supermarkets or from King Arthur Flour, listed in the mail order information on page 224. ❦ These almond horns have a 1-inch thickness, so they remain moist on the inside after they bake. *To Freeze:* Place the bottoms of 2 almond horns together and wrap in plastic wrap. Place in a metal or plastic freezer container and cover tightly. Label with the date and contents. Freeze up to 3 months. *To Serve:* Defrost the wrapped cookies at room temperature. Serve within 4 days.

Toasted Almond Meringues

I wondered what would happen to a sweet, sugary meringue if I added so many nuts to it that the nut flavor would dominate. I found out when I made these cookies, which have more toasted almonds than sugar and a pure almond flavor. Using toasted almonds produces a crisp meringue rather than the chewy one that untoasted almonds would.

MAKES 36 COOKIES

1½ cups toasted blanched almonds, chopped or slivered
¼ cup powdered sugar
2 tablespoons unbleached all-purpose flour
4 large egg whites
¼ teaspoon cream of tartar
¾ cup superfine sugar
½ teaspoon vanilla extract
¼ teaspoon almond extract
Powdered sugar

1. Position 2 oven racks in the middle and upper middle of the oven. Preheat the oven to 325°F. Line 2 heavy baking sheets with parchment paper or a nonstick liner.

2. Put the almonds, powdered sugar, and flour in the work bowl of a food processor fitted with the steel blade and process with a few short bursts to combine. Process the mixture about 2 minutes until the almonds are finely ground.

3. Put the egg whites and cream of tartar in the clean large bowl of an electric mixer and beat on low speed until frothy. Increase the speed to medium-high and beat until soft peaks form. Reduce the speed to medium and slowly beat in the superfine sugar, 1 tablespoon every 30 seconds. Mix in the vanilla and the almond extract. Remove the bowl from the mixer and use a rubber spatula to fold in the almond mixture. Drop well-rounded teaspoons of the meringue mixture 1 inch apart on the prepared baking sheets.

4. Bake 5 minutes. Decrease the oven temperature to 275°F and bake another 15 minutes, until the tops of the meringues feel firm and dry. The edges and bottoms of the cookies will be golden. Cool the cookies on the baking sheet for 5 minutes. Use a metal spatula to transfer the cookies to a wire rack. (The cookies will crisp as they cool.) Dust lightly with powdered sugar.

Good Advice: Since superfine sugar is more finely ground than regular granulated sugar, it dissolves easily and helps produce a crisp, dry meringue. To Freeze: Place the bottoms of 2 cookies together and wrap them in plastic wrap. Put the wrapped cookies in a metal or plastic freezer container and cover tightly. Label with the date and contents. Freeze up to 3 months. To Serve: Defrost the wrapped cookies at room temperature. Serve within 3 days.

Beacon Hill Cookies

hese are chocolate meringues with a difference. Melted chocolate, rather than cocoa powder, makes them crisp on the outside and soft and fudgelike on the inside. I did a double take when I saw the 10-minute baking time, but it's correct, and the cookies do bake crisp. 🏃 I feel lucky that so many people share their treasured family recipes with me, but this was the first time I received one by e-mail. Rich Frino, who works with my husband in the technical department of the University of Maine at Augusta, e-mailed this recipe from his Aunt Nancy to me.

MAKES ABOUT 32 COOKIES

> 6 ounces semisweet chocolate, chopped
> 2 large egg whites
> $1/8$ teaspoon cream of tartar
> $1/2$ cup sugar
> $1/2$ teaspoon vanilla extract
> $1/2$ teaspoon white vinegar
> $3/4$ cup walnuts, chopped fine

1. Position 2 racks in the middle and upper third of the oven. Preheat the oven to 175°F. Place the semisweet chocolate in a small ovenproof container and melt it in the oven, about 12 minutes. Remove the chocolate from the oven as soon as it is melted and stir it smooth. Set aside.

2. Increase the oven temperature to 350°F. Line 2 large baking sheets with parchment paper.

3. Put the egg whites and cream of tartar in the clean large bowl of an electric mixer and beat on low speed until foamy. Increase the speed to medium and beat until soft peaks form. Slowly beat in the sugar, 1 tablespoon every 30 seconds. Mix in the vanilla and vinegar. Remove the bowl from the mixer and use a rubber spatula to fold the nuts into the mixture. In 2 additions, add the melted chocolate, folding it in gently until no white specks remain. Drop heaping teaspoons of the mixture $1^{1}/_{2}$ inches apart on the prepared baking sheets.

4. Bake about 10 minutes until the tops of the cookies are firm, shiny, and crackled. Reverse the baking sheets after 5 minutes, front to back and top to bottom, to ensure that the cookies bake evenly. (Watch the cookies carefully toward the end of the baking time to prevent the bottoms from burning.) Cool the cookies on the baking sheet; they will crisp as they cool.

Good Advice: Watch the meringues carefully toward the end of their baking time, as the bottoms can burn if they are even slightly overbaked. 🏃 Rich advised that these should not be attempted on rainy or humid days, but I find that if I wrap and freeze the cookies as soon as they are cool, they're not affected by the humidity. **To Freeze:** Place the bottoms of 2 cookies together and wrap them in plastic wrap. Put the wrapped cookies in a metal or plastic freezer container and cover tightly. Label with the date and contents. Freeze up to 3 months. **To Serve:** Defrost the wrapped cookies at room temperature. Serve within 2 days.

Almond Macaroon Sandwiches

As my daughter, Laura, would say, I'm "way proud" of these cookies. On a long-ago trip to Paris, I discovered the many-flavored macaroon sandwiches that French pastry shops sell. These perfectly formed puffy rounds with soft insides and crisp outsides are sandwiched together with a complementary filling. 🏃 On our most recent trip to Paris I decided that I would try to reproduce them at home, and I bought boxes of macaroons from every Paris pastry shop we passed in all the flavors I could find. We went back to the hotel, ordered big pots of tea, and had a macaroon marathon to determine the best flavor combinations and most desirable qualities of each. My whole family humored me and didn't seem to mind tasting dozens of cookies. 🏃 Now I had the flavors I wanted to re-create, but producing them at home was another matter. At first, I baked a lot of flat, soggy macaroons until I worked out the right proportion of nuts to sugar and realized the importance of letting the cookies rest before they bake. This recipe is simple, but it looks like something from a fancy French bakery.

MAKES ABOUT 60 PLAIN MACAROONS OR 30 MACAROON SANDWICHES

> 1 cup slivered or sliced blanched almonds
> 2 cups powdered sugar
> 4 large egg whites, at room temperature for 30 minutes
> 1/4 teaspoon cream of tartar
> 1/4 cup superfine sugar
> 1/2 teaspoon almond extract

Almond Praline Buttercream

> 8 tablespoons (1 stick) soft unsalted butter
> 1/3 cup powdered sugar
> 3 tablespoons almond Nut Pralines powder (page 26)
> 1/2 teaspoon vanilla extract

Chocolate Truffle Filling (alternative filling)

> 1 cup Chocolate Truffle Sauce (page 20), warmed just until spreadable

MAKE THE COOKIES

1. Position 2 oven racks in the lower middle and upper third of the oven. Preheat the oven to 400°F. Line 2 heavyweight baking sheets with parchment paper. Have ready 2 flat baking sheets without raised sides.

2. Put the almonds and powdered sugar in the work bowl of a food processor fitted with the steel blade and process with a few short bursts to combine. Process the mixture about 3 minutes until the almonds are finely ground. Put the nut mixture in a large bowl and set aside.

3. Put the egg whites and cream of tartar in the clean large bowl of an electric mixer and beat on low speed until frothy. Increase the speed to medium-high and beat until soft peaks form. Reduce the speed to medium and slowly beat in the superfine sugar, 1 tablespoon every 30 seconds. Mix in the almond extract. Remove the bowl from the mixer and, use a rubber spatula to fold the egg whites in 2 additions into the almond mixture.

4. Spoon the macaroon mixture into a large pastry bag fitted with a $^1/_2$-inch plain pastry tip. Hold the pastry bag upright and pipe cookies about 1 inch in diameter and 1 inch apart on the lined baking sheets. Let the cookies sit uncovered for 30 to 60 minutes at room temperature. The tops will look smooth and the cookies may flatten slightly. Put each baking sheet on top of an empty flat baking sheet to insulate the top sheet.

5. Put the baking sheets in the oven and immediately lower the oven temperature to 350°F. Bake about 10 minutes, reversing the baking sheets after 6 minutes, front to back and top to bottom, to ensure that the cookies bake evenly. The tops of the cookies will be smooth, firm, and light golden, and the bottoms will have formed a soft crust.

6. As soon as you remove the baking sheets from the oven carefully lift the parchment paper, one end at a time, and sprinkle about 2 tablespoons of water under the paper. The steam will loosen the cookies. Be careful that the steam doesn't burn you and that water doesn't splash on the cookies. After 3 minutes lift the parchment paper off the baking sheets and peel the cookies from the paper. Cool the macaroons thoroughly on a wire rack. If any cookies stick to the paper, loosen them with a metal spatula.

MAKE THE FILLING AND FILL THE COOKIES

Stir the butter and powdered sugar in a medium bowl until smooth. Mix in the almond praline powder and vanilla. Spread a thin layer of buttercream, about 1 teaspoon, on the flat bottom of half the cookies. Gently press another cookie, bottom side down, onto each frosted cookie.

Or, spread about $1^1/_2$ teaspoons Chocolate Truffle Sauce on the flat bottom of half the cookies. Press another cookie, bottom side down, onto each filled cookie.

Good Advice: Let the unbaked cookies sit at room temperature for 30 minutes before they are baked. This will produce the traditional crusty tops. Cool the warm Chocolate Truffle Filling until firm enough to hold its shape and it does not run off the cookie when spread. To fill half the cookies with the praline buttercream and half with the chocolate truffle, just prepare half a recipe of each filling. **Doubling the Recipe:** Prepare the macaroon mixture in 2 batches. You will need 4 baking sheets. Double the ingredients for the filling. **To Freeze:** Place 2 cookies side by side and wrap in plastic wrap. Put the wrapped cookies in a metal or plastic freezer container and cover tightly. Label with the date and contents. Freeze up to 2 months. **To Serve:** Defrost the wrapped cookies at room temperature. Serve within 2 days.

Lemon Sandwich Macaroons

efreshing and light—that's what lemons bring to mind. These macaroons have fewer nuts in proportion to egg whites than my other macaroon recipes, so the cookies have a moist yet light meringuelike texture. A lemon curd filling enhances the lemon flavor.

MAKES ABOUT 62 PLAIN MACAROONS OR 31 MACAROON SANDWICHES

Powdered sugar
1 cup slivered or sliced blanched almonds
2 cups powdered sugar
4 large egg whites, at room temperature for 30 minutes
$^1/_4$ teaspoon cream of tartar
$^1/_4$ cup superfine sugar
$^1/_2$ teaspoon almond extract
1 tablespoon grated lemon zest

$^2/_3$ cup Lemon Curd (page 24), frozen or cold

1. Position 2 oven racks in the lower middle and upper third of the oven. Preheat the oven to 400°F. Line 2 heavyweight baking sheets with parchment paper. Dust the paper lightly with powdered sugar. Have ready 2 flat baking sheets without raised sides.

2. Put the almonds and 2 cups powdered sugar in the work bowl of a food processor fitted with the steel blade and process with a few short bursts to combine. Process the mixture about 3 minutes, or until the nuts are finely ground. Put the nut mixture in a large bowl and set aside.

3. Put the egg whites and cream of tartar in the clean large bowl of an electric mixer and beat on low speed until frothy. Increase the speed to medium-high and beat until soft peaks form. Reduce the speed to medium and slowly beat in the superfine sugar, 1 tablespoon every 30 seconds. Mix in the almond extract and lemon zest. Remove the bowl from the mixer and use a rubber spatula to fold the egg whites in 2 additions into the almond mixture.

4. Spoon the macaroon mixture into a large pastry bag fitted with a $^1/_2$-inch plain pastry tip. Hold the pastry bag upright and pipe cookies about 1 inch in diameter and 1 inch apart on the lined baking sheets. Let the cookies sit uncovered for 30 minutes at room temperature. If after 15 minutes the points on top of some cookies have not flattened, wet your finger and smooth the tops. Put each baking sheet on top of an empty flat baking sheet to insulate the top baking sheet.

5. Put the baking sheets in the oven and immediately lower the oven temperature to 350°F. Bake about 10 minutes, reversing the baking sheets after 6 minutes, front to back and top to bottom, to ensure that the cookies bake evenly. The tops of the cookies will be firm and light golden and the bottoms will have formed a soft crust. Let the macaroons cool 10 minutes on the baking sheets. Lift the cookies from the paper and cool them thoroughly on a wire rack. If any cookies stick to the paper, loosen them with a metal spatula.

6. Spread about 1 teaspoon of the Lemon Curd on the flat bottom of half of the cookies. Gently press another cookie, bottom side down, onto each filled cookie.

Good Advice: These macaroons do not need steam to release them from the baking sheet. I dust the parchment paper with powdered sugar and the macaroons lift off easily. ✻ Store thawed macaroons in the refrigerator to preserve the lemon curd filling. **Doubling the Recipe:** Prepare the macaroon mixture in 2 batches. You will need 4 baking sheets. Double the ingredients for the filling. *To Freeze:* Place 2 cookies side by side and wrap in plastic wrap. Put the wrapped cookies in a metal or plastic freezer container and cover tightly. Label with the date and contents. Freeze up to 2 months. *To Serve:* Defrost the wrapped cookies in the refrigerator. Store leftover macaroons in the refrigerator and serve within 2 days.

Coffee Hazelnut Macaroons with Chocolate Truffle Filling

hese sophisticated macaroons for grown-ups have a warm tan color from coffee and a rich flavor from the hazelnut and coffee combination. Chocolate is my classic choice for the filling, but these cookies are quite good served without filling.

MAKES ABOUT 66 PLAIN MACAROONS OR 33 MACAROON SANDWICHES

1 cup blanched hazelnuts, toasted in a 325°F oven for 12 minutes and cooled
2 cups powdered sugar
4 large egg whites, at room temperature for 30 minutes
¹/₄ teaspoon cream of tartar
¹/₄ cup superfine sugar
2 tablespoons instant decaffeinated coffee granules dissolved in 1 tablespoon plus
    2 teaspoons hot water

³/₄ cup Chocolate Truffle Sauce (page 20), warmed just until spreadable

1. Position 2 oven racks in the lower middle and upper third of the oven. Preheat the oven to 400°F. Line 2 heavyweight baking sheets with parchment paper. Have ready 2 flat baking sheets without raised sides.

2. Put the hazelnuts and powdered sugar in the work bowl of a food processor fitted with the steel blade and process with a few short bursts to combine. Process the mixture about 3 minutes until the hazelnuts are finely ground. Put the nut mixture in a large bowl and set aside.

3. Put the egg whites and cream of tartar in the clean large bowl of an electric mixer and beat on low speed until frothy. Increase the speed to medium-high and beat until soft peaks form. Reduce the speed to medium and slowly beat in the superfine sugar, 1 tablespoon every 30 seconds. Mix in the dissolved coffee. Remove the bowl from the mixer and use a rubber spatula to fold the egg whites in 2 additions into the hazelnut mixture.

4. Spoon the macaroon mixture into a large pastry bag fitted with a ¹/₂-inch plain pastry tip. Hold the pastry bag upright and pipe cookies about 1-inch in diameter and 1 inch apart on the lined baking sheets. Let the cookies sit, uncovered, for 30 to 60 minutes at room temperature. The tops will look smooth and the cookies may flatten slightly. Put each baking sheet on top of an empty flat baking sheet to insulate the top baking sheet.

5. Put the baking sheets in the oven and immediately lower the oven temperature to 350°F. Bake about 12 minutes, reversing the baking sheets after 7 minutes, front to back and top to bottom, to ensure that the cookies bake evenly. The tops of the cookies will be firm, light brown, and slightly crackled. The bottoms should form a soft crust.

6. As soon as you remove the baking sheets from the oven, carefully lift the parchment paper, one end at a time, and sprinkle about 2 tablespoons of water under the paper. The steam will loosen the cookies from the paper. Be careful that the steam doesn't burn you and that water doesn't splash on the cookies. After 3 minutes lift the parchment paper off the baking sheet and peel off the cookies from the paper. Cool the macaroons thoroughly on a wire rack. If any cookies stick to the paper, loosen them with a metal spatula.

7. Spread about 1 teaspoon of the Chocolate Truffle Sauce on the flat bottom of half the cookies. Gently press another cookie, bottom side down, onto each filled cookie. Or, leave the macaroons unfilled.

Good Advice: Sprinkle the instant coffee on top of the hot water to dissolve it. ✗ Buy blanched hazelnuts if they are available. The hazelnuts should be lightly toasted until they begin to change color. If the hazelnuts toast too long, they dry out and add little of the desired moistness to the macaroons. Defrost frozen hazelnuts before toasting them. ✗ This particular macaroon mixture is quite thick (probably caused by the coffee), so the macaroons will not spread much during baking. These macaroons have cracked tops rather than smooth ones. ✗ Cool the warm Chocolate Truffle Sauce filling until it is firm enough to hold its shape and does not run off the cookie when it is spread. **Doubling the Recipe:** Prepare the macaroon mixture in 2 batches. You will need 4 baking sheets. Double the ingredients for the filling. **To Freeze:** Place 2 cookies side by side and wrap in plastic wrap. To freeze the macaroons without filling, put the bottoms of 2 cookies together and wrap them in plastic wrap. Put the wrapped cookies in a metal or plastic freezer container and cover tightly. Label with the date and contents. Freeze up to 2 months. **To Serve:** Defrost the wrapped cookies at room temperature. Serve within 2 days.

Raspberry Macaroon Sandwiches

 These pastel-pink cookies add a touch of spring to any cookie platter. Raspberry purée tints these macaroons a soft pink, while raspberry jam makes a simple, colorful filling that adds intense flavor.

MAKES ABOUT 50 SINGLE MACAROONS OR 25 MACAROON SANDWICHES

1 cup fresh raspberries or ³/₄ cup unsweetened frozen raspberries, defrosted and drained
1 cup slivered or sliced blanched almonds
2 cups powdered sugar
3 large egg whites, at room temperature for 30 minutes
¹/₄ teaspoon cream of tartar
¹/₄ cup superfine sugar
¹/₂ teaspoon almond extract

7 tablespoons seedless raspberry jam

1. Position 2 oven racks in the lower middle and upper third of the oven. Preheat the oven to 375°F. Line 2 heavyweight baking sheets with parchment paper. Have ready 2 flat baking sheets without raised sides.

2. Put the raspberries in a strainer set over a small bowl, and, with the back of a spoon, press them to make ¹/₄ cup strained seedless raspberry purée. Set aside.

3. Put the almonds and powdered sugar in the work bowl of a food processor fitted with the steel blade and process with a few short bursts to combine. Process the mixture about 3 minutes until the almonds are finely ground. Put the nut mixture in a large bowl and set aside.

4. Put the egg whites and cream of tartar in the large bowl of an electric mixer and beat on low speed until frothy. Increase the speed to medium-high and beat until soft peaks form. Reduce the speed to medium and slowly beat in the superfine sugar, 1 tablespoon every 30 seconds. Blend in the almond extract. Remove the bowl from the mixer and use a rubber spatula to fold the raspberry purée into the egg white mixture. In 2 additions, fold the egg white mixture into the almond mixture.

5. Spoon the macaroon mixture into a large pastry bag fitted with a ¹/₂-inch plain pastry tip. Hold the pastry bag upright and pipe cookies about 1 inch in diameter and 1 inch apart on the lined baking sheets. Let the cookies sit uncovered for about 60 minutes at room temperature. The tops will look smooth and the cookies may flatten slightly. Put each baking sheet on top of an empty flat baking sheet to insulate the top baking sheet.

6. Put the baking sheets in the oven and immediately decrease the oven temperature to 325°F. Bake about 10 minutes, reversing the baking sheets after 6 minutes, front to back and top to bottom, to ensure the cookies bake evenly. The tops of the cookies will be smooth, firm, and light pink with some golden highlights and the bottoms will have formed a soft

crust. As soon as you remove the baking sheets from the oven carefully lift the parchment paper, one end at a time, and sprinkle about 2 tablespoons of water under the paper. The steam will loosen the cookies from the paper. Be careful that the steam doesn't burn you and that water doesn't splash on the cookies. After 3 minutes lift the parchment paper off the baking sheets and peel the cookies from the paper. Cool the macaroons thoroughly on a wire rack. If any cookies stick to the paper, loosen them with a metal spatula.

FILL THE COOKIES

Gently spread a thin layer of jam, about ³/₄ teaspoon, on the flat bottom of half the cookies. Gently press another cookie, bottom side down, onto each filled cookie.

Good Advice: These macaroons should sit at room temperature for 60 minutes rather than the usual 30 minutes before being baked. The longer resting time forms the desired shiny, crisp top. 🔆 The cookies will not dry properly if baked on a humid or rainy day. The raspberry purée makes the centers of these cookies especially moist, so take extra care when removing them from the parchment paper. Gently peel the paper from the cookies and use a thin metal spatula to loosen any cookies that stick to the paper. 🔆 To prevent their browning and losing the pink color, bake these macaroons at a lower oven temperature than the other macaroon sandwiches in this chapter. 🔆 Fresh raspberries will usually produce less purée than frozen raspberries, so more are required to make ¹/₄ cup purée. **Doubling the Recipe:** Prepare the macaroon mixture in 2 batches. You will need 4 baking sheets. Double the amount of jam. **To Freeze:** Place 2 cookies side by side and wrap in plastic wrap. Put the wrapped cookies in a metal or plastic freezer container and cover tightly. Label with the date and contents. Freeze up to 2 months. **To Serve:** Defrost the wrapped cookies at room temperature. Store in the refrigerator and serve within 2 days.

Dark Chocolate Truffle Macaroon Sandwiches

I t sounds impossible, but these macaroons are light and fudgy at the same time. Cocoa powder, which contains some fat, adds richness to this chocolate macaroon mixture while the truffle filling carries the fudge theme from top to bottom. The batter is a light brown color before baking, but baking changes it to a lush chocolate brown.

MAKES ABOUT 23 MACAROON SANDWICHES OR 46 PLAIN MACAROONS

1 cup blanched hazelnuts, toasted in a 325°F oven for 12 minutes and cooled
2^1/$_2$ cups powdered sugar
^{1}/$_4$ cup unsweetened Dutch process cocoa powder
4 large egg whites, at room temperature for 30 minutes
^{1}/$_4$ teaspoon cream of tartar
^{1}/$_4$ cup superfine sugar
1 teaspoon vanilla extract

^{3}/$_4$ cup Chocolate Truffle Sauce (page 20), warmed just until spreadable

1. Position 2 oven racks in the lower middle and upper third of the oven. Preheat the oven to 400°F. Line 2 heavyweight baking sheets with parchment paper. Have ready 2 flat baking sheets without raised sides.

2. Put the hazelnuts, powdered sugar, and cocoa powder in the work bowl of a food processor fitted with the steel blade and process with a few short bursts to combine. Process the mixture about 3 minutes until the hazelnuts are finely ground. Put the nut mixture in a large bowl and set aside.

3. Put the egg whites and cream of tartar in the clean large bowl of an electric mixer and beat on low speed until frothy. Increase the speed to medium-high and beat until soft peaks form. Reduce the speed to medium and slowly beat in the superfine sugar, 1 tablespoon every 30 seconds. Blend in the vanilla.

4. Remove the bowl from the mixer and use a rubber spatula to fold the egg whites in 2 additions into the hazelnut mixture. Spoon the macaroon mixture into a large pastry bag fitted with a ^{1}/$_2$-inch plain pastry tip. Hold the pastry bag upright, and pipe cookies about 1 inch in diameter and 1 inch apart on the lined baking sheets. Let the cookies sit uncovered for 30 minutes at room temperature. The tops will look smooth and the cookies will flatten. Put each baking sheet on top of an empty flat baking sheet to insulate the top baking sheet.

5. Put the baking sheets in the oven and immediately lower the oven temperature to 350°F. Bake about 12 minutes, reversing the baking sheets after 7 minutes, front to back and top to bottom, to ensure that the cookies bake evenly. The tops of the cookies will be

shiny and firm, and the bottoms will have formed a soft crust. As soon as you remove the baking sheets from the oven carefully lift the parchment paper, one end at a time, and sprinkle about 2 tablespoons of water under the paper. The steam will loosen the cookies. Be careful that the steam doesn't burn you and that water doesn't splash on the cookies. After 3 minutes lift the parchment paper off the baking sheet and peel the cookies from the paper. Cool the macaroons thoroughly on a wire rack. If any cookies stick to the paper, loosen them with a metal spatula.

6. Spread about 1 teaspoon of the Chocolate Truffle Sauce on the flat bottom of half the cookies. Gently press another cookie, bottom side down, onto each filled cookie.

Good Advice: Cool the warm Chocolate Truffle Sauce filling until firm enough to hold its shape and it does not run off the cookie when spread. *Doubling the Recipe:* Prepare the macaroon mixture in 2 batches. You will need 4 baking sheets. Double the ingredients for the filling. *To Freeze:* Place 2 cookies side by side and wrap in plastic wrap. To freeze unfilled macaroons, put the bottoms of 2 cookies together and wrap them in plastic wrap. Put the wrapped cookies in a metal or plastic freezer container and cover tightly. Label with the date and contents. Freeze up to 2 months. *To Serve:* Defrost the wrapped cookies at room temperature. Serve within 2 days.

Tassies, Tea Cakes, and Truffles

hese cookies are bite-size versions of pies, cakes, or candy. "Tassie" is the name southerners give to little pies baked in a mini-muffin tin. Pecan is the classic flavor for tassies, but the miniature crusts can be baked using almost any pie filling.

Tassies bake in twelve-cup mini-muffin tins that have individual holes with a capacity of two tablespoons of batter. I bought nonstick tins in a hardware store over twenty years ago. The nonstick finish hasn't scratched yet and the baked tassies remove easily. I do not recommend using metal tins that don't have a nonstick finish.

I keep tins of unbaked tassie crusts in my freezer ready to fill and bake, and keep baked frozen crusts available for fillings that don't require baking. Lemon Curd can be spooned into the baked crusts straight from the freezer, and the Caramel Filling and chocolate truffle topping for the Caramel Pecan Truffle Tassies (page 183) need only a quick warming before being spooned into baked tassie crusts.

In England, tea cakes refer to most individual pastries that are served with tea. Some cookies made with ground nuts and rolled in powdered sugar are also called tea cakes. My tea cakes are actually little cakes that bake in the mini-muffin tins. Tea cakes are fairly plain, but moist, and they are often topped with a glaze or frosting. Since I line the tins with paper liners, each cake releases smoothly, and the pans are easily cleaned up. The paper liners can be removed before serving, but are best left on during freezer storage for additional protection. There are two sizes of mini-muffin liners in my supermarket—1⅝ inches and 1¾ inches in diameter. The smaller 1⅝-inch liner fits the openings perfectly, while the 1¾-inch liner wrinkles when placed in each opening and causes ridges on the baked cakes.

Truffles are made by melting chocolate and cream to a smooth mixture, chilling it, and rolling it into soft chocolate balls. Truffle centers can be coated with melted chocolate, ground nuts, or praline, or they can be dusted with cocoa powder. The sizes vary from tiny balls to golf-ball size. I prefer the small ones containing a rounded teaspoonful of filling.

Lemon Tassies

 hese tiny cups of butter crust pastry are filled with Lemon Curd. I make them two ways and can never decide which one I prefer, so I've included both here. In one version the Lemon Curd bakes in the crust, but in the second version, cold Lemon Curd is spooned into the baked crusts, then served. My husband said that everyone would probably choose to make the easier unbaked version, but baking the tassies is simple. When baked, the Lemon Curd thickens to a firm custard with a deep golden color. I serve cold Lemon Tassies in the summer and baked tassies when the weather turns cool.

MAKES 12 TASSIES

12 dough circles of Butter Pastry for Tassies (page 23), pressed into a mini-muffin tin and baked blind
²/₃ cup (approximately) cold Lemon Curd (page 24)
12 candied violets, optional

PREPARE THE BAKED LEMON TASSIES

1. Position a rack in the middle of the oven. Preheat the oven to 325°F.

2. Put about 2 teaspoons Lemon Curd in each baked tassie crust, about ¼ inch below the top of the crust.

3. Bake 15 minutes. Remove the tin from the oven and cool the tassies in the pan. Cool and serve, or freeze. Top with a candied violet before serving, if desired.

PREPARE THE UNBAKED LEMON TASSIES

Have ready 12 baked and cooled tassie pastry shells. Fill each shell with 1 scant tablespoon cold Lemon Curd. Top with a candied violet, if desired. Serve, or cover and refrigerate to serve later the same day.

VARIATION   Whip 1 cup cold whipping cream with 1 tablespoon powdered sugar and 1 teaspoon vanilla extract until soft peaks form. Top the baked or unbaked Lemon Tassies with a spoonful of whipped cream before serving. If using candied violets, put them on top of the whipped cream.

Good Advice: These small tarts bake quickly and the curd shouldn't cook longer than 15 minutes. When curd is baked too long, it will bubble up out of the crust and may become grainy. ❀ Candied violets can be found in cookshops and, during the holiday season, they can be ordered from the Williams-Sonoma catalog (page 224). **Doubling the Recipe:** Use 24 tassie shells and double the amount of Lemon Curd. **To Freeze Baked Lemon Tassies:** Wrap each tassie in plastic wrap. Put the wrapped tassies in a single layer in a metal or plastic freezer container and cover tightly. Label with the date and contents. Freeze up to 2 weeks. **To Serve:** Defrost the wrapped tassies in the refrigerator. Serve cold or at room temperature. Serve within 2 days.

Mom's Brown Sugar Pecan Tassies

I remember that one of the first baking tasks I was allowed to do by myself was filling mini-muffin tins with pastry for these tiny pecan tarts. The cream cheese dough isn't adversely affected by some extra handling, and my little fingers were perfect for spreading the dough evenly in each small opening. Using brown sugar produces a crunchy filling rather than the usual syrupy type that is typical of pecan pies. The unsweetened cream cheese crust complements the sweet filling.

MAKES 24 TASSIES

Cream Cheese Crust

8 tablespoons (1 stick) unsalted butter, softened slightly
3 ounces cream cheese, softened slightly
1 cup unbleached all-purpose flour, sifted

Brown Sugar Pecan Filling

1 large egg
3/4 cup packed light brown sugar
1 tablespoon unsalted butter, melted
1 teaspoon vanilla extract
Pinch salt
2/3 cup (about 3 ounces) coarsely chopped pecans

MAKE THE CREAM CHEESE CRUST

1. Position a rack in the middle of the oven. Preheat the oven to 325°F. Have ready 2 mini-muffin tins. If the tins don't have a nonstick finish, butter each opening.

2. Put the butter and cream cheese in the large bowl of an electric mixer and beat on low speed until they are thoroughly blended, about 45 seconds. Mix in the flour until a smooth dough forms. Roll scant tablespoons of dough into smooth 1-inch balls. Put 1 ball of dough into each muffin cup. Press down into the center to make an indentation, then press the dough up the sides of each opening until it is even with the top edge of the tin. Check to see that the bottom of each tin is covered completely with dough and that the thickness of the sides is even. The crusts can now be filled and baked or frozen without filling.

MAKE THE PECAN FILLING

1. Put the egg in a small bowl and beat with a whisk to combine the yolk and white. Whisk in the brown sugar, butter, vanilla, and salt until smooth, or 30 seconds. Use a large spoon to stir in 1/3 cup of the pecans.

2. Fill each pastry-lined muffin cup with a scant 2 teaspoons filling. Sprinkle the remaining 1/3 cup pecans evenly over the top of each tassie. Wipe any drips off the pan.

3. Bake until the top is puffed and the crust is light brown, about 25 minutes. Cool the tassies in the baking pan until firm, about 20 minutes. Use a small knife to loosen the crust from the sides of the pan. Transfer the tassies to a wire rack to cool thoroughly.

Good Advice: Soften the butter and cream cheese just until they are cool but not rock hard, about 30 minutes. The mixing process further softens the butter and cream cheese, and using cold butter and cream cheese makes a cool dough that is easy to handle. ✿ Rolling the dough into smooth balls produces crusts with smooth edges. **To Freeze Tassie Pastry Without Filling:** Wrap each pastry-filled tin tightly with plastic wrap, then with heavy aluminum foil. Label with the date and contents. Freeze up to 2 months. Once the pastry is frozen, the tins can be stacked. The crust does not need to defrost before it is filled and baked. **To Freeze Filled Tassies:** Wrap each tassie in plastic wrap. Put the wrapped tassies in a single layer in a metal or plastic freezer container and cover tightly. Label with the date and contents. Freeze up to 2 weeks. **To Serve:** Defrost the wrapped tassies at room temperature. Serve within 3 days.

Caramel Pecan Truffle Tassies

ith their caramel pecan filling and Chocolate Truffle Sauce topping, these tassies are a cross between classic turtle candy and tiny candy bars. I would choose either one.

MAKES 24

1/2 cup Caramel Filling (page 25), cooled, or defrosted and warmed just to pouring consistency

1/3 cup coarsely chopped pecans, toasted (pages 3–4)

24 Butter Pastry for Tassies (page 23), pressed into mini-muffin tins, baked blind and cooled

6 tablespoons Chocolate Truffle Sauce (page 20), warmed just until spreadable

Put the caramel filling and pecans in a small bowl and stir together. With a small spoon, place about 1 teaspoon of the filling in each of the baked crusts. Spread about 3/4 teaspoon truffle sauce over the caramel mixture.

Doubling the Recipe: Use 48 tassie shells and double the remaining ingredients. **To Freeze:** Refrigerate the tassies to firm the chocolate topping. Wrap each tassie in plastic wrap. Put the wrapped tassies in a single layer in a metal or plastic freezer container and cover tightly. Label with the date and contents. Freeze up to 2 weeks. **To Serve:** Defrost the wrapped tassies in the refrigerator. Unwrap and let sit at room temperature for about 30 minutes to soften before serving. Store leftover tassies in the refrigerator. Serve within 3 days.

Almond-Drenched True Tea Cakes

he British call most cookies served with tea, tea cakes, but I always imagine them to be tiny, moist, buttery cakes, not crisp cookies. These small tea cakes flavored with almond paste, almond extract, and soaked with an almond-flavored glaze are the real thing.

MAKES 24

Tea Cakes

1/4 cup (about 2 1/2 ounces) firmly packed almond paste, at room temperature
1/2 cup cake flour
1/2 cup unbleached all-purpose flour
6 tablespoons packed dark brown sugar
3 tablespoons granulated sugar
1/4 teaspoon salt
1/4 cup plus 1 tablespoon canola or corn oil
1/2 cup sour cream
1 large egg
1/2 teaspoon vanilla extract
1/4 teaspoon almond extract
1/2 teaspoon baking powder
1/4 teaspoon baking soda

Almond Glaze

4 tablespoons (1/2 stick) soft unsalted butter
1 cup powdered sugar, sifted
1 tablespoon milk
1/8 teaspoon almond extract

PREPARE THE TEA CAKES

1. Position a rack in the middle of the oven. Preheat the oven to 350°F. Line with paper liners 2 mini-muffin tins that have 12 openings each.

2. Place the almond paste, both flours, brown sugar, granulated sugar, and salt in the large bowl of an electric mixer and mix on low speed until crumbs form, about 1 minute. Add the oil and mix until large crumbs coated with oil form, about 1 minute.

3. Put the sour cream, egg, vanilla, and almond extract in a small bowl and stir until the egg is incorporated. Gently stir in the baking powder and baking soda. Mix the sour cream mixture into the crumb mixture, stirring until the batter is evenly moistened.

4. Put 1 rounded teaspoon batter in each cup of the prepared tins, filling each to 1/4 inch from the top. Bake just until a toothpick inserted in the center comes out clean, about 15 minutes. Prepare the glaze while the tea cakes bake.

PREPARE THE GLAZE

Use a large spoon to stir the butter, powdered sugar, milk, and almond extract in a small bowl until smooth.

GLAZE THE TEA CAKES

Remove the tea cakes from the oven. Immediately use a toothpick to poke 5 or 6 holes in the top of each tea cake. Spread about 1 teaspoon glaze over the top of the warm cakes. Cool the tea cakes for 10 minutes. Transfer to a wire rack to cool thoroughly and let the glaze firm.

Good Advice: Soft, moist dark brown sugar is best for making these tea cakes. Dry brown sugar doesn't combine completely with the batter and produces specks of brown sugar in the baked tea cakes. ❦ Use small paper baking liners that are 1⅝ inches in diameter rather than 1¾ inches. They fit the mini-muffin tin openings perfectly. **Doubling the Recipe:** Double the ingredients and use 4 mini-muffin tins. **To Freeze:** Wrap each tea cake in plastic wrap. Put the wrapped tea cakes in a single layer in a metal or plastic freezer container and cover tightly. Label with the date and contents. Freeze up to 1 month. **To Serve:** Defrost the wrapped tea cakes at room temperature. Serve within 3 days.

Morning Glory Tea Cakes

I n early mornings in Camden, Maine, people line up at our local market for fresh morning glory muffins that have more apples, raisins, carrots, walnuts, and coconut in them than you'd think they could hold. My Morning Glory Tea Cakes have all the glory and more. They include the same fruit and nut combination in a spicy cake batter and are baked in small muffin tins, but they're topped with swirls of cream cheese frosting.

MAKES 42 TEA CAKES

Morning Glory Tea Cakes

1 cup unbleached all-purpose flour
1 teaspoon baking soda
$^1/_2$ teaspoon salt
1 teaspoon ground cinnamon
1 cup sugar
$^1/_2$ cup canola or corn oil
2 large eggs
1 cup peeled, finely chopped carrots
$^1/_2$ cup peeled, grated apple (1 small apple)
$^1/_4$ cup seedless raisins
$^1/_2$ cup finely chopped walnuts
$^1/_4$ cup shredded sweetened coconut

Cream Cheese Frosting

8 tablespoons (1 stick) soft unsalted butter
6 ounces soft cream cheese
2 teaspoons vanilla extract
3 cups powdered sugar

PREPARE THE TEA CAKES

1. Position 2 racks in the lower middle and upper middle of the oven. Preheat the oven to 350°F. Line with paper liners 4 mini-muffin tins that have 12 openings each. One tin will have 6 openings that are empty. Do not line these. Fill these openings half full with water.

2. Sift the flour, baking soda, salt, and cinnamon into the large bowl of an electric mixer. Add the sugar and mix on low speed just to combine. Blend in the oil. (The mixture will look crumbly.) Add the eggs, blending until smooth, about 30 seconds. Stir in the carrots, apple, raisins, walnuts, and coconut. Fill each paper liner with batter to $^1/_4$ inch from the top, using about 1 level tablespoon each. Bake just until a toothpick inserted in the center comes out clean and the top is golden, about 15 minutes. Reverse the baking sheets after 10 minutes, top to bottom and front to back, to ensure that the tea cakes bake evenly. Cool the tea cakes for 5 minutes in the pan. Transfer the tea cakes in their paper liners to a wire rack to cool completely.

Put the butter, cream cheese, and vanilla in the large bowl of an electric mixer and beat on medium-low for about 1 minute, until the mixture is smooth and the butter and cream cheese are combined thoroughly. Decrease the speed to low and mix in the powdered sugar in 2 additions. Beat until the powdered sugar is incorporated and the frosting is smooth. Spoon the frosting into a large pastry bag fitted with a large star pastry tip. Leaving a $1/4$-inch plain edge, pipe swirls of frosting over the tops of the cakes. (Plain frozen tea cakes can be frosted while still frozen.)

Good Advice: Small paper baking liners that are listed on the box as $1^5/8$ inches in diameter rather than $1^3/4$ inches fit the mini-muffin tin openings perfectly. The larger $1^3/4$-inch liners wrinkle when put in the small muffin tins. ❦ Piping swirls of frosting on top of the tea cakes is not only a fancy touch, it's also a fast way to frost them. **To Freeze Plain Tea Cakes:** Wrap each cooled tea cake tightly with plastic wrap. Place them in a single layer in a metal or plastic freezer container. Cover tightly and label with the date and contents. Freeze up to 2 months. **To Freeze Frosted Tea Cakes:** Freeze the tea cakes uncovered for about $1/2$ hour, or until the frosting is firm. Wrap each tea cake in plastic wrap. Place them in a single layer in a metal or plastic freezer container and cover tightly. Label with the date and contents. Freeze up to 1 month. **To Serve:** Defrost the wrapped tea cakes at least 5 hours or overnight in the refrigerator. Unwrap and let sit at room temperature for 1 hour before serving. Store leftover tea cakes up to 3 days in the refrigerator, but serve them at room temperature.

Strawberry Tea Cakes

azie MacKay, who lived up the street from us in Florida during my childhood, was a working mother long before careers became routine for southern women. She ran a lumberyard by day, but somehow managed to have home-baked cakes for her daughter Maggie Jane and me after school. These tea cakes were reserved for special occasions. 🎄 Strawberries tint the cakes and frosting pink. When the tea cakes are turned upside down and spread with frosting, they look like pink bonbons.

MAKES 48 TEA CAKES

Strawberry Tea Cakes

One 16-ounce box sweetened frozen strawberries, defrosted, juice reserved for another use
1¼ cups plus 2 tablespoons unbleached all-purpose flour
½ teaspoon baking powder
¼ teaspoon salt
3 large egg whites
1 cup sugar
½ cup canola or corn oil
1 teaspoon vanilla extract
½ teaspoon almond extract
½ teaspoon baking soda
½ cup sour cream

Strawberry Cream Cheese Frosting

8 tablespoons (1 stick) soft unsalted butter
6 ounces soft cream cheese; do not use reduced-fat cream cheese
1 teaspoon vanilla extract
¼ teaspoon almond extract
3 cups powdered sugar

MAKE THE TEA CAKES

1. Position 2 racks in the lower middle and upper middle of the oven. Preheat the oven to 350°F. Line with paper liners 4 mini-muffin tins that have 12 openings each.

2. In a food processor, process the strawberries and remaining juice just until the strawberries are coarsely chopped. Set aside.

3. Sift the flour, baking powder, and salt together and set aside. Put the egg whites and sugar in the large bowl of an electric mixer and beat on medium speed until smooth, 1 minute. Decrease the speed to low and mix in the oil, vanilla, and almond extract until the oil is incorporated. Rub any lumps out of the baking soda and gently mix it into the sour cream. Stir the sour cream mixture into the batter. Add the flour mixture and mix just until it is incorporated. Blend in 1 cup of the reserved chopped strawberries. Fill each paper liner to $\frac{1}{4}$ inch from the top, using about 1 level tablespoon for each.

4. Bake just until a toothpick inserted in the center comes out clean and the top begins to turn golden, about 17 minutes. Reverse the baking sheets after 10 minutes, top to bottom and front to back, to ensure that the tea cakes bake evenly. Cool the tea cakes for 5 minutes in the pan. Transfer the tea cakes in their paper liners to a wire rack to cool completely.

FROST THE TEA CAKES

1. Line 2 baking sheets with wax paper. Put the butter, cream cheese, vanilla, and almond extract in the large bowl of an electric mixer and beat on medium-low speed for about 1 minute, until the mixture is smooth and the butter and cream cheese are combined thoroughly. Decrease the speed to low and add the powdered sugar in 2 additions. Beat until the powdered sugar is incorporated and the frosting is smooth. Add the remaining chopped strawberries and beat 1 minute (the frosting will be pink).

2. Remove the paper liners from the tea cakes and turn the cakes upside down. Spread the frosting over the bottom and sides of each tea cake. Place the frosted tea cakes 1 inch apart on the prepared baking sheets. If plain tea cakes have been frozen, they can be frosted while still frozen, but the paper liners must be removed before frosting.

Good Advice: Use full-fat cream cheese for the frosting; low-fat cream cheese produces a frosting that is softer than desired. *To Freeze Plain Tea Cakes:* Wrap each cooled tea cake tightly with plastic wrap. Place them in a single layer in a metal or plastic freezer container. Cover tightly and label with the date and contents. Freeze up to 2 months. *To Freeze Frosted Tea Cakes:* Freeze the tea cakes uncovered for about $\frac{1}{2}$ hour until the frosting is firm. Wrap each tea cake in plastic wrap. Place them in a single layer in a metal or plastic freezer container and cover tightly. Label with the date and contents. Freeze up to 1 month. *To Serve:* Defrost the wrapped tea cakes at least 5 hours or overnight in the refrigerator. Serve cold. Store leftover tea cakes up to 3 days in the refrigerator.

Cappuccino and Walnut Truffles

 innamon plays a dual role in these truffles. Combined with coffee and white chocolate it creates the cappuccino filling and it tints the decoration for the white chocolate coating. The walnut nestled inside each truffle provides a discreet foil for the creamy filling.

MAKES ABOUT 36 TRUFFLES

Cappuccino Truffle Filling

1/2 cup heavy whipping cream
4 tablespoons (1/2 stick) unsalted butter, cut in 2 pieces
12 ounces white chocolate, chopped (preferably Callebaut or Lindt)
2 teaspoons instant decaffeinated coffee dissolved in 2 teaspoons water
1 teaspoon ground cinnamon
1 teaspoon vanilla extract
36 walnut halves

White Chocolate Coating

12 ounces white chocolate, chopped (preferably Callebaut or
    Baker's Premium)
2 tablespoons canola or corn oil

1/2 to 3/4 teaspoon ground cinnamon

PREPARE THE TRUFFLE FILLING

1. Put the cream and butter in a small saucepan and heat just until the cream is hot and the butter is melted. The hot cream mixture will form tiny bubbles and measure about 160°F on a food thermometer. Do not let the mixture boil. Remove from the heat, add the chopped white chocolate, and let the white chocolate melt in the cream for 1 minute. Return the saucepan to low heat for 1 minute to melt the white chocolate completely, stirring constantly. Add the coffee, cinnamon, and vanilla. Stir the mixture until smooth. Pour the mixture into the large bowl of an electric mixer and press plastic wrap onto the surface. Refrigerate the filling until firm and cold to the touch, about 3 hours or overnight. Stir occasionally to ensure that the mixture chills completely.

2. Line 2 baking sheets with wax paper or parchment paper. Place the walnut halves 3 inches apart on the baking sheets. Set aside.

3. Use an electric mixer to whip the cold truffle mixture on high speed until the mixture lightens in color, or about 20 seconds. The mixture will look very smooth. Use a teaspoon to drop rounded teaspoons of the truffle mixture onto each walnut half. With another small spoon, scrape the mixture off the teaspoon, if necessary. Smooth the tops slightly with the teaspoon (the mounds will not be completely smooth). Freeze the truffle filling until firm, about 45 minutes.

PREPARE THE WHITE CHOCOLATE COATING

Put the white chocolate and the oil in a heatproof container and place it over, but not touching, a saucepan of barely simmering water. Stir the mixture until the white chocolate is melted and the mixture is smooth. Pour the coating into a small bowl (a soup bowl works well) and let it sit about 5 minutes to cool slightly. The mixture should feel barely warm to the touch.

COAT THE TRUFFLES

1. Remove 1 baking sheet from the freezer. Lift the truffles and paper from the baking sheet. If any stick to the paper, use a thin metal spatula to loosen them. Line the baking sheet with a clean piece of wax paper or parchment paper.

2. Slide a two- or three-pronged candy-dipping fork, or a small two-pronged fondue fork or pickle fork, under the bottom of a cold truffle mound. Dip the truffle in the white chocolate coating and spoon the coating over the truffle. Lift out the coated truffle and let the coating drip back into the bowl, tapping the fork over the rim of the bowl to remove the excess. Use the metal spatula to slide the truffle off the fork and onto the paper-lined baking sheet, flat walnut bottom side down. Repeat the process to coat all the truffles. Remove any excess coating that forms around the bottom edge of the truffle with the spatula. The coating will firm quickly. Refrigerate the coated truffles while you coat the second baking sheet of truffles.

3. Stir the cinnamon into the remaining white chocolate coating. Use enough cinnamon to color the white chocolate to a tan color. The amount of cinnamon depends on the quantity of white chocolate remaining. Dip a clean fork in the cinnamon coating and wave it over each truffle to form thin lines crisscrossing back and forth over the top. Move the fork quickly to create thin lines. If the coating has become too firm to drizzle easily, pour it back in the heatproof container and warm it over hot water.

4. Refrigerate or freeze the truffles to firm the coating thoroughly, about 30 minutes. Cover and refrigerate any leftover coating up to 1 week. Leftover coating can be warmed over hot water and poured over ice cream (it will form a crisp shell).

Good Advice: Cool the white chocolate coating for a few minutes before trying to dip the truffles. Warm coating will melt the filling and slide off it. ✱ I use a small two-pronged fork to hold the truffle filling while I dip it in the white chocolate. A fondue fork or a pickle fork also both work well. Large two-pronged meat forks are too cumbersome for dipping small pieces of candy. *To Freeze:* Wrap each truffle in plastic wrap. Place the truffles in a single layer in a metal or plastic freezer container and cover tightly. Label with the date and contents. Freeze up to 1 month. *To Serve:* Defrost the wrapped truffles for 4 hours or overnight in the refrigerator. Unwrap and let sit at room temperature for 30 minutes before serving. Cover leftover truffles with plastic wrap and store in the refrigerator up to 3 days.

Milk Chocolate and
Almond Praline Truffles

Swiss chocolatiers realized long ago the superiority of truffles that combine nut pralines and milk chocolate. The Swiss make truffles in many shapes and sizes, but most of the fillings are a praline and milk chocolate combination. I've put almond praline powder in these milk chocolate truffles and rolled them in additional praline for a quick, shimmering coating.

MAKES 24 TRUFFLES

> $^2/_3$ cup whipping cream
> 4 tablespoons ($^1/_2$ stick) unsalted butter, cut in 4 pieces
> 10 ounces milk chocolate, chopped
> 1 tablespoon Amaretto (or other almond-flavored liqueur)
> $^1/_4$ teaspoon almond extract
> $^3/_4$ cup almond Nut Pralines powder (page 26)

1. Put the cream and butter in a small saucepan and heat just until the cream is hot and the butter is melted. The hot cream mixture will form tiny bubbles and measure about 160°F on a food thermometer. Do not let the mixture boil. Remove from the heat, add the chopped milk chocolate, and let the milk chocolate melt in the cream for 1 minute. Stir the mixture until smooth. Return the saucepan to low heat for 1 minute, if necessary, to melt the milk chocolate completely, stirring constantly. Add the amaretto and almond extract and stir until smooth. Pour the mixture into the large bowl of an electric mixer and press plastic wrap onto the surface. Refrigerate the mixture until firm around the edges and cold to the touch, about 1 hour, stirring occasionally to ensure the mixture chills throughout.

2. Line a baking sheet with wax or parchment paper. Add 2 tablespoons of the almond praline powder to the cold chocolate mixture and beat with an electric mixer on high speed until the color lightens slightly, about 20 seconds (the mixture will look smooth). Roll 2 teaspoon-size portions of the truffle mixture between the palms of your hand to form a ball about $^3/_4$ to 1 inch in diameter. If the mixture becomes too sticky, chill it just until firm. Refrigerate the truffles to firm them, about 30 minutes. Spread the remaining almond praline powder on wax paper. Roll the truffles in the praline to coat them evenly.

Good Advice: Cool the truffle mixture before adding the almond praline powder. This keeps the praline crunchy by preventing the caramelized sugar from melting. Use a good-quality milk chocolate, such as Callebaut or Lindt, for the best flavor. *To Freeze:* Wrap each truffle in plastic wrap. Place the truffles in a single layer in a metal or plastic freezer container and cover tightly. Label with the date and contents. Freeze up to 1 month. *To Serve:* Defrost the wrapped truffles for 4 hours or overnight in the refrigerator. Unwrap and let sit at room temperature for 30 minutes before serving. Cover leftover truffles with plastic wrap and store in the refrigerator up to 5 days.

Especially for
Holidays

I t happens to me at the same time ever year. Around the middle of November, a little cookie alarm goes off in my head. I don't set it; it's automatic. I dig out my traditional cookie recipes, as well as the envelope stuffed with the new recipes that I've clipped throughout the year, and bake cookies. Occasionally on a rainy weekend, I'll have an all-day cookie baking event, but most cookies are short-term projects. Whenever I can snatch a couple of hours, I bake a batch or two. Cookie yields are measured in dozens, and a hundred cookies take a surprisingly short time to prepare. My freezer quickly fills with Eggnog Bars for parties, cookies cut into holiday designs, gift tins holding traditional lebküchen and rugelach, and Gingerbread People for children of all ages. Even the new year doesn't slow me down. Stars and moons turn into hearts, four-leaf clovers, and bunnies; and the clipping envelope fills up again.

Family cookie customs often develop from a holiday cookie that's passed from generation to generation. The group of cookies in this chapter has many traditional recipes contributed by my friends or their mothers and grandmothers. They incorporate many ingredients associated with winter holidays—peppermint candy, cranberries, and plenty of ginger and spices. There are cookies for children to cut out and decorate as they please. Grandma Theresa's sugar cookie dough is one that kids enjoy baking because it doesn't stick to rolling surfaces and isn't affected if little hands play with it or roll it out repeatedly. The cookie cutters produce the perfect shapes that make baking such fun and every cookie a success.

Grandma Theresa's
Sugar Cookie Cutouts

W hen Janet Roberts suggested that I try her Grandmother Theresa's famous-in-her-family sugar cookies, she emphasized that they must be rolled until very thin. Although Janet doesn't bake, her brother-in-law, Billy Singer, does. He sent me the recipe, repeating that the cookies should be rolled as thinly as possible. Billy told me that Grandma Theresa always kept a stash of them in her cookie jar, and she had cookie cutters for every holiday.

MAKES ABOUT 84 COOKIES

8 tablespoons (1 stick) slightly softened margarine
1 cup plus 2 tablespoons sugar
2 teaspoons vanilla extract
$^1/_2$ teaspoon salt
1 large egg
$^1/_4$ cup whole milk
$3^3/_4$ cups unbleached all-purpose flour
3 tablespoons sugar mixed with $^1/_2$ teaspoon ground cinnamon for sprinkling

1. Position 2 racks in the lower middle and upper middle of the oven. Preheat the oven to 375°F. Line 2 or 4 baking sheets with parchment paper. Spray the paper with vegetable oil spray.

2. Put the margarine, sugar, vanilla, and salt in the large bowl of an electric mixer and beat on medium speed until smooth, about 2 minutes. Add the egg and beat until blended into the creamed mixture, about 30 seconds. Mix in the milk until it is incorporated. (The mixture may look curdled.) Stop the mixer and scrape the sides of the bowl once during the mixing. On low speed, mix in the flour until a firm dough forms that comes away from the sides of the bowl. The dough will not be smooth but will form large clumps.

3. Divide the dough into 2 parts. Knead each piece with the heel of your hand until smooth. Knead by pressing down on the dough to flatten it, then folding it over onto itself. Form the dough into 4 balls, wrap each piece in plastic wrap, and let rest in the refrigerator for 4 hours or up to 2 days.

4. Remove the dough from the refrigerator, and let it sit until it softens slightly and is easy to roll, about 1 hour. Unwrap 1 ball of dough. Flouring the rolling surface and rolling pin very lightly, roll the dough out until it is $^1/_{16}$ inch thick. Slide a thin metal spatula under the dough to loosen it from the rolling surface. Use a 2- to $2^1/_2$-inch cookie cutter to cut out hearts, trees, stars, shamrocks, or any desired shape. Place the cookies $^1/_2$ inch apart on a prepared baking sheet. Wrap the scraps in plastic wrap and set aside.

5. Roll and cut out another piece of dough. Transfer the cookies to another baking sheet. Press all the dough scraps together until smooth and repeat the rolling and cutting process, rolling the dough to a $^1/_{16}$-inch thickness. Discard any remaining scraps. Transfer the cookies

to a baking sheet. Sprinkle cinnamon sugar over the center of each cookie. One teaspoon of the sugar mixture will cover about 10 cookies.

6. Bake 6 to 7 minutes, reversing the baking sheets, top to bottom and back to front, after 3 minutes of baking. Bake the cookies just until the edges begin to turn light brown. Cool the cookies 5 minutes on the baking sheets. Transfer them to a wire rack to cool thoroughly. Roll and cut the 2 remaining pieces of dough and bake on 2 cooled baking sheets for 6 to 7 minutes.

VARIATION   Sprinkle granulated sugar or colored sugar crystals over the unbaked cookies. You could use red for Valentine's Day or green for St. Patrick's Day.

Good Advice: This is a firm dough that doesn't become sticky when it is rolled to the desired $1/16$-inch thickness. Flour the rolling surface and rolling pin lightly with just a few pinches of flour. 🍪 I use cookie cutters that are 2 to $2^1/2$ inches long to produce about 84 cookies. Use smaller cutters for more cookies or larger cutters for fewer cookies. 🍪 One batch of cookies requires 4 baking sheets. I bake 2 sheets of cookies, then cool the baking sheets, and reuse the cooled pans to bake the remaining cookies. **Doubling the Recipe:** Mix the dough in separate batches. **To Freeze Unbaked Dough:** Wrap pieces of plastic-wrapped dough tightly in heavy aluminum foil and freeze up to 2 months. When ready to use it, defrost the dough overnight in the refrigerator. **To Freeze Baked Cookies:** Stack 6 cookies together and wrap them in plastic wrap. Put the wrapped cookies in a metal or plastic freezer container and cover tightly. Label with the date and contents. Freeze up to 3 months. **To Serve:** Defrost the wrapped cookies at room temperature. These cookies can be stored in a clean metal tin at room temperature up to 10 days.

Cranberry Walnut Rugelach

My friend Alan Roberts is a cookbook writer's dream come true. Until Alan began baking from my first book, *Bake and Freeze Desserts*, he had never baked anything before. Now his wife, Janet, says there's nothing he won't try, and he's sharing recipes with me. His cranberry rugelach have a crisp cream cheese pastry, lightened somewhat by using low-fat cream cheese, and an original chopped cranberry, nut, and spiced sugar filling. Alan came up with the idea of adding the filling after cutting the rugelach dough into wedges. If you've ever tried to cut neatly through a fruit and nut filling in a soft dough, you'll appreciate what a good idea this is.

MAKES 64 RUGELACH

Cream Cheese Dough
    $1/2$ pound (2 sticks) soft unsalted butter
    8 ounces low-fat cream cheese, softened about 1 hour
    $1/2$ teaspoon salt
    $1/2$ cup sugar
    2 cups unbleached all-purpose flour

Spiced Cranberry Walnut Filling
    1 cup sugar
    1 tablespoon plus $1^1/2$ teaspoons ground cinnamon
    1 cup finely chopped walnuts
    1 cup (about 5 ounces) dried cranberries, chopped
    1 teaspoon ground allspice
    8 tablespoons (1 stick) unsalted butter, melted

    1 large egg, beaten, for glazing

PREPARE THE DOUGH

Put the butter, cream cheese, and salt in the large bowl of an electric mixer and blend on low speed until smooth. Add the sugar and mix until fluffy, 1 minute. Add the flour, blending until all the flour is incorporated, about 45 seconds. (The dough will be soft and sticky.) Divide the dough into 2 pieces, form each piece into a ball, then flatten it to a 6-inch-round disk. Wrap each disk in plastic wrap and refrigerate until firm, at least 2 hours or overnight.

PREPARE THE FILLING

1. Put the sugar and cinnamon in a medium bowl and stir until mixed. Remove 3 tablespoons of the sugar mixture and set aside. Stir in the walnuts, cranberries, and allspice, then stir in the melted butter.

2. Position 2 oven racks in the middle and upper third of the oven. Preheat the oven to 350°F. Line 3 baking sheets with parchment paper.

1. Remove 1 dough package from the refrigerator and unwrap it. Cut it into 4 pieces and roll each piece into a smooth ball. Lightly flour the rolling surface and rolling pin. Roll 1 piece of dough into a circle approximately 10 inches in diameter and trim the edges evenly. The trimmed circle will be about $9\frac{1}{2}$ inches in diameter. Cut the circle into 8 wedges. Leaving a $\frac{3}{4}$-inch plain border, put 1 teaspoon of filling on each wedge of dough. Roll each wedge up tightly from the wide edge to the point. Place, point side down, about $1\frac{1}{2}$ inches apart, on the prepared baking sheets. Bend the edges slightly to curve them. Repeat with the remaining dough to form 64 small rugelach. Brush the top of each lightly with beaten egg. Sprinkle lightly with the reserved sugar mixture.

2. Bake for about 20 minutes until the tops are golden. Reverse the baking sheets after 10 minutes, front to back and top to bottom, to ensure even browning. Slide a metal spatula under the rugelach to loosen them from the parchment paper and transfer them immediately to a wire rack to cool thoroughly.

TO FREEZE UNBAKED RUGELACH

Do not brush with beaten egg or sprinkle with cinnamon sugar until you are ready to bake. Bend the edges of each rugelach slightly and wrap each in plastic wrap. Place in a plastic freezer container and cover tightly. Label with the date and contents. Freeze up to 1 month.

TO BAKE FROZEN RUGELACH

1. Position 2 oven racks in the middle and upper third of the oven. Preheat the oven to 350°F. For every 22 rugelach you want to bake, line a baking sheet with parchment paper.

2. Place the frozen rugelach, point side down, about $1\frac{1}{2}$ inches apart, on the prepared baking sheet. Brush the top of each lightly with beaten egg. Sprinkle lightly with 3 tablespoons cinnamon sugar mixture.

3. Bake for about 23 minutes until the tops are golden. Reverse the baking sheets after 10 minutes, front to back and top to bottom, to ensure even browning. Slide a metal spatula under the rugelach to loosen them from the parchment paper and transfer immediately to a wire rack to cool thoroughly.

Good Advice: Low-fat cream cheese softens more quickly than full-fat cream cheese. ✻ Cut the dried cranberries with a large, sharp knife into approximate $\frac{1}{4}$-size pieces. Whole dried cranberries tend to poke out of the dough and burn during baking. **Doubling the Recipe:** Double the ingredients for the filling and mix the dough in 2 batches. **To Freeze Baked Rugelach:** Place the bottoms of 2 rugelach together and wrap them in plastic wrap. Place in a metal or plastic freezer container and cover tightly. Label with the date and contents. Freeze up to 3 months. **To Serve Baked Rugelach:** Remove the quantity desired from the freezer and defrost the wrapped pastries at room temperature about 3 hours. To return the just-baked taste to the rugelach, unwrap them and heat them in an oven preheated to 225°F until warm, about 10 minutes. Leftover rugelach may be covered with plastic wrap and stored at room temperature up to 3 days.

Eggnog Bars

t our house instead of drinking eggnog we toast the holidays with these Eggnog Bars. The cream cheese filling is just as velvety as any liquid eggnog, while rum and a sprinkling of nutmeg add the traditional touches.

MAKES 12 BARS

Nutmeg Graham Cracker Crust

2³/4 cups graham cracker crumbs
³/4 teaspoon ground cinnamon
¹/4 teaspoon ground nutmeg
8 tablespoons (1 stick) unsalted butter, melted

Eggnog Filling

12 ounces cream cheese, softened 3 to 4 hours at room temperature
¹/2 cup sugar
1 tablespoon unbleached all-purpose flour
1 large egg, at room temperature
1 large egg yolk, at room temperature
1 teaspoon vanilla extract
2 tablespoons dark rum
¹/4 cup whipping cream
¹/2 teaspoon ground nutmeg

MAKE THE CRUMB CRUST

1. Position a rack in the middle of the oven. Preheat the oven to 325°F. Line a 13 × 9 × 2-inch pan with heavy aluminum foil, letting the foil extend over the ends of the pan. Butter the bottom and sides of the aluminum foil.

2. Put the graham cracker crumbs, cinnamon, and nutmeg in a large bowl and mix together. Add the melted butter and stir until the crumbs are evenly moistened with the butter. Transfer the crumbs to the prepared pan. Using your fingers, press the crumbs evenly over the bottom and ¹/2 inch up the sides of the aluminum foil. Bake the crust for 8 minutes. Cool the crust while you make the filling.

MAKE THE FILLING

1. Increase the oven temperature to 350°F.

2. Put the cream cheese in the large bowl of an electric mixer. Mix on low speed until smooth, about 1 minute, and blend in the sugar and flour. Add the egg and egg yolk and blend in until smooth. Stop the mixer and scrape the sides of the bowl. Mix in the vanilla, rum, and whipping cream. Pour the filling into the crumb crust. Sprinkle the nutmeg evenly over the top.

3. Bake about 25 minutes, or until the filling looks set when you give the pan a gentle shake.

4. Cover the pan loosely with paper towels and cool for 1 hour at room temperature. Discard the paper towels and refrigerate for 1 hour. Cover with plastic wrap and chill thoroughly in the refrigerator, at least 6 hours or overnight.

Good Advice: These bars taste rich, so I make them thinner than most bars; they are about $3/4$ inch thick. ❀ To sprinkle the batter evenly with ground nutmeg, grate a piece of whole nutmeg directly over the top of the batter. A light coating of nutmeg equals the $1/2$ teaspoon nutmeg called for in the filling. **Doubling the Recipe:** Use 2 pans and double the remaining ingredients. **To Freeze:** Use the overhanging ends of aluminum foil to lift the cold bars out of the pan. Cut into 12 pieces. Use a wide spatula to slide each bar off the aluminum foil. Wrap individual bars in plastic wrap. Place in a metal or plastic freezer container and cover tightly. Label with the date and contents. Freeze up to 1 month. **To Serve:** Defrost the wrapped bars in the refrigerator for 5 hours or overnight. Store the bars in the refrigerator up to 5 days. Serve cold.

Orange, Cranberry, and Toasted Almond Bars

hese bars have a crisp crust that is just thick enough to support the moist brown sugar and maple syrup filling; the chopped almonds are held in place by the sticky filling; and bright red cranberries peek out through the crisp topping.

MAKES 12 TO 16 BARS

1 Press-in Butter Crust for Bars (page 21), prepared with brown sugar and unbaked (if frozen, don't defrost). Use the ingredients listed for a 13 × 9 × 2-inch pan, but press them into a 9 × 9 × 2-inch pan.
2 large eggs
³/₄ cup packed dark brown sugar
¹/₂ cup granulated sugar
¹/₄ cup pure maple syrup
3 tablespoons unsalted butter, melted and cooled
1 teaspoon grated orange zest
¹/₄ teaspoon salt
1 teaspoon vanilla extract
1¹/₄ cups fresh or previously frozen and defrosted unsweetened cranberries, chopped
1 cup toasted almonds, chopped coarsely (pages 3–4)

1. Position a rack in the middle of the oven. Preheat the oven to 350°F. Bake the prepared crust until the top is light golden, about 20 minutes. If the crust is frozen, bake it 25 minutes.

2. Put the eggs in a large bowl and whisk the yolks and whites together. Add the brown sugar and granulated sugar, and whisk until the eggs and sugar are smoothly blended. Mix in the maple syrup, butter, orange zest, salt, and vanilla. Use a large spoon to stir in the chopped cranberries and chopped almonds. Spread the filling evenly over the baked crust.

3. Bake until the filling is set when you give it a gentle shake and the center remains firm, about 30 minutes. Cool thoroughly at room temperature.

Good Advice: Chop the almonds and cranberries separately in a food processor, using the steel blade and a few quick on/off pulses. This results in a mixture of finely chopped and coarsely chopped almonds that works well for this recipe. Chop the almonds first, remove them, then, without washing the work bowl, process the cranberries with just a few short bursts until most of the pieces are halves and quarters. If using frozen whole cranberries, defrost them before chopping them. To Freeze: Use a small, sharp knife to loosen the bars from the edges of the pan. Cut into 12 or 16 individual bars. Carefully slide a metal spatula under the bars to loosen them from the bottom of the pan. Wrap the individual bars in plastic wrap, place in a metal or plastic freezer container, and cover tightly. Label with the date and contents. Freeze up to 1 month. To Serve: Defrost the wrapped bars at room temperature. Serve within 3 days.

Gingerbread People

I may be the gingerbread baker in my house, but my husband, Jeff, and my daughter, Laura, are the gingerbread eaters. They've been buying commercial gingerbread cookies for years in their search for the perfect cookie. So when I wanted to produce Gingerbread People that tasted as good as they looked, I had two specialists ready to judge my baking efforts and they pronounced these as having the perfect blend of spices, the correct crisp texture, and just the right thickness. 🏃 This dough is easy to mix, and a vigorous stirring by hand produces a smooth, firm dough that is easy to roll out. A combination of maple syrup and molasses softens the flavor of the cookies and eliminates any bitterness that too much molasses can cause. Use several sizes of cookie cutters to produce a family of Gingerbread People and an anything-goes attitude when you decorate each one.

MAKES ABOUT ELEVEN 5- TO 6-INCH ADULT-SIZE COOKIES AND
TWENTY-FIVE SMALL 2- TO 3-INCH–LONG CHILD-SIZE COOKIES

Gingerbread Cookies
> 3 cups unbleached all-purpose flour
> 1 teaspoon baking soda
> 1 teaspoon ground cloves
> 1 teaspoon ground cinnamon
> 2 teaspoons ground ginger
> $1/2$ teaspoon ground mace
> 8 tablespoons (1 stick) margarine
> $1/2$ cup packed light brown sugar
> $1/4$ cup molasses
> $1/4$ cup pure maple syrup
> 1 large egg
> Raisins and currants for decorating

Powdered Sugar Frosting
> $1^1/2$ cups powdered sugar, sifted
> $3/4$ teaspoon vanilla extract
> 2 tablespoons plus 1 to 3 teaspoons water

MAKE THE GINGERBREAD COOKIES

1. Position 2 oven racks in the middle and upper third of the oven. Preheat the oven to 325°F. Line 2 baking sheets with open sides with parchment paper.

2. Sift the flour, baking soda, cloves, cinnamon, ginger, and mace into a large bowl and set aside. Put the margarine, brown sugar, molasses, and maple syrup in a medium saucepan. Cook over low heat until the margarine and sugar are melted, stirring

occasionally. Increase the heat to medium-high and bring to a boil. Remove the mixture from the heat and cool for 10 minutes.

3. Put the egg in a medium bowl and whisk to blend. Whisking constantly, slowly pour the warm mixture over the egg. Make a well in the center of the flour mixture and pour in the liquid mixture. Use a large spoon to stir the mixture together until a smooth dough forms, about 1 1/2 minutes.

4. Divide the dough in half and form into 2 smooth disks about 6 inches in diameter. Wrap 1 disk in plastic wrap. Lightly flour the rolling surface and rolling pin. Roll the remaining disk into a rectangle measuring about 11 × 9 inches and 3/16 inch thick. Slide a thin metal spatula under the dough to loosen it from the rolling surface. With a large 5-inch gingerbread man or woman cookie cutter, cut out 4 people. Fold the arms over the chest of each and slide the cookies onto a baking sheet, placing them about 1/2 inch apart. Spread the arms flat. Use a small 2 to 3-inch cutter to cut out about 9 small people shapes. Slide them onto a baking sheet. Wrap the scraps in plastic wrap and set aside. Unwrap the second piece of dough and repeat the rolling and cutting process. Transfer the cookies to a baking sheet. Press all the dough scraps together to form a smooth disk. Repeat the rolling and cutting process, rolling the dough 3/16 inch thick. Transfer the cookies to the baking sheet. Firmly press raisins in the large cookies and currants in the small cookies to form eyes and a nose and 3 or 4 buttons down the middle of the body.

Bake about 12 minutes, reversing the sheets, top to bottom and back to front, after 7 minutes of baking. The tops of the cookies will feel firm and the edges will just begin to darken slightly. Cool the cookies 5 minutes on the baking sheet. Transfer the cookies to a wire rack to cool completely. While the cookies are warm, use a toothpick to poke a hole in the top of a cookie so that it can be hung later as an ornament.

MAKE THE FROSTING AND DECORATE THE COOKIES

In a bowl, blend the powdered sugar, vanilla, and enough water to form a stiff frosting. Spoon the frosting into a small pastry bag fitted with a small, round writing tip. Hold the pastry tip about 1 inch above the cookie and pipe hair, a mouth, and shoes on each cookie. You can also draw a frosting bow or bow tie at the neck and outline a dress or jacket around the edge of the body. Feel free to create any design with the frosting decoration; it will look whimsical. (I sometimes look at a picture of a decorated gingerbread cookie and try to copy it.) Let the cookies sit until the frosting is firm. Place the cookies in a tin between layers of wax paper, tightly covered, and store up to 2 weeks at room temperature.

Good Advice: Stir the dough by hand or with an electric mixer on low speed until it is smooth. Smooth dough bakes into smooth cookies. 🐵 During baking, these cookies do not spread, but they do rise slightly. 🐵 I use currants to decorate the small cookies and raisins to decorate the larger cookies. Jeff prefers raisins for flavor, but it's difficult to place several raisins on a 2-inch-long Gingerbread person. ☃ Rolling the scraps more than twice produces hard gingerbread, so I cut out the Ginger-bread People carefully to make as many as possible. After rolling the dough twice, discard the remaining scraps. If you place 2 small cookie people with hands touching, they will stick together and hold hands when baked. Use baking sheets with open sides so that the cookies slide off easily. ☃ The flavor of these cookies improves after 1 day. **Doubling the Recipe:** Double the ingredients and use an electric mixer to combine them. **To Freeze:** Wrap large cookies in plastic wrap. Place the bottoms of 2 small cookies together and wrap them in plastic wrap. Place in a metal or plastic freezer container and cover tightly. Label with the date and contents. Freeze up to 3 months. **To Serve:** Defrost the wrapped cookies at room temperature. Store leftover cookies, wrapped in plastic wrap, up to 5 days at room temperature or up to 2 weeks in a tightly covered tin.

White Christmas Cranberry Florentines

lassic florentines are thin, lace-textured cookies flavored with honey, sliced almonds, and candied fruit, with dark chocolate covering the bottoms. For the holidays I deck out these florentines by replacing the candied fruit with cranberries and trimming the cookies with melted white chocolate.

MAKES ABOUT 45 COOKIES

> 3/4 cup dried cranberries, ground or finely chopped
> 1/4 cup unbleached all-purpose flour
> 5 tablespoons unsalted butter, cut in pieces
> 1/4 cup whipping cream
> 1/2 cup sugar
> 2 tablespoons honey
> 3/4 cup sliced almonds
> 4 ounces white chocolate, chopped (preferably Callebaut, Lindt, or Baker's Premium)

MAKE THE COOKIES

1. Position 2 oven racks in the middle and upper third of the oven. Preheat the oven to 325°F. Line 2 or 4 baking sheets with parchment paper.

2. Mix the ground cranberries and flour together in a small bowl and set aside.

3. Put the butter, whipping cream, sugar, and honey in a medium saucepan and cook, stirring often, over low heat until the butter melts and the sugar dissolves. Increase the heat to medium-high and boil the mixture, stirring often, until the syrup measures 240°F on a candy thermometer, about 5 minutes. The mixture should not become brown, but will become thick and syrupy. Remove it from the heat and stir in the sliced almonds. Stir in the cranberry mixture. Drop teaspoons of batter 3 inches apart on 4 baking sheets. Press the top of each cookie with the back of the teaspoon to flatten it.

4. Bake 2 baking sheets of cookies 9 to 10 minutes, or until they are evenly light brown. Reverse the baking sheets after 5 minutes, front to back and top to bottom, to ensure that the cookies bake evenly. (One baking sheet may be ready 1 minute sooner than the other one.) If any cookies have spread into each other or have spread unevenly, use a fork to separate them or gently push in the edges to shape them. Bake the remaining 2 sheets of cookies. If using the same baking sheets, cool them before baking more cookies on them. Reverse the baking sheets after 5 minutes.

5. Cool the cookies on the baking sheets until they are firm, about 10 minutes. Transfer the cookies to a wire rack to cool completely.

MAKE THE WHITE CHOCOLATE TOPPING

1. Preheat the oven to 175°F. Place the chopped white chocolate in a nonreactive, ovenproof container and melt the chocolate in the oven, about 10 minutes. As soon as the white chocolate is melted, remove it from the oven and stir it smooth.

2. Arrange the cookies so they are touching on the wire rack. Dip a fork in the melted white chocolate and drizzle thin crisscrossing lines of white chocolate back and forth over the tops of the cookies. Use all of the white chocolate to generously coat the cookies with thin lines. Let the cookies sit until the white chocolate is firm or refrigerate them to firm the white chocolate quickly.

Good Advice: I once baked these cookies using whole dried cranberries and slivered almonds. The cookies spread across the baking sheet, had large holes, and fell apart when I took them off the baking sheet. It's the finely chopped cranberries and thinly sliced almonds that thicken the batter and hold it together. It takes about 30 seconds to grind the dried cranberries in a food processor. ✻ I prefer to bake the cookies on parchment paper rather than on a nonstick liner. The cookies spread quite thin when baked on a nonstick liner and can break easily. ✻ This recipe requires 4 baking sheets or 2 baking sheets used twice. If you are working with 2 baking sheets, let them cool before adding another batch of cookies. ✻ If the batter stiffens as it sits and cools, warm it gently to soften it. **To Freeze:** Place the bottoms of 2 cookies together and wrap them in plastic wrap. Put the wrapped cookies in a metal or plastic freezer container and cover tightly. Label with the date and contents. Freeze up to 3 months. **To Serve:** Defrost the wrapped cookies at room temperature. Serve within 2 days.

Holiday Lebküchen

ne of my favorite things about Christmas is sharing different family traditions with our friends. For our first Christmas in Maine, our friend Mrs. Thomas gave us a tin of her festive lebküchen, which really brightened up what might have been a lonely Christmas in a new home. Her lebküchen are soft and spicy bars, filled with bits of candied fruit and pecans, and topped with a white glaze gaily decorated with colored sugar and edible silver dragées. Mrs. Thomas's daughter, Harriet DeHoff, shared the recipe with me. 🐿 Mrs. Thomas used to cut up large red and green gumdrops and form them into candlesticks and wreaths on the top of each bar. When those gumdrops became difficult to find, simpler red and green sugar or sprinkles and little balls of silver dragées were used instead. You can use any holiday candy that appeals to you to decorate the bars.

MAKES ABOUT 24 BARS

Lebküchen dough

2³/₄ cups unbleached all-purpose flour
¹/₂ teaspoon baking soda
¹/₂ teaspoon salt
¹/₂ teaspoon ground cloves
1 teaspoon ground cinnamon
1 teaspoon ground allspice
1 cup molasses
³/₄ cup sugar
1 large egg
1 teaspoon grated lemon zest
1 cup diced candied fruit, mixed choice of orange, lemon, and citron
¹/₂ cup chopped pecans

Frosting

2 cups powdered sugar, sifted
3 tablespoons unsalted butter, melted
1 tablespoon fresh lemon juice
2 tablespoons plus 1 to 2 teaspoons whipping cream
Red and green sugar or sprinkles and silver dragées, optional

BAKE THE LEBKÜCHEN

1. Sift the flour, baking soda, salt, cloves, cinnamon, and allspice and set aside.

2. Put the molasses in a large saucepan and bring to a boil. Remove the molasses from the heat, stir in the sugar, and let sit for about 5 minutes, just until it is cool enough not to cook the egg when it is added, and would not burn your hand if you touched it. Use a large spoon to beat in the egg. Add the lemon zest and stir in the flour mixture in 3 additions.

Mix in the candied fruit and the pecans. Put the dough in a large bowl, press plastic wrap against the dough, and refrigerate overnight.

3. Position an oven rack in the middle of the oven. Preheat the oven to 400°F. Lightly oil 2 baking sheets that have open ends.

4. Remove the dough from the refrigerator and let it sit 30 minutes to soften. Divide the dough in half. Roll 1 piece of dough into a 9 × 5-inch rectangle. Slide a metal spatula under the dough to loosen it and put it on a baking sheet. Press the dough into a 12 × 6-inch rectangle, using a rolling pin to help smooth the dough and your fingers to press it into shape. The dough will be ½ inch thick. Form the second piece of dough into a 12 × 6-inch rectangle on another baking sheet.

5. Bake 1 baking sheet at a time, 9 to 10 minutes, until the lebküchen puffs slightly and the edges brown. Reverse the baking sheet after 5 minutes to ensure even browning. Remove from the oven and cool 5 minutes. Bake the second baking sheet of lebküchen. Use a large, sharp knife to cut off about ½ inch of the crisp edges from the warm lebküchen and discard. Cut the lebküchen in half lengthwise, then into 6 slices crosswise. Each pan will give you 12 bars measuring about 2¾ × 1¾ inches. Cool the bars thoroughly on the baking sheet, about 1 hour.

PREPARE THE FROSTING

Put the powdered sugar in a medium bowl. Stir in the melted butter and lemon juice. Add enough of the cream that the frosting has a good spreading consistency. Spread about 1½ teaspoons frosting evenly over the top of each bar. If desired, sprinkle lightly with colored sugar or sprinkles and dragées and press them in gently to adhere. Let the bars sit until the frosting is firm.

Good Advice: This dough must chill overnight before it is baked. ✲ Cool the molasses only about 5 minutes, so that it won't cook the egg when it is added; the molasses should be a pourable syrup. I once cooled the molasses until it was almost firm; the dough became stiff and hard to handle, and the bars were less moist than usual. ✲ It's not necessary to dust the rolling surface with additional flour when rolling out the lebküchen. ✲ The bars bake at a high temperature, so you must watch them carefully. When they are baked for 10 minutes they will be crisper and firmer on the outside than when baked for 9 minutes. The bars should become light brown around the edges, but not all over. Try baking a sheet each way and choose what you prefer. ✲ Cutting the lebküchen into bars when warm will create neat, sharp-edged slices. Bake on open-ended cookie sheets so the bars cut easily on the sheets. I have used a baking sheet with 1-inch sides and burned my hands when I tried to cut the warm bars. ✲ You can buy a mixture of diced candied lemon peel, orange peel, and citron in the supermarket. King Arthur Flour, in the mail order section on page 224, ships the candied fruit in separate flavors. **To Freeze:** Place 2 bars side by side and wrap them in plastic wrap. Place in a metal or plastic freezer container and cover tightly. Label with the date and contents. Freeze up to 3 months. **To Serve:** Defrost the wrapped bars at room temperature. Store leftover bars wrapped in plastic wrap in a tightly covered tin for up to 1 week at room temperature.

Hanukkah Stars, Christmas Moons, and Holiday Cutouts

hese versatile lemon-flavored sugar cookies will become your all-occasion holiday treat. The soft dough rolls out smoothly and is easy to cut into different designs. Since the cookies hold their shape during baking, they can be adapted to any holiday just by changing cookie cutters. The topping can be a mixture of egg white and sugar, added before baking, or a glaze of powdered sugar frosting, added after baking. These thin, crisp cookies store especially well at room temperature or in the freezer. 🏃 I used to wonder why few stores stocked half moon–shaped cookie cutters until I realized that an ordinary round cookie cutter can be used to create half-moons. Simply use only half of the round cutter. A six-pointed star is traditional for a Hanukkah cookie, but any star cookie cutter is fine. During the holiday season, I bake stars and moons from one batch of dough and have them ready for both Hanukkah and Christmas.

MAKES ABOUT 80 COOKIES

$^{1}/_{2}$ **pound (2 sticks) soft unsalted butter**
1 cup sugar
1$^{1}/_{2}$ teaspoons grated lemon zest
1 large egg, separated
1 tablespoon lemon juice
2 teaspoons vanilla extract
$^{1}/_{2}$ teaspoon almond extract
$^{1}/_{8}$ teaspoon salt
2$^{1}/_{4}$ cups unbleached all-purpose flour
2 tablespoons granulated or 3 tablespoons colored sugar for sprinkling

1. Position 2 oven racks in the middle and upper third of the oven. Preheat the oven to 350°F. Line 3 baking sheets with parchment paper.

2. Put the butter in a large mixing bowl and mix with an electric mixer on low speed for 15 seconds. Add the sugar and lemon zest and beat on medium speed for 2 minutes, until the mixture lightens in color and looks fluffy. Stop the mixer and scrape the sides of the bowl once during the mixing. Add the egg yolk, lemon juice, vanilla, almond extract, and salt. Decrease the speed to low and mix in the flour until the dough holds together and comes away from the sides of the bowl, about 1 minute. Stop the mixer and scrape the bowl and the beaters. Pat the dough into two 5-inch disks. Wrap each disk in plastic wrap and chill them in the refrigerator for 1 hour, or until the dough is firm.

3. Remove 1 piece of dough from the refrigerator. Lightly flour the rolling surface and rolling pin. Roll the dough until it is $^{3}/_{16}$ inch thick. Slide a thin metal spatula under the dough to loosen it from the rolling surface. With a 2- to 2$^{1}/_{2}$-inch cookie cutter cut out stars, half-moons, or any desired shape. Place half of a round cookie cutter on the dough to cut half-moons. (Using more than half the cutter makes larger half-moons and less than half the cutter makes smaller crescent moons.) Place the cookies ¹/₂ inch apart on a prepared baking sheet. Wrap the scraps in plastic wrap and set aside.

4. Roll and cut out the second piece of dough. Transfer the cookies to another baking sheet. Press all the dough scraps together until smooth and repeat the rolling and cutting process, rolling the dough to a ³/₁₆-inch thickness. Transfer the cookies to a baking sheet. Put the egg white in a small bowl and whisk until foamy. Brush the top of each cookie lightly with slightly beaten egg white. Sprinkle granulated sugar or colored sugar lightly over the egg white. Or, omit the egg white and leave the top of the cookies plain, then glaze the warm baked cookies with a powdered sugar glaze as directed below.

5. Bake 2 baking sheets at a time 10 to 12 minutes, reversing the sheets, top to bottom and back to front, after 6 minutes of baking. The tops of the cookies will be golden and the edges light brown. Bake the remaining sheet of cookies on the middle rack of the oven for 10 to 12 minutes. Cool the cookies 5 minutes on the baking sheet. Transfer them to a wire rack to cool thoroughly.

VARIATION   Omit the egg white and sugar topping and bake the cookies as directed. Make a powdered sugar glaze by mixing 1¹/₄ cups sifted powdered sugar and 2 tablespoons plus 1 to 2 teaspoons of lemon juice or water until a thin glaze forms. Use a thin metal spatula to spread a thin layer of glaze over the tops of the warm cookies. The glaze will firm as the cookies cool thoroughly.

Good Advice: Chill the dough before rolling it, and it will not stick. Before cutting out any cookies, loosen the rolled-out dough from the counter with a thin metal spatula. *To Freeze:* Stack 6 cooled cookies together and wrap them in plastic wrap. Put the wrapped cookies in a metal or plastic freezer container and cover tightly. Label with the date and contents. Freeze up to 3 months. *To Serve:* Defrost the wrapped cookies at room temperature. Serve within 1 week.

Chocolate Peppermint Crunch Sandwiches

aybe it's the white chocolate and crunchy peppermint filling or the bright crushed candy topping on the dark chocolate cookie itself, but whatever it is, these cookies look as if you've spent a lot of time on them. The simple dough is a pleasure to work with and can be rolled right after mixing, no chilling required, while melted white chocolate and crushed peppermint candy are all you need for the fancy filling. These cookies keep their shape during baking and can also be cut into stars, trees, or hearts.

MAKES ABOUT 30 SANDWICHES

2 cups plus 2 tablespoons all-purpose flour
6 tablespoons unsweetened Dutch process cocoa powder, such as Droste or
    Hershey's European
^{1}/$_2$ teaspoon salt
^{1}/$_2$ pound (2 sticks) soft unsalted butter
^{3}/$_4$ cup sugar
1 teaspoon instant decaffeinated coffee granules dissolved in 1 teaspoon water
1 teaspoon vanilla extract

8 ounces white chocolate, chopped (preferably Callebaut)
4 ounces semisweet chocolate, chopped
^{3}/$_4$ cup (about 6 ounces) peppermint candy, crushed into small pieces

1. Position 2 oven racks in the middle and upper third of the oven. Preheat the oven to 325°F. Line 2 baking sheets with parchment paper.

2. Sift the flour, cocoa powder, and salt together and set aside.

3. Put the butter in a large mixing bowl and mix with an electric mixer on medium speed for 15 seconds. Add the sugar, dissolved coffee, and vanilla and beat for 1 minute. Slowly add the flour mixture. Mix until blended completely and the dough holds together, about 45 seconds.

4. Divide the dough in half. Lightly flour the rolling surface and rolling pin. Roll out 1 piece of dough ^{1}/$_8$ inch thick. Use a 2-inch cookie cutter to cut out circles or other desired shapes. Slide a thin metal spatula under the cookies to loosen them from the rolling surface. Place the cookies 1 inch apart on a prepared baking sheet. Wrap the scraps in plastic wrap and set aside. Roll and cut out the second piece of dough. Transfer the cookies to another baking sheet. Press all the dough scraps together until smooth and repeat the rolling and cutting process, rolling the dough ^{1}/$_8$ inch thick. Transfer the cookies to the baking sheet. Bake until the tops feel firm, about 15 minutes, reversing the baking sheets after 10 minutes, front to back and top to bottom, to ensure that the cookies bake evenly. Check the cookie bottoms toward the end of the baking time. Transfer the cookies to a wire rack to cool completely.

5. While the cookies cool, preheat the oven to 175°F. Place the white chocolate in a small nonreactive ovenproof container and the semisweet chocolate in a separate ovenproof container and melt them in the oven for 10 to 12 minutes. Remove the chocolates from the oven as soon as they are melted and stir them smooth. Let the white chocolate sit about 5 minutes to thicken slightly.

6. Turn half of the cookies bottom side up and, leaving a ¼-inch plain edge, spread a thin layer, about 1 teaspoon, of white chocolate over them. Sprinkle a generous ½ teaspoon crushed peppermint candy over the white chocolate. Press the flat bottoms of the remaining cookies on the peppermint candy filling. Let the filling firm for 10 minutes. Use a thin metal spatula to spread a thin layer of melted semisweet chocolate over half the top of each cookie sandwich. For other shapes, spread the chocolate topping appropriately—in the center of stars and trees or over one side of a heart. Sprinkle about ½ teaspoon of the remaining crushed peppermint candy over the dark chocolate.

Good Advice: Flour the rolling surface as lightly as possible so as not to leave any white flour residue on the cookie. If you notice any flour on unbaked cookies, brush it off with a pastry brush. ❧ Using larger or smaller cookie cutters yields a different number of cookie sandwiches. I use an assortment of star cutters that make a festive mix of different-size star cookies. **To Freeze:** Chill the cookies, uncovered, until the chocolate is firm. Wrap each cookie sandwich in plastic wrap. Put the wrapped cookies in a metal or plastic freezer container and cover tightly. Label with the date and contents. Freeze up to 1 month. **To Serve:** Defrost the wrapped cookies at room temperature. Leftover cookies can be covered with plastic wrap and stored at room temperature up to 3 days.

Savory Cookies

avory cookies are the flip side of the cookie coin. Although I never realized it, I had been baking them for many years. I've long used Cheese Crispies as my standard hors-d'oeuvre wafer. I realized that many categories of cookies could become savory appetizers, crackers, crisp breads, or snacks; I was off and running—or baking, to be precise.

The categories of cookies that made the successful changeover from sweet to savory were ones that didn't include a lot of sugar. They contained spices that could be exchanged for herbs, and their sweet fruit fillings could be replaced with ones with cheese, potatoes, and onions. I made tuiles with basil and rosemary, seasoned cheesecake bars with sun-dried tomatoes and bread crumb crusts, and stuffed strudel with cream cheese and onions.

Although I serve most savory cookies as appetizers or in place of bread, I've also found them to be good picnic fare. Served at room temperature, Sun-Dried Tomato and Chive Cheesecake Bars make an interesting alternative to the usual potato salad. When crushed, Cheese Crispies make a good accompaniment to soups or a crunchy topping for casseroles.

Onion Caraway Shortbread

S avory rather than sweet, this buttery shortbread is seasoned with sautéed onions and caraway seeds. Onion and caraway have such an affinity for each other that they seem to form their own third flavor, and people often ask me what the seasoning is as they pick up their third or fourth piece.

MAKES 24 RECTANGULAR PIECES

2 teaspoons unsalted butter
1 cup finely chopped onion (1 medium)
1¼ cups unbleached all-purpose flour
1 tablespoon powdered sugar
½ teaspoon baking powder
¼ teaspoon salt
12 tablespoons (1½ sticks) soft unsalted butter
1 teaspoon caraway seed
1 large egg white, slightly beaten
½ teaspoon kosher salt

1. Melt the 2 teaspoons butter in a medium frying pan over medium heat. Add the onion and cook until it is soft and the edges are brown, stirring occasionally. Put in a small bowl and set aside to cool thoroughly.

2. Position a rack in the middle of the oven. Preheat the oven to 350°F. Butter a 9 × 9 × 2-inch square pan.

3. Sift the flour, powdered sugar, baking powder, and salt together. Set aside. Put the soft butter in the large bowl of an electric mixer and mix on low speed for 15 seconds. Add the caraway seed and cooled onions and beat on medium-high for 1 minute. Stop the mixer and scrape the sides of the bowl. Decrease the speed to low and add the flour mixture. Mix until the dough holds together and all of the flour is incorporated. Stop the mixer and scrape the bowl and the beaters during the mixing. Press the dough evenly into the prepared pan. Dip your fingers lightly in flour to prevent the dough from sticking to them when pressing it into the pan. Brush the top of the dough with egg white (you will not use all of it). Sprinkle the salt evenly over the egg white.

4. Bake about 25 minutes, until the top is pale golden and the edges light brown. Remove from the oven and cut 6 rows in one directions and 4 rows across, cutting through to the bottom. Cool the shortbread thoroughly in the pan.

Good Advice: Cool the cooked onions thoroughly before mixing them with the soft butter so the butter doesn't melt. ❦ Kosher salt, found in the spice section of the supermarket, is a coarse salt that has a pure, clean taste. *To Freeze:* Place the bottoms of 2 shortbread pieces together and wrap them in plastic wrap. Put the wrapped shortbread in a metal or plastic freezer container and cover tightly. Label with the date and contents. Freeze up to 3 months. *To Serve:* Defrost the wrapped shortbread at room temperature. Serve as appetizers, snacks, or in place of bread. Store leftover shortbread, wrapped in plastic wrap, up to 3 days at room temperature.

Camden Cheese Ribbons

ummer in Camden, Maine, is a time for parties. Old friends sail into the harbor or arrive on our doorstep. Every long sunny day is an excuse for celebration after the short quiet days of winter when every invitation depended on the track of the latest snowstorm. One thing that is sure to show up at every summer party are these thin cheese crackers, which are always the first to disappear. There can never be enough of them, so I just bake as many as I can and resign myself to running out. They are exceptionally thin, rectangular cheese crackers, rich with butter and cheese and topped with a sprinkling of salt.

MAKES 40 CHEESE RIBBONS

$^3/_4$ cup unbleached all-purpose flour
$1^1/_3$ cups (about 5 ounces) grated sharp white cheddar cheese
Pinch salt
4 tablespoons ($^1/_2$ stick) soft unsalted butter
1 teaspoon Worcestershire sauce
$^1/_8$ teaspoon ground cayenne pepper or hot Hungarian paprika
1 teaspoon kosher salt

1. Stir the flour, cheddar cheese, and pinch of salt together in a small bowl. Set aside.

2. Put the butter in the large bowl of an electric mixer and beat on low speed for 30 seconds. Mix in the Worcestershire sauce and cayenne pepper. Add the flour mixture and mix just to incorporate the flour. Increase the speed to medium and beat until a smooth dough forms that holds together and pulls away from the sides of the bowl, about 1 minute. You will see specks of cheese in the dough. Divide the dough in half and press each piece into a square about $^3/_4$ inch thick. Wrap each piece in plastic wrap and refrigerate until firm, about 30 minutes.

3. Position an oven rack in the middle of the oven. Preheat the oven to 400°F. Line 2 baking sheets with parchment paper.

4. Remove 1 piece of dough from the refrigerator and unwrap it. Flour the rolling surface and rolling pin lightly. Roll the dough into a rectangle that measures 12 × 5 inches and is $^1/_8$ inch thick. Trim the edges. Use a large, sharp knife or fluted pastry wheel to cut 20 strips 3 inches long and 1 inch wide. Cut 20 strips by cutting 5 rows lengthwise and 4 rows crosswise. Slide a thin metal spatula under the dough to loosen it from the rolling surface. Separate each strip and roll it until it is 4 inches long and about $^1/_{16}$ inch thick. Use the spatula to loosen the strips from the rolling surface and transfer the strips to the baking sheet, placing them 1 inch apart. Repeat with the second piece of dough. Sprinkle the strips lightly with the kosher salt. Each strip will have only a few grains of salt on it.

5. Bake 1 sheet at time until the edges of the cheese ribbons are light brown and the centers are just golden, about 6 minutes. The ribbons should not become brown all

over. Bake the remaining baking sheet of cheese ribbons about 6 minutes. Cool the cheese ribbons 5 minutes on the baking sheets. Transfer them to a wire rack to cool thoroughly.

Good Advice: To achieve a rich butter and cheese flavor, these crackers must be prepared with a full-fat cheddar cheese rather than a reduced-fat kind. ☘ The best way to make this thin cracker is to roll it twice. After I roll the dough into a square about $^1/_8$ inch thick, I cut it into strips and roll each strip even thinner. ☘ These cheese crackers can have a straight edge if cut with a knife or a zigzag edge if cut with a fluted pastry wheel. ☘ Use coarse-grained kosher salt for the topping. Kosher salt can be found in the spice section of the supermarket. *To Freeze:* Stack 6 cheese ribbons together and wrap them in plastic wrap. Put the wrapped cheese ribbons in a metal or plastic freezer container and cover tightly. Label with the date and contents. Freeze up to 3 months. *To Serve:* Defrost the wrapped cheese ribbons at room temperature. They can be stored in a clean metal tin at room temperature up to 5 days.

Flaky Cheese Batons

he same Aunt Alice who brought you crisp gingersnaps (page 87) created these flaky cheddar crackers. They have all of the richness and multilayers of puff pastry, but without any of the time-consuming work.

MAKES ABOUT SEVENTY-TWO 2 BY $^3/_4$-INCH BATONS

1 cup unbleached all-purpose flour
$^1/_4$ teaspoon salt
8 tablespoons (1 stick) cold unsalted butter, cut in 8 pieces
1 cup (about 4 ounces) grated sharp cheddar cheese

1. Position an oven rack in the middle of the oven. Preheat the oven to 400°F. Line 2 baking sheets with parchment paper.

2. Sift the flour and salt into the large bowl of an electric mixer and mix on low speed just to blend. Add the butter and mix just until the butter pieces are the size of peas. Add 2 tablespoons ice water and mix until the dough forms large clumps and holds together, about 30 seconds. Gather the dough into a ball; then pat it into a flat disk. Flour the rolling surface and rolling pin very lightly. Roll the dough into a 10 × 5-inch rectangle. The shorter end of the dough should be parallel to the edge of the counter. Sprinkle $^1/_3$ cup of the cheese evenly over the dough. Fold the bottom third of the dough to the center, then fold the top third of the dough to the opposite edge. Press the edges to seal. (There will be 3 layers in the dough package.)

3. Turn the dough so an open end faces you. Roll into another 10 × 5-inch rectangle. Sprinkle with $^1/_3$ cup of the cheese and repeat the folding procedure. Roll the dough into another 10 × 5-inch rectangle. Sprinkle with the remaining cheese and repeat the folding. Cut the dough package in half. Roll a piece of dough out $^1/_8$ inch thick, about 9 × 8 inches. Trim the edges even. Cut strips of dough $^3/_8$ inch wide (a pizza cutter works well here). Cut each strip into thirds, about 2$^1/_2$ inches long, to make 36 long, thin strips. Place the strips 1 inch apart on a baking sheet. Repeat the rolling and folding procedure with the remaining piece of dough, forming 36 more batons on the second baking sheet.

4. Bake 1 sheet of crackers at a time until their bottoms are light brown, 7 to 8 minutes. Reverse the baking sheets after 4 minutes to ensure that the crackers bake evenly. The tops should not become brown. Bake the remaining pan 7 to 8 minutes, reversing the pan after 4 minutes. Cool the batons 5 minutes on the baking sheets. Transfer them to a wire rack to cool thoroughly.

VARIATION   The rolled dough can be cut into 1$^1/_4$-inch circles with a round metal cutter. Roll out any dough scraps and cut out more circles. Bake about 8 minutes until the bottoms are light brown. This will make about 60 round crackers.

Good Advice: Use a full-fat cheddar cheese. The butter, water, and cheese must be cold for the flaky layers to form.   The unbaked dough can be refrigerated up to 2 days. **To Freeze:** Line a freezer container with plastic wrap. Fill the container with the cooled crackers, press plastic wrap onto them, and cover tightly. Label with the date and contents. Freeze up to 3 months. **To Serve:** Remove as many crackers as you need from the freezer, cover the crackers with plastic wrap, and defrost at room temperature. Serve within 4 days.

Cheese Crispies

We used to canoe a mile for these cheese wafers. When we had a summer home on a lake in Maine, our friends the Mayers lived on the opposite shore. Summer evenings often found us paddling across to their cottage for beer and these cheese crispies. Rice Krispies are the secret to the crunch, and Tabasco sauce plus mustard add the zing. They're worth that mile of canoeing.

MAKES 24 CRACKERS

1 cup (about 4 ounces) grated sharp cheddar cheese
8 tablespoons (1 stick) soft margarine
1 cup unbleached all-purpose flour
1/2 teaspoon salt
1/2 teaspoon garlic powder
1/2 teaspoon powdered mustard
1 teaspoon Worcestershire sauce
1/2 teaspoon Tabasco sauce
2 cups Rice Krispies

1. Position an oven rack in the middle of the oven. Preheat the oven to 350°F. Line a baking sheet with parchment paper.

2. Put the cheddar cheese and margarine in the large bowl of an electric mixer and blend on low speed until smooth, 30 seconds. Mix in the flour, salt, garlic powder, powdered mustard, Worcestershire, and Tabasco until a smooth dough forms that comes away from the sides of the bowl, 1 minute. Stop the mixer and scrape the sides of the bowl once during the mixing. Stir in the Rice Krispies just until they are incorporated. (There will be a few loose ones in the bottom of the bowl.) Roll slightly rounded tablespoons of dough into 1 1/4-inch balls. Place the balls 1 1/2 inches apart on the baking sheet. Use a fork to press the balls into 1/2-inch-thick wafers. If any edges crack, use your fingertips to press them smooth.

3. Bake until the edges and bottoms are golden, about 18 minutes. Cool the wafers 5 minutes on the baking sheet. Transfer them to a wire rack to cool thoroughly.

Good Advice: Stir the Rice Krispies into the dough just to incorporate them. Overmixing will break the cereal into tiny bits, and the crackers will lose some of their crunch. Flattening the top of the crackers with a fork produces a nice ridged pattern. **To Freeze:** Place the bottoms of 2 wafers together and wrap them in plastic wrap. Put the wrapped wafers in a metal or plastic freezer container and cover tightly. Label with the date and contents. Freeze up to 3 months. **To Serve:** Defrost the wrapped wafers at room temperature. They can be stored in a clean metal tin at room temperature up to 5 days.

Basil and Rosemary Tuiles

This is an herb-seasoned version of thin, crisp French tuile cookies. Since the batter contains a small amount of flour, it's easy to spread into the desired thin rounds. Grated Parmesan cheese creates a crisp topping and freshly ground black pepper adds the zip. Traditionally, tuiles are formed into a curved roof-tile shape, but I prefer these flat. They can be served as an hors d'oeuvre or in the place of bread. 🏃 Try to use imported Italian Parmigiano-Reggiano cheese for these crackers to add a sweet rather than a sharp flavor.

MAKES ABOUT TEN 4-INCH CRACKERS

1 large egg white
2 teaspoons sugar
¹/₄ cup grated Parmesan (preferably Parmigiano-Reggiano)
1 teaspoon finely chopped fresh basil
¹/₂ teaspoon finely chopped fresh rosemary or ¹/₄ teaspoon dried and crushed rosemary
¹/₂ teaspoon dried chopped onion
¹/₄ teaspoon salt
3 tablespoons unsalted butter, melted and cooled
¹/₃ cup unbleached all-purpose flour
Freshly ground black pepper

1. Position a rack in the middle of the oven. Preheat the oven to 350°F. Line 2 baking sheets with nonstick liners or parchment paper.

2. Put the egg white, 3 tablespoons water, sugar, 2 tablespoons of the Parmesan, basil, rosemary, dried onion, and salt in a medium bowl and beat with a fork until frothy, about 20 seconds. Add the melted butter and flour and mix until all the flour is incorporated.

3. Using 1 tablespoon of batter for each tuile, with a thin metal spatula, spread five 4-inch thin circles of batter on a prepared baking sheet. The batter looks translucent and there will be some holes in it. Sprinkle a few grindings of black pepper and 1 tablespoon of the Parmesan over the tops of the 5 wafers.

4. Bake until the edges of the tuiles are evenly brown and the centers are light golden, about 8 minutes. Prepare the second sheet of tuiles while the first sheet bakes. Remove the first baking sheet from the oven and cool the tuiles on the sheet for 5 minutes. Transfer to a wire rack to cool thoroughly. Bake the remaining pan of tuiles.

Good Advice: Use a nonstick liner or parchment paper to line the baking sheets so the crackers don't stick. This batter is thicker than a sweet tuile batter, so parchment paper works just as well as a nonstick liner. Using dried onion rather than fresh onion helps keep the tuiles crisp. The batter should be spread thin enough to look translucent. There will be holes in it, but they will close during baking. *To Freeze:* Stack 3 or 4 tuiles together and wrap in plastic wrap. Carefully put the wrapped tuiles in a single layer in a metal or plastic freezer container and cover tightly. Label with the date and contents. Freeze up to 1 month. *To Serve:* Defrost the wrapped tuiles at room temperature. Store in a sealed container and serve within 2 days. If the tuiles soften, warm them for about 10 minutes in a 225°F oven. They will crisp as they cool.

Cream Cheese and Onion Strudel

 hese hot appetizers of crisp phyllo pastry, filled with onions, cream cheese, and Swiss cheese, can go straight from the freezer to the oven, ready to bake at a moment's notice.

MAKES 36 PIECES OF STRUDEL

8 tablespoons (1 stick) unsalted butter
4 cups onions (3 medium), thinly sliced
6 ounces cream cheese, softened
1³/₄ cups (about 8 ounces) grated Swiss cheese
1 teaspoon caraway seed
Salt and freshly ground black pepper
12 sheets (18 by 14 inches) phyllo pastry, defrosted if frozen

PREPARE THE CREAM CHEESE FILLING

Melt 1 tablespoon of the butter in a medium frying pan over low-medium heat. Add the onions and cook for about 15 minutes until the onions soften, stirring often. Put the onions in a medium bowl and set aside to cool thoroughly. Use a large spoon to mix the cream cheese, Swiss cheese, and caraway seed into the onions. Add salt and pepper to taste.

ASSEMBLE THE STRUDEL

Melt the remaining 7 tablespoons butter. Stack the phyllo sheets on a work surface and cover them with plastic wrap and a damp dish towel. Place 1 phyllo sheet on a work surface with the short side of the pastry facing you. Brush lightly with melted butter. Repeat the layering with 2 more phyllo sheets. Top with a fourth phyllo sheet. Leaving a 1-inch plain edge along the bottom and sides of the pastry, spoon a third of the cheese filling (about ³/₄ cup) in a 1¹/₂-inch-wide strip along the bottom edge of the top sheet of pastry. Fold the sides of the pastry in to enclose the edges of the filling, and roll up tightly. Brush the top lightly with melted butter. Place the strudel seam side down and use a sharp knife to mark 1-inch pieces on the top of the pastry. Repeat to form 2 more strips of strudel.

Good Advice: Keep the phyllo sheets covered with plastic wrap and a clean, damp dish towel once you unwrap the package. Left uncovered, phyllo pastry dries out quickly and becomes brittle. 🏃 The finished strudel strip is rolled up in a piece of heavy aluminum foil. The foil makes a tight seal around the strudel, so plastic wrap is unnecessary. **To Freeze:** Roll each strudel strip tightly in heavy aluminum foil. Label with the date and contents. Freeze up to 3 months. **To Bake and Serve:** Position an oven rack in the middle of the oven and preheat the oven to 375°F. Unwrap as many strudel strips as desired. Line a baking sheet with the aluminum foil used to wrap the strudel. Place the strudel, seam side down, on the baking sheet. If baking more than 1 strip of strudel, place the strips 2 inches apart. Bake until the top is golden, about 30 minutes, reversing the baking sheet, front to back, after 15 minutes to ensure even browning. Cold, defrosted strudel takes about 25 minutes to bake. Cool the strudel 10 minutes on the baking sheet. With a sharp knife slice the strudel into individual pieces. Serve warm. 🏃 If you are making the strudel for a party, bake the rolls one at a time so you have a continuous supply of warm strudel. Or, cover the baked strudel with aluminum foil and keep it warm for up to 1 hour in a 200°F oven or on an electric warmer tray.

Onion Rugelach

hen I was a child, these hot onion appetizers were the best part of family weddings. They had a puff pastry crust filled with sweet sautéed onions that dissolved with a crunch when you bit into them. I managed to gorge myself with quite a few pastries during the cocktail hour. In this recipe a rich cream cheese dough substitutes for time-consuming puff pastry. The result is just as buttery and flaky as the pastry but can be mixed in minutes.

MAKES 32 SMALL PASTRIES

Cream Cheese Dough

> 1 cup unbleached all-purpose flour
> 2 teaspoons sugar
> 1/4 teaspoon salt
> 6 ounces cream cheese, softened
> 6 tablespoons (3/4 stick) soft unsalted butter
> 2 tablespoons sour cream

Onion Filling

> 1 tablespoon plus 1 teaspoon unsalted butter
> 2 cups chopped onion
> Salt and freshly ground black pepper
>
> 2 tablespoons unsalted butter, melted, for brushing the dough

Egg Wash and Sesame Topping

> 1 egg, beaten with 2 tablespoons whipping cream
> 1 1/2 teaspoons sesame seeds, not toasted

PREPARE THE CREAM CHEESE DOUGH

Put the flour, sugar, and salt in the large bowl of an electric mixer and mix on low speed just to blend the ingredients. Add the cream cheese and butter and mix until all of the flour is incorporated and a soft dough forms, about 45 seconds. Add the sour cream and mix until a sticky dough forms, about 15 seconds. Divide the dough into 4 equal pieces and form each piece into a round disk. Wrap each disk in plastic wrap and refrigerate until firm, for at least 1 hour or overnight.

PREPARE THE ONION FILLING

Melt the butter in a medium frying pan over medium heat. Add the onions and cook for about 10 minutes, until the onions soften and the edges turn brown, stirring often. Put the onions in a small bowl. Add salt and freshly ground black pepper to taste. Set aside to cool thoroughly.

1. Position an oven rack in the middle of the oven. Preheat the oven to 375°F. Line a baking sheet with parchment paper.

2. Remove the dough packages from the refrigerator and unwrap them. If the dough has become cold and hard, let it sit at room temperature for about 5 minutes until it is easy to roll. Lightly flour the rolling surface and rolling pin. Roll 1 piece of dough into an 8-inch circle. Trim the edges evenly. The trimmed circle will be about 7$\frac{1}{2}$ inches in diameter. Brush lightly with melted butter.

3. Leaving a $\frac{3}{4}$-inch plain border, use a thin spatula to spread $\frac{1}{4}$ cup of the cooled onion mixture evenly over the dough. Press the onions lightly into the dough. Use a large knife to cut the dough evenly into 8 wedges. Roll each wedge up tightly from the wide edge to the point. Place, point side down, 1 inch apart, on the prepared baking sheet. Repeat with the remaining dough to form 32 small rugelach. With pastry brush lightly brush the top of each rugelach with egg wash, then sprinkle with sesame seeds.

4. Bake about 20 minutes until the pastry is golden brown. After 10 minutes, reverse the baking sheet, front to back, to ensure even browning. Transfer the rugelach immediately to a wire rack to cool thoroughly.

VARIATION   Make a mushroom and onion filling: Cook 1$\frac{1}{2}$ cups chopped fresh crimini or button mushrooms and $\frac{1}{2}$ cup chopped onion in 1 tablespoon butter until the onions soften and the moisture evaporates from the mushrooms. Stir in 1 tablespoon whipping cream. Remove from the heat and add salt and pepper to taste. Cool the mixture, then use it to fill the rugelach.

Good Advice: Check any smaller-size rugelach toward the end of the baking time, as they may be done and need to be removed sooner than the larger rugelach. ✻ Cool the onion filling before spreading it on the dough. Hot onion filling will melt the dough. ✻ Freezing the rugelach unbaked, then baking them as needed, ensures that they will be fresh and crisp. **Doubling the Recipe:** Mix the dough in 2 batches. Double the ingredients for the filling. **To Freeze:** Place the bottoms of 2 rugelach together and wrap them in plastic wrap. Put the wrapped pastries in a metal or plastic freezer container and cover tightly. Label with the date and contents. Freeze up to 3 months. **To Serve:** Defrost the wrapped pastries at room temperature, about 3 hours. Uncover and bake in a preheated 225°F oven for about 10 minutes until warm. Serve warm. Store leftover rugelach at room temperature up to 3 days, but warm them in the oven before serving.

Sun-Dried Tomato and Chive Cheesecake Bars

I spent several years baking cheesecakes for a restaurant in Camden. The flavors changed often, and I baked at least fifty varieties. I discovered the versatility of a cream cheese filling, and a savory cheesecake was the natural next step. These bars have a toasted bread crumb and pecan crust that holds a cream cheese filling seasoned with a generous quantity of sun-dried tomatoes. The bars make a hearty hors d'oeuvre, and their golden-orange color flecked with green chives brightens any table.

MAKES 12 TO 16 BARS

Bread Crumb and Pecan Crust
1¹/₃ cups coarsely ground bread crumbs
¹/₂ cup chopped pecans
3 tablespoons unsalted butter, melted

Cream Cheese Filling
¹/₄ cup chopped packed fresh chives
¹/₂ cup drained oil-packed sun-dried tomatoes, thinly sliced
1 tablespoon olive oil
2 peeled halved garlic cloves, green centers removed
1 large egg, at room temperature
1 large egg yolk, at room temperature
1 tablespoon unbleached all-purpose flour
¹/₄ teaspoon salt
¹/₄ teaspoon freshly ground black pepper
10 ounces cream cheese, softened about 2 hours at room temperature
1 cup sour cream

MAKE THE BREAD CRUMB AND PECAN CRUST

1. Position a rack in the middle of the oven. Preheat the oven to 350°F. Line a 9 × 9 × 2-inch pan with heavy aluminum foil, letting the foil extend over the ends of the pan. Butter the bottom and sides of the aluminum foil.

2. Put the bread crumbs and pecans in the work bowl of a food processor fitted with the steel blade. Begin with a few on/off bursts, then process until the nuts are finely ground, about 20 seconds. Add the melted butter and process just until incorporated, about 10 seconds. Transfer the crumbs to the prepared pan. Use your fingers to press the crumbs evenly over the bottom. Bake the crust for 10 minutes.

MAKE THE CREAM CHEESE FILLING

1. Reserve 1 tablespoon of the chives and put the remaining chives, sun-dried tomatoes, olive oil, and garlic in the work bowl of a food processor fitted with the steel blade. Begin with a few on/off bursts, then process until finely chopped, about 30 seconds. Add the egg, egg yolk, flour, salt, and pepper, and process just to blend the eggs into the mixture. Add the cream cheese and process until smooth, 1 minute. Add the sour cream and process just until it is incorporated and no white streaks remain. Pour the batter over the baked crust and smooth the top. Sprinkle the reserved chives over the top.

2. Bake until the top looks firm, about 20 minutes. Cool 1 hour in the pan. Cover with plastic wrap and chill thoroughly in the refrigerator, at least 3 hours or overnight. Lift the aluminum foil and the rectangle from the baking pan. Loosen the aluminum foil from the sides. Cut into 12 to 16 pieces. Use a wide spatula to slide the bars off the aluminum foil.

Good Advice: When I have bread that is about to become stale, I use the food processor to grind it into crumbs. Then I seal it tightly in a plastic freezer bag and freeze it for up to 2 months. ❀ You can substitute the green tops of finely chopped green onions for the chives. An easy way to cut chives is to snip them with scissors. *To Freeze:* Wrap individual bars in plastic wrap. Place in a metal or plastic freezer container and cover tightly. Label with the date and contents. Freeze up to 2 weeks. *To Serve:* Defrost in the refrigerator for 4 hours or overnight. The wrapped bars can be stored in the refrigerator up to 3 days. Serve cold or at room temperature.

Mail Order Sources

American Spoon Foods
P.O. Box 566, Petoskey, MI 49770
(888) 735-6700, Fax: (800) 847-2512

Dried fruits, including sweetened Montmorency cherries

B & L Specialty Foods
P.O. Box 80068, Seattle, WA 98108-0068
(800) 328-7278, Fax: (800) 366-3746

Callebaut chocolate and Guittard chocolate chips

Bridge Kitchenware
214 East 52nd Street, New York, NY 10022,
(800) 274-3435, Fax: (212) 758-5387

Large selection of kitchen equipment and many imported kitchen utensils

Buchanan Hollow Nut Company
6510 Minturn Road, Le Grand, CA 95333
(800) 532-1500, Fax: (209) 389-4321

Shelled pistachio nuts, walnuts, and pecans

Hadley Fruit Orchards
P.O. Box 495, Cabazon, CA 92230
(800) 854-5655, Fax: (909) 849-1663

Dried fruits and nuts, including unsweetened Bing cherries and unsalted macadamia nuts

King Arthur Flour Baker's Catalogue
P.O. Box 876, Norwich, VT 05055
(800) 827-6836, Fax: (800) 343-3002

Equipment and baking ingredients, including unbleached all-purpose flour, peeled hazelnuts, and nonstick liners

Penzey's, Ltd.
P.O. Box 933, Muskego, WI 53150
(414) 679-7207, Fax: (414) 679-7878

Complete selection of fresh spices and dried herbs. Source for two high-quality cinnamons, ground extra-fancy China Tunghing cassia cinnamon, and extra-fancy Vietnamese cassia cinnamon

Previn
2044 Rittenhouse Square, Philadelphia, PA
19103, (215) 985-1996

Quality baking equipment

Simpson and Vail
P.O. Box 765, Quarry Road, Brookfield, CT
06804, (800) 282-8327, Fax: (203) 775-0462

Key lime juice

Sunnyland Farms
P.O. Box 8200, Albany, GA 31706
(800) 999-2488, Fax: (912) 432-1358

Nuts, including unsalted macadamia nuts, and some dried fruit

**Sweet Celebrations Division of
Maid of Scandinavia**
P.O. Box 39426, Edina, MN 55439-0426
(800) 328-6722, Fax: (612) 943-1688

Baking equipment, including cardboard cake circles, pastry bags, and pastry tips, and Callebaut chocolate

Walnut Acres Organic Farms
Penns Creek, PA 17862
(800) 433-3998, Fax: (717) 837-1146

Dried fruits, nuts, and toasted almond butter

Williams-Sonoma
10000 Covington Cross Drive, Las Vegas, NV
89134, (800) 541-2233, Fax: (702) 360-7091

Baking equipment and ingredients

Zingerman's
422 Detroit Street, Ann Arbor, MI 48104
(888) 636-8162, Fax: (734) 769-1260

Callebaut chocolate; ships for 2-day delivery

Bibliography

BOOKS

Bridge, Fred, and Jean F. Tibbetts. *The Well-Tooled Kitchen.* New York: William Morrow and Company, Inc., 1991.

Desrosier, Norman W., and Donald K. Tressler. *Fundamentals of Food Freezing.* Connecticut: AVI Publishing Company, Inc., 1977.

Gates, June. *Basic Foods.* New York: Holt, Rinehart, and Winston, 1976.

Gortner, Willis, Frederick Erdman, and Nancy Masterman. *Principles of Food Freezing.* New York: John Wilson and Sons, Inc., 1948.

Herbst, Sharon Tyler. *Food Lover's Companion.* New York: Barron's, revised 1995.

Labensky, Steven, Gaye G. Ingram, and Sarah R. Labensky. *Webster's New World Dictionary of Culinary Arts.* New Jersey: Prentice Hall, 1997.

McGee, Harold. *The Curious Cook.* San Francisco: North Point Press, 1990.

McGee, Harold. *On Food and Cooking.* New York: Macmillan Publishing Company, 1984.

Sultan, William. *Practical Baking*, 3rd ed. Connecticut: AVI Publishing Company, Inc., 1983.

Whitman, Joan, and Dolores Simon. *Recipes into Type.* New York: HarperCollins, 1993.

HANDBOOKS

Sugar's Functional Roles in Cooking and Food Preparation, The Sugar Association, Inc., Washington, D.C.

Index

A

Almond
Butter, Roasted, Brownies, 112
-Drenched True Tea Cakes, 184
Lace Cookies, Chocolate-
Filled, 147
Macaroon Horns, 166
Macaroon Sandwiches, 170
Meringues, Toasted, 168
and Milk Chocolate Praline
Truffles, 192
Raspberry Tall Bars, New York
Bakery, 128; variation, 129
Toasted, Orange, and Cranberry
Bars, 200
Toasted, and White Chocolate
Bars, 127
Tuiles, 80; variations, 80
Amish Raisin Cookies, 92
Apple Raisin Rugelach, 158
Apricot Bars, 132
Avenue "J" Butter Cookies, 48

B

baking
equipment, 6–11. *See also*
equipment
ingredients, 11–15. *See also*
ingredients
techniques, 2–6. *See also*
techniques
Banana
Caramel Brownies, 116
Date Bars with Cinnamon
Cream Cheese Frosting, 136
Bars. *See also* Brownies
about pans for, 7
Almond Raspberry Tall, New
York Bakery, 128; variation,
129
Apricot, 132
Banana Date, with Cinnamon
Cream Cheese Frosting, 136
Berry Picnic, Summer, 143
Blueberry Crisp Squares, 144
Butterscotch Chip, Uncle
Howie's Extraordinary, 35
Caramel Cashew Triangles,
118

Cheesecake, Sun-Dried Tomato
and Chive, 222
Chocolate Chip, 95
Chocolate Fudge Soufflé, 122
Chocolate Truffle Squares, 36
Coconut Pecan Southland, 125
Coffee Toffee, 123
Cookie Crumb Crusts for, 22
Double Deckers, 121
Eggnog, 198
Fruit Jelly Squares, 142
Graham Cracker Chocolate
Chip, 34
Key Lime, 134
Mango Macadamia, Marvelous,
131
Oatmeal, My Sister's, 37
Oatmeal Toffee, D.C., 120
Orange, Cranberry, and Toasted
Almond, 200
Pecan Cinnamon Crisps, 126
Pine Nut Toffee, Pure, 124;
variations, 124
Press-in Butter Crust for, 21
Raisin Spice, with Simple
Caramel Glaze, New
England, 138
Spice Leather, 140
Sticky Tiffin, 28
White Chocolate and Toasted
Almond, 127
Basil and Rosemary Tuiles, 218
Beacon Hill Cookies, 169
Berry Picnic Bars, Summer, 143
The Best of Everything Chocolate
Chip Cookies, 98
Birthday Cookie, A Big Chocolate
Chip, 96
Black and White Hazelnut Cookie
Tarts, 152
Blueberry Crisp Squares, 144
Breakaway Chocolate Chip
Cookie Crunch, 101
Brown Sugar
Pecan Shortbread, 65
Pecan Tassies, Mom's, 182
Brownie(s), 107–116. *See also*
Bars
about pans for, 7
Almond Butter, Roasted, 112
Banana Caramel, 116

Cappuccino, 111
Chocolate Chip, 100
Chocolate Chubbies, 105
Peanut Butter Chocolate
Chunk, 113
Pecan Praline, 110
Peppermint Patty, 109
A Really Good, 108
White Chocolate and Raspberry
Ripple, 114
Butter
Crust for Bars, Press-in, 21
Pastry for Tassies, 23
Pecan Crisps, 79
shortening, and oils, 11–12
Butter Cookies, 68–80. *See also*
Crisps; Shortbread
Almond Tuiles, 80; variations, 80
Avenue "J," 48
Butter Nuggets, 69
Caramel Crunch, 76
Cherry Orange Flaky Flats, 70
Swedish Chocolate, 72;
variation, 72
Triple-Chocolate-Topped
Chocolate, 74
Butterscotch Chip Bars, Uncle
Howie's Extraordinary, 35

C

Camden Cheese Ribbons
(crackers), 214
Cappuccino
Brownies, 111
and Walnut Truffles, 190
Caramel
Banana Brownies, 116
Cashew Triangles, 118
Crunch Butter Cookies, 76
Filling, 25; variation, Coffee
Caramel Sauce, 25
Pecan Truffle Tassies, 183
Carrot Strudel, 160
Cashew
Caramel Triangles, 118
Lace Crisps, 77
Checkerboards and Stripes,
Mocha, 39
Cheese
Batons, Flaky, 216; variation, 216

Crispies, 217
Ribbons (crackers), Camden, 214
Cheesecake Bars, Sun-Dried Tomato and Chive, 222
Cherry
    Chocolate Chip Oatmeal Cookies, 104
    Orange Flaky Flats, 70
Chocolate. *See also* Brownies; Chocolate Chip; White Chocolate
    about melting, 4
    about varieties (bittersweet, semisweet, white, etc.), 12–13
    Beacon Hill Cookies (meringues), 169
    Butter Cookies, Triple -Chocolate-Topped, 74
    Chubbies, 105
    Chunk Peanut Butter Brownies, 113
    Dark, Truffle Macaroon Sandwiches, 178
    -Filled Almond Lace Cookies, 147
    Fudge Soufflé Bars, 122
    and Hazelnut Praline Cookie Tarts, 150; variation, 151
    Milk, and Almond Praline Truffles, 192
    Milk, Toasted Hazelnut Shortbread Hearts Dipped in, 66
    Mocha Checkerboards and Stripes, 39
    Peppermint Crunch Sandwiches, 210
    Sticky Tiffin Bars, 28
    Swedish, Butter Cookies, 72
    Truffle Sauce, Filling and Glaze, 20
    Truffle Squares, 36
Chocolate Chip(s). *See also* Butterscotch Chips
    Bars, 95
    The Best of Everything Cookies, 98
    Birthday Cookie, A Big, 96
    Breakaway, Cookie Crunch, 101
    Brownies, 100
    Cherry, Oatmeal Cookies, 104
    Chocolate Chubbies, 105
    Galettes, 106

Graham Cracker Bars, 34
Millionaire's Shortbread, 60
Raisin Crunch, 102
Sticky Tiffin Bars, 28
Super S'mores, 30
Chocolate Chip Cookies and Bars, 94–106
Christmas Moons, 208; variation, 209
Cinnamon
    Pecan Crisps, 126
    Spiral Crisps, 44
    Sugar Mandel Bread, 84
citrus and citrus zest, 13
Coconut
    Pecan Southland Bars, 125
    Swahili Shortbread, 46
Coffee
    Caramel Sauce, 25
    Hazelnut Macaroons with Chocolate Truffle Filling, 174
    Toffee Bars, 123
cookie cutters, 9
cookies. *See* equipment; freezing and shipping; ingredients; techniques
cooling racks, 9
Cranberry
    Orange, and Toasted Almond Bars, 200
    Walnut Rugelach, 196
    White Christmas Florentines, 204
Cream Cheese and Onion Strudel, 219
cream and milk, 13
creaming fats and sugar, 2
Crisp(s). *See also* Butter Cookies; Shortbread
    Butter Pecan, 79
    Cashew Lace, 77
    Cinnamon Spiral, 44
    Parisian Toffee, 78
    Pecan Cinnamon, 126
Crispies, Cheese, 217
Crumb
    Crusts, Cookie, for Bars, 22
    -Topped Lemon Cream Sandwiches, 148; variations, 149
Cutouts,
    Gingerbread People, 201
    Holiday, 208; variation, 209
    Sugar Cookie, Grandma Theresa's, 194; variation, 195

D
D.C. Oatmeal Toffee Bars, 120
Dark Chocolate Truffle Macaroon Sandwiches, 178
Date
    Banana Bars with Cinnamon Cream Cheese Frosting, 136
    Maple, and Walnut Chews, 50
    Oatmeal Cookie Sandwiches, 154
Double Deckers (brown sugar-pecan meringue), 121

E
Eggnog Bars, 198
eggs, beating, 23; using whites and yolks, 13–14
electric mixers, 7
English Shortbread Batons, 52
equipment, cookie baking, 6–11
    electric mixers, 7
    food processors, 7
    freezers, 8
    ovens, 8
    pans (baking sheets/cookie sheets), 6–7
    pans for brownies and bars, 7
    pie pans, 7
    saucepans and double boilers, 8
    scales, 8
    thermometers, 8
    utensils, 9–11. *See also* utensils

F
Fig Cookies, Sicilian, 162
Filled Cookies. See Sandwiches and Filled Cookies
Filling. *See* Sauce
Flaky
    Cheese Batons, 216; variation, 216
    Flats, Cherry Orange, 70
flavorings and spices, 14
Florentines, White Christmas, Cranberry, 204
flour, types of, 14
folding ingredients, 3
food processors, 7
Freezer Cookies, Slice and Bake, 38–50
    Butter Cookies, Avenue "J," 48
    Cinnamon Spiral Crisps, 44
    Maple, Date, and Walnut Chews, 50

Mocha Checkerboards and Stripes, 39
Raspberry and Lemon Pinwheels and Whirlybirds, 42
Swahili Shortbread, 46
freezers, 8; temperature for, 16
freezing and shipping cookies, 15–18
best ones for, 17
defrosting, 17
preventing crumbles, 17
wrapping and labeling for, 16–17
Frozen Pantry, 19–26
Butter Pastry for Tassies, 23
Caramel Filling, 25; variation, 25
Chocolate Truffle Sauce, Filling, and Glaze, 20
Cookie Crumb Crusts for Bars, 22
Lemon Curd, 24; orange variation, 24
Nut Pralines, 26
Press-in Butter Crust for Bars, 21
Fruit(s)
Bars with, 130–45
Jelly Squares, 142
and nuts, Morning Glory Tea Cakes, 186
Fudge. *See* Chocolate

G

Galettes, Chocolate Chip, 106
Ginger
Molasses Cookies, Big, 88
Shortbread, Grasmere Crisp, 56
Gingerbread People, 201
Gingersnaps, 87
Graham Cracker Chocolate Chip Bars, 34
Grasmere Crisp Ginger Shortbread, 56
graters, 9

H

Hanukkah Stars, 208; variation, 209
Hazelnut
and Chocolate Praline Cookie Tarts, 150; variation, 151
Coffee Macaroons with Chocolate Truffle Filling, 174

Cookie Tarts, Black and White, 152
Toasted, Shortbread Hearts Dipped in Milk Chocolate, 66
Holiday Cookies, 193–210
Chocolate Peppermint Crunch Sandwiches, 210
Cranberry Walnut Rugelach, 196
Cutouts, Hanukkah Stars, Christmas Moons, 208; variation, 209
Eggnog Bars, 198
Gingerbread People, 201
Lebküchen, 206
Orange Cranberry, and Toasted Almond Bars, 200
Shortbread Rounds, 64
Sugar Cookie Cutouts, Grandma Theresa's, 194; variation, 195
White Christmas Cranberry Florentines, 204
Horns, Almond Macaroon, 166

I

ingredients for cookies, 11–15
butter, shortening, and oils, 11–12
chocolate, 12–13
citrus, citrus zest, 13
cream and milk, 13
eggs, 13–14
flavorings and spices, 14
flour, 14
leavening agents, 14
nuts, 15
sugars, 15

J

Jelly Fruit Squares, 142

K

Key Lime Bars, 134
Kid Easy Cookies, 27–37
Butterscotch Chip Bars, Uncle Howie's Extraordinary, 35
Chocolate Truffle Squares, 36
Graham Cracker Chocolate Chip Bars, 34
Oatmeal Bars, My Sister's, 37
Peanut Thinsies, 32
Rafiki Oatmeal, 33

Shortbread, Mistake, 31
Super S'mores, 30
Tiffin Bars, Sticky, 28
kitchen temperatures, 5–6
knives, 9

L

Lace Cookies
Chocolate-Filled Almond, 147
Crisps, Cashew, 77
Leather, Spice, 140
leavening agents, 14–15
Lebküchen, Holiday, 206
Lemon
Cream Sandwiches, Crumb-Topped, 148; variations, 149
Curd (sauce), 24
-Glazed Shortbread Wedges, 62
and Raspberry Pinwheels and Whirlybirds, 42
Sandwich Macaroons, 172
Tassies, 181

M

Macadamia Mango Bars, Marvelous, 131
Macaroon(s), 165. *See also* Meringues
Almond Horns, 166
Almond, Sandwiches, 170
Coffee Hazelnut, with Chocolate Truffle Filling, 174
Dark Chocolate Truffle Sandwiches, 178
Lemon Sandwich, 172
Raspberry Sandwiches, 176
Mandel Bread, Cinnamon Sugar, 84
Mango Macadamia Bars, Marvelous, 131
Maple, Date, and Walnut Chews, 50
measuring spoons and cups, 9
Meringue(s), 165. *See also* Macaroons
Beacon Hill Cookies, 169
Toasted Almond, 168
topping, brown sugar-pecan, Double Deckers, 121
Milk Chocolate. *See also* Chocolate
and Almond Praline Truffles, 192
milk and cream, 13

Millionaire's Shortbread, 60
Mistake Shortbread, 31
mixing bowls and spoons, 10
Mocha Checkerboards and
    Stripes, 39
Molasses Ginger Cookies, Big, 88
Morning Glory Tea Cakes, 186

N

New England Raisin Spice Bars,
    with Simple Caramel Glaze,
    138
New York Bakery Almond
    Raspberry Tall Bars, 128;
    variation, 129
Nut(s). *See also* Almond; Cashew;
    Hazelnut; Macadamia;
    Peanut; Pecan; Pine Nut;
    Walnut
    about, 15; peeling, toasting, and
        grinding, 3–4
    D.C. Oatmeal Toffee Bars, 120
    Double Deckers (bars), 121
    and fruits, Morning Glory Tea
        Cakes, 186
    Pralines, 26; powder, 26

O

Oatmeal
    Bars, My Sister's, 37
    Cherry Chocolate Chip
        Cookies, 104
    Cookies, Rafiki, 33
    Date Cookie Sandwiches, 154
    Toffee Bars, D.C., 120
oils, butter, and shortening, 11–12
Old-Fashioned Sugar Cookies, 83
Onion
    Caraway Shortbread, 213
    and Cream Cheese Strudel, 219
    Rugelach, 220; mushroom
        variation, 221
Orange
    Cranberry, and Toasted Almond
        Bars, 200
    Curd, 24
ovens, 8

P

pans (baking sheets/cookie sheets,
    for brownies and bars, pie
    pans), 6–7
Parisian Toffee Crisps, 78
pastry bags, tips, brushes, 10

Peanut
    Butter Chocolate Chunk
        Brownies, 113
    Thinsies, 32
Pecan(s)
    Brown Sugar Shortbread, 65
    Brown Sugar Tassies, Mom's,
        182
    Butter, Crisps, 79
    Caramel Truffle Tassies, 183
    Cinnamon Crisps, 126
    Cinnamon Sugar Mandel
        Bread, 84
    Coconut Southland Bars, 125
    Crescents, 86
    Double Deckers, 121
    Praline Brownies, 110
    Super S'mores, 30
Peppermint Patty Brownie, 109
Petticoat Tails, 58
Pine Nut Toffee Bars, Pure, 124;
    variations, 124
Pinwheels and Whirlybirds,
    Raspberry and Lemon, 42
Praline(s)
    Brownies, Pecan, 110
    Cookie Tarts, Chocolate and
        Hazelnut, 150; variation, 151
    Nut, 26
    Truffles, Milk Chocolate and
        Almond, 192
Press-in Butter Crust for Bars, 21
Pumpkin Whoopie Pies, 156

R

Rafiki Oatmeal Cookies, 33
Raisin
    Apple Rugelach, 158
    Chocolate Chip Cookies, 102
    Cookies, Amish, 92
    Spice Bars with Simple
        Caramel Glaze, New
        England, 138
Raspberry
    Almond Tall Bars, New York
        Bakery, 128; variation, 129
    and Lemon Pinwheels and
        Whirlybirds, 42
    Macaroon Sandwiches, 176
    Ripple and White Chocolate
        Brownies, 114
A Really Good Brownie, 108
rolling pins and surfaces, 10
Rugelach
    Apple Raisin, 158
    Cranberry Walnut, 196

Onion, 220; variation,
    mushrooms, 221

S

S'mores, Super, 30
Sandwich(es) and Filled Cookies,
    146–62
    Almond Macaroon, 170
    Apple Raisin Rugelach, 158
    Black and White Hazelnut
        Cookie Tarts, 152
    Carrot Strudel, 160
    Chocolate-Filled Almond Lace,
        147
    Chocolate and Hazelnut
        Praline Cookie Tarts, 150;
        variation, 151
    Chocolate Peppermint Crunch,
        210
    Crumb-Topped Lemon Cream,
        148; variations, 149
    Dark Chocolate Truffle
        Macaroon, 178
    Fig, Sicilian, 162
    Lemon, Macaroons, 172
    Oatmeal Date, 154
    Pumpkin Whoopie Pies, 156
    Raspberry Macaroon, 176
Sauce
    Chocolate Truffle (Filling and
        Glaze), 20
    Coffee Caramel, 25
    Lemon Curd, 24
    Orange Curd, 24
saucepans and double boilers, 8
Savory Cookies, 212–22
    Basil and Rosemary Tuiles, 218
    Cheese Batons, Flaky, 216;
        variation, 216
    Cheese Crispies, 217
    Cheese Ribbons (crackers)
        Camden, 214
    Cream Cheese and Onion
        Strudel, 219
    Onion Caraway Shortbread,
        213
    Onion Rugelach, 220; variation,
        221
    Sun-Dried Tomato and Chive
        Cheesecake Bars, 222
scales, 8
A Scot's Favorite Shortbread, 55
Scottish Shortbread/Shortcake,
    Thick, 54
Shortbread, 51–66. *See also* Butter
    Cookies; Crisps

about butter in, 51
Batons, English, 52
Brown Sugar Pecan, 65
Crisp Ginger, Grasmere, 56
Hearts Dipped in Milk
    Chocolate, Toasted
    Hazelnut, 66
Millionaire's, 60
Mistake, 31
Onion Caraway, 213
Petticoat Tails, 58
Rounds, 64
A Scot's Favorite, 55
Shortcake, Thick Scottish, 54
Swahili, 46
Wedges, Lemon-Glazed, 62
shortening, butter, and oils, 11–12
Sicilian Fig Cookies, 162
Slice and Bake Cookies from the
    Freezer, 38–50. *See also*
    Freezer Cookies
softening ingredients, 3
Soufflé Bars, Chocolate Fudge,
    122
spatulas, 11
Spice. *See also* Sugar and Spice
    Cookies, 90
    Lebküchen, Holiday, 206
    Leather, 140
    Raisin Bars with Simple
        Caramel Glaze, New
        England, 138
spices and flavorings, 14
Sticky Tiffin Bars, 28
strainers and sifters, 11
Strawberry Tea Cakes, 188
Strudel
    Carrot, 160
    Cream Cheese and Onion,
        219
Sugar
    about powdered, for coating, 6;
        types of, 15
    Cookie Cutouts, Grandma
        Theresa's, 194; variation, 195
Sugar and Spice Cookies, 82–93
    Amish Raisin, 92
    Cinnamon Sugar Mandel
        Bread, 84
    Gingersnaps, 87
    Molasses Ginger, Big, 88
    Old-Fashioned Sugar, 83
    Pecan Crescents, 86
    Spice, 90
Summer Berry Picnic Bars, 143
Sun-Dried Tomato and Chive
    Cheesecake Bars, 222

Swahili Shortbread, 46
Swedish Chocolate Butter
    Cookies, 72; variation, 72

T

Tassies, 180
    Brown Sugar Pecan, Mom's,
        182
    Butter Pastry for, 23
    Caramel Pecan Truffle, 183
    Lemon, 181
Tea Cakes, 180
    Almond-Drenched True, 184
    Morning Glory, 186
    Strawberry, 188
techniques, cookie baking, 2–6
    baking times, 6
    beating eggs, 2–3
    coating with powdered sugar, 6
    creaming fats and sugar, 2
    folding mixtures together, 3
    kitchen temperatures, 5
    melting chocolate, 4
    peeling, toasting, and grinding
        nuts, 3–4
    preparing baking pans, 4–5
    proper baking temperatures, 5
    softening ingredients, 3
thermometers, kinds of, 9
Tiffin Bars, Sticky, 28
Toasted
    Almond Meringues, 168
    Almond, Orange, and
        Cranberry Bars, 200
    Almond and White Chocolate
        Bars, 127
    Hazelnut Shortbread Hearts
        Dipped in Milk Chocolate,
        66
Toffee
    Coffee Bars, 123
    Crisps, Parisian, 78
    Oatmeal Bars, D.C., 120
    Pine Nut Bars, Pure, 124
Triple-Chocolate-Topped
    Chocolate Butter Cookies, 74
Truffle(s), 180
    Cappuccino and Walnut, 190
    Macaroon Sandwiches, Dark
        Chocolate, 178
    Praline, Milk Chocolate and
        Almond, 192
    Sauce, Filling, and Glaze,
        Chocolate, 20
    Squares, Chocolate, 36
    Tassies, Caramel Pecan, 183

Tuiles
    Almond, 80; variations, 80
    Basil and Rosemary, 218

U

utensils, cookie baking, 9–11. *See
    also* equipment
    baking pan liners, 10
    cookie cutters, 9
    cooling racks, 9
    graters, 9
    knives, 9
    measuring cups and spoons,
        9–10
    mixing bowls and spoons, 10
    pastry bags and tips, 10
    pastry brushes, 10
    rolling pins and rolling surfaces,
        10–11
    spatulas, 11
    strainers and sifters, 11
    whisks, 11

W

Walnut
    and Cappuccino Truffles, 190
    Cranberry Rugelach, 196
    Maple, and Date Chews, 50
Whirlybirds. *See* Pinwheels
whisks, 11
White Chocolate
    Black and White Hazelnut
        Cookie Tarts, 152
    Cappuccino Brownies, 111
    Cappuccino and Walnut
        Truffles, 190
    Caramel Cashew Triangles, 118
    Chocolate Peppermint Crunch
        Sandwiches, 210
    and Hazelnut Praline Cookie
        Tarts, 151
    and Raspberry Ripple Brownies,
        114
    and Toasted Almond Bars, 127
    Triple-Chocolate-Topped
        Chocolate Butter Cookies, 74
    White Christmas Cranberry
        Florentines, 204
Whoopie Pies, Pumpkin, 156